JUVENILE RIGHTS SINCE 1967

AN ANNOTATED, INDEXED BIBLIOGRAPHY OF SELECTED ARTICLES AND BOOKS

by
HELENA P. von PFEIL, B.A., B.S., M.L.S.
Assistant Law Librarian
University of Oregon School of Law

FOREWORD by
Dean Monrad Paulsen
University of Virginia School of Law

PREFACE by
Judge William Fort
Oregon Court of Appeals

Senator Bette Browne
Oregon State Senator

FRED B. ROTHMAN & CO. 1974 South Hackensack, N.J.

Library of Congress card #74-83233
ISBN 0-8377-1000-6

MIGNON and ENZIO

CONTENTS

FOREWORD

This bibliography of recently published articles and books is an extraordinarily useful research tool for persons interested in the rights of children and the law relating to the juvenile court. Mrs. Helena von Pfeil, with a librarian's expertise, has gathered nearly 1100 periodical references and listed almost 350 books on these subjects.

In most cases the article or book is briefly summarized. The result enhances the usefulness of the bibliography greatly. We need no longer depend solely upon the title of a book or article as the indicators of relevance to a particular line of inquiry. The summaries will save a good bit of time in the library. Further, the summaries may offset any tendency a researcher might have to limit reading to pieces published in well-established journals or to articles by authors who are widely known.

The bibliography has two additional important advantages. Articles listed are taken from some periodicals not included in the Index to Legal Periodicals, including a substantial number of foreign listings (the number of German entries is especially large.) The book references frees a scholar from the card catalogue of a particular library's holdings.

The entries of articles and books respectively are arranged in alphabetical order according to the author's surname. A subject-matter breakdown is provided by an extensive index. Thus, anyone wishing to read articles on a particular topic can quickly find the entires in the alphabetical listing.

Finally, looking over the entire list one gets a sense of where the scholarly work has been done and where more needs to be done. The past six to seven years have produced a great amount of work respecting due process in delinquency juvenile court cases. There has been much less attention given to neglect matters (though the problem of "child abuse" has received a great deal of play), to matters of children rebelling against adult authority ("PINS" or "ungovernables"), and to questions of juvenile correction.

We are all in Mrs. von Pfeil's debt for the impressive amount of skillful work she has done.

MONRAD G. PAULSEN
John B. Minor Professor and Dean
University of Virginia Law School

PREFACE

After the United States Supreme Court's decisions in Kent (1966) and Gault (1967), the rights of juveniles who were brought within the juvenile justice system came sharply into focus. Kent and Gault admonished that paternal concern by the state for a child's welfare could not bypass the "due process" of the Fourteenth Amendment which, under those decisions, extended many of the rights, previously established for adults under the Bill of Rights, to children.

Prior to those decisions, literature and cases concerning children before the court for delinquency, dependency, neglect or abuse were virtually non-existent. Subsequent to those decisions, the literature has burgeoned at a greatly accelerated rate concerning all aspects of the juvenile process, thus well justifying the author in limiting her compilation to the post-Gault era.

Mrs. von Pfeil has well served the juvenile justice field by her exhaustive annotated collection of relevant material, world-wide in scope. Nowhere else is such a handy tool available to the worker in the vineyard of all the included disciplines of juvenile justice to be found. Mrs. von Pfeil's bibliography will save hours of research time. The author's interest in this field and her perception of the need for this bibliography is to be highly commended. Whether one's special interest in children is national or international, whether oriented to law, sociology, education, psychiatry or social work, this bibliography will be an essential tool to teacher, student, researcher, writer, or practitioner in the field. We strongly commend this book to every toiler in the realm of rights and needs of children.

ELIZABETH W. BROWNE
Editor, Juvenile Court Digest
President-elect, Western Conference of Council of State Governments
Oregon State Senator

WILLIAM S. FORT
Judge, Oregon Court of Appeals
Executive Director, National Council of Juvenile Court Judges
Chairman, ABA Joint Committee on Juvenile Justice Standards
Chairman, Oregon State Bar Committee on Family and Juvenile Law

INTRODUCTION

This annotated bibliography is concerned with informative materials regarding trends in the juvenile court in the United States and abroad since 1967. It is designed expressly for the widest possible variety of interests and professions -- for judges, attorneys, law and other students, juvenile justice planners, police and probation officers, academicians, social control agency workers and administrators, juvenile department counselors, juvenile court intake officers, child and family social welfare workers, school principals, corrections officers, and anyone interested in what is happening to children and their parents in the courts since the Kent and Gault decisions.

Abstracts of selected articles and books written since 1967 covering the five to six official agencies of the juvenile justice system are included -- the courts, the juvenile department, the child welfare agency, probation, corrections, and police. About 14 indexes, legal as well as social work, police, corrections, and medicine were searched for pertinent material. 1073 articles and 343 books were chosen from over 2000 examined. As far as possible, author summaries were used in the abstracts. An explanation of the use of the index is included at the end of this introduction.

Research in juvenile rights was commenced in 1970 when I was completing undergraduate work in political science and in sociology and public affairs. These two departments at the University of Oregon provided funds to conduct two surveys, one on the impact of Gault on judges and attorneys in Oregon, and one on the attitudes of the child welfare agency caseworkers and juvenile department counselors in seven large counties in Oregon. I quickly found that much was being written as a result of Gault. Since I have been exposed to the juvenile court system in a custody matter first in Germany, then in London, England, and subsequently in this country, I know that our present system has much to learn from other countries whose personnel appear to have far deeper insight and show greater concern for families. It is hoped that students will research foreign materials.

During the course of the survey I was able to observe in many juvenile court settings and in judges' chambers, and to talk to judges, district attorneys, social caseworkers, and juvenile counselors in various counties. Several points were mentioned repeatedly. Child welfare supervisors deplored the fact that their caseworkers would not read and educate themselves in their field even when time was made available on the job for such study. They stated that there is a large turnover in caseworkers. The reason given was that people are interested only in short-term work while finishing their university studies. Responses to the questionnaires noted the lack of training of judges and attorneys in juvenile matters, and the fact that in some counties cases are rotated amongst the various circuit court judges who thus have minimal contact with actual juvenile court processes, instead of an appointed, specialized judge experienced in juvenile and family matters. A juvenile court judge in one county particularly stressed the point that the practice of assigning juvenile cases on a rotating basis among attorneys resulted in a disservice to the young clients and their families. He stated that the attorneys assigned juvenile cases should have at least ten years experience at the bar. The district attorney confirmed this, and observed that in said county only certain attorneys are assigned by the court to represent juveniles. Some caseworkers severly criticize the emphasis attorneys place on "winning" the case. In family matters no one wins. Everyone loses when a family is separated. Attorneys and judges expressed great concern because of the difficulties encountered in trying to remove supervision of a child from child welfare agencies that are reluctant to release children from their custody. They also expressed displeasure with the practice of these agencies, of passing a child from one foster home to another, and for their lack of sensitivity in placing children in homes different from the social milieu to which the child is accustomed. Child welfare agencies are also severly criticized for not endeavoring to preserve families, and for their lack of accountability. The need was expressed for better judicial supervision of these agencies and for restriction of their power.

Most of the material read and abstracted refers to the impact of the various Supreme Court decisions, Gault, Kent, Miranda, Winship, Tinker, McKeiver. As to Gault, its many facets, the six basic rights allegedly denied the respondent, and its far-reaching consequences, special reference should be made to an article by Judge Harlow Lenon (#604). He states that it is his hope that in the final bibliography on Gault there will be one writer who has been adversely critical, and who will have expressed a small, mild, shy doubt about the Court's sociology, its notions of child psychology, its view of the plight of urban adolescents, its statistics, its practical grasp of the juvenile court process, the intimacy of its acquaintance with the low income family, its sense of the incompetence of social workers, its view of the contribution which the Miranda device may make to the child's proud acceptance of the trial process, and a host of other issues it may be considered to have stirred up. Some such articles are included.

The law, the role of the attorney, the interpretation of the rights of the child and the remedies for problems of the child and the family have changed. These and other points are considered such as the process of public intervention into the parent-child relationship. Important questions are raised about the role of judges, child welfare services, probation services, state intervention, foster care, adoption, etc. (Katz, B162). Several articles on the actual procedural practices of the juvenile court and the juvenile justice system are included. (Faust, B91). Some other points examined are as follows:

ADVERSARY PROCESS. The pros and cons of the adversary process are discussed by several authors. A belief is expressed that the adversary process has no place in family, parent/child disputes. However close family members are, the examination and cross-examination, and the admonitions and accusations thrown by opposing attorneys, finally drive families further apart. (Arthur, 26). (Sidman, 901). Attorneys are urged to seek alternative ways of dispute settlement if the juvenile court is to fulfill one of its important promises, i.e. to preserve families. The general belief appears to be that actions involving dependent and neglected children and runaways, should be handled in a manner different from the present practice. Gault places all these in the same category, but the above should be handled differently.

ATTORNEY'S ROLE. The enlarged role of the attorney is analyzed by various authors; some discuss a single-minded adversary stance (Kay, 548), that requires the attorney to do anything within ethical bounds to "win" the case, versus the view that the juvenile attorney's role should be that of participant in a non-adversary, open and conciliatory activity. The attorney may tend to occupy too large a role in the juvenile's life. (Lockwood, 624). Much attention is focused on the need for the attorney to seek alternative dispute settlement in child/parent conflicts. (Coulson, 191). (Isaac, 495). In the narrowest terms, it would seem reasonable to conclude that Gault guarantees the right to counsel only to the juvenile and not to his parents. (Skoler, 908). At the treatment phase, which is perhaps more sociologically oriented than any other phase, whether it concerns treatment of the child or of the family, the attorney must be prepared to participate in the decision-making process. He must also realize that he is in the best position to prod the welfare workers and others to follow their legislated responsibilities. (Murphy, 695). Many articles stress the great need for training in juvenile law and specialization in juvenile court proceedings so that the attorney may be in a better position to represent his client and better able to challenge social and psychological reports. Articles on attorney representation in waiver proceedings are included. (Croxton, 210).

CHILD ABUSE AND PROTECTION. The material on this subject is extensive. Dean Monrad Paulsen has written widely on the subject and researchers should read his earlier articles also: "The legal framework for child protection." Columbia Law Review 66:679-717 (1966), "Child abuse reporting laws - some legislative history." George Washington Law Review 34:482-506 (1966), "The licensing of child-care facilities a look at the law." Alabama Law Review 21 (1):1-24 (1968). Some authors criticize the vague statutes governing child neglect trials and the simultaneous delegation of power to the judiciary which allows the courts to impose on parents their individual notions of child care and morality. (Sullivan, 949). (Katz, B163). Many authors urge that more time be given by investigators to discovering the reason for the abuse and to assisting parents to overcome the problem instead of immediately removing children. (Brown, 96). Frequently the economic adversities, the social pressure and the non-acceptance by neighbors of families whose background is different causes the problem, and the parents may be crying out for help. Social control agencies, such as child welfare agencies, and police, are inclined to identify with the child and criminalization of parents results. Those in the service of protecting children and helping preserve families must seek a better balance between responsibility to the community and responsibility to the family in crisis. Child neglect and delinquency are frequently related to poverty. More control should be asserted over delegate agencies of the juvenile justice system serving the poor. (Katz, B163). (Wheeler, 1044). The policing of families is discussed and the vulnerability of the one-parent family to the charge of child neglect and abuse. (Watts, 1026). Dean Paulsen raises questions about the competency, and skill of the judge and the protective service worker to bring about significant changes in the quality of family life. Some authors discuss the prosecutor's interest in his evidence to "win" the case. (Eger and Popeck, 290). Studies are included on public knowledge and opinions about child abuse. Some authors suggest that the problem is exaggerated when it concerns the older child. (Gil, 380). According to some of the authors, lawmakers need to learn where to draw the line between child abuse and discipline.

CHILD WELFARE AGENCY. Many authors severly criticize child welfare agencies and advocate stronger judicial supervision. The suggestion is advanced that children and families find themselves in captor-captive settings once they become involved with the state welfare agency. (Wineman, 1054). Articles also discuss the dangers of giving authority to inexperienced caseworkers, and the reluctance of intake personnel to relinquish cases to the proper authorities. Authors suggest that certain standards should be set by the courts to prevent such problems. (Watts, 1026).

Court or welfare personnel are too often assumed to be endowed with superior wisdom which empowers them to dictate the modes and goals of living of those they presumably serve. (Sulzer, 950). Social workers need to develop a viable relationship with abusive parents and to seek ways to remedy the family situation. (Court, 193). They should explore ways for positive work with families; breaking them up is not the only solution. The attitude of the welfare agency toward foster parents, and the agency's "authority" over the child is also discussed. (Katz, 545). It is submitted that foster parents be chosen with great care -- the fact that they might be physicians or lawyers does not mean they do not also have internal family problems which might be their reason for wanting a foster child. Some authors believe that intake departments have a strong intimidating effect on parents and tend to elicit false or hurried admissions from them and from children. (Dobson, 245). Caseworkers and supervisors might do families a great service by learning approaches from agencies in other countries. In at least one country, caseworkers are chosen with great care to fit the situation so that the worker is able to communicate with the family members. Caseworkers are matched to a family and to a situation instead of being assigned geographically. The changing of caseworkers at various stages of a case should be avoided at all cost so as to ensure continuity of reporting and stability. The dangers of social reports are discussed by many authors, especially the problem of "hearsay." Some writers suggest that reports be limited. Because of the policy of allowing the caseworker more authority than he/she actually possesses, and without judicial review of possible duress, parents frequently sign away their children. Harsh judgment is passed on the nation's child welfare agencies. (Levine, 615). Welfare laws need to be changed in order to promote family stability. (Foster, 335).

CORRECTIONS. Some selected articles on this subject are included. So much has been written that a bibliography devoted entirely to corrections would be necessary for comprehensive coverage. Some criticism is made of the manner in which the $75 million federal appropriation for juvenile crime prevention is being spent. (McCarty, 633).

DELINQUENCY. This is another subject that needs a bibliography of its own. References to delinquency appear in almost every article. Specific discussions of the juvenile offender and the criminal juvenile offender are included, as well as articles on the etiology and the varieties of delinquency. Authors discuss the "middle-class" delinquent who might be captive to the obligation to go along with the mores and dictates of his peers and his neighborhood, whose behavior is condoned by his parents, and who, therefore, adopts an unserious attitude towards delinquency and thinks himself immune. (Cressey, B65). Articles on the control and prevention of delinquency in this country and in foreign countries are included. (Gukovskaja, 421). (Reifen, 790). (Rowe, 824).

DISCRIMINATION. This subject, in its various forms, arises in the areas of police, child welfare agencies, correctional care, probation and the juvenile court. The agencies of the juvenile justice system are accused especially of discriminating against the child or family of poor social standing, one not wanting to go along with neighborhood norms, one of a different ethnic or cultural background.

DISPOSITION. Disposition is the heart beat of the juvenile court, (Arthur, 22). Training is badly needed in this important phase of the juvenile court proceeding for judges and for attorneys as participant decision-makers.

FAMILY PROBLEMS. A trend seems to appear toward an all-encompassing family court with combined jurisdiction in all child and family matters. A trend is forming toward establishing specialized forums where family matters can be settled instead of in court. (Andrews, B11). (Sidman, 901). (Orlando, 721). More attempts should be made towards conciliation. Ofttimes courts and agencies insist on applying middle-class American standards to low class or non-conforming families, and to families of other cultural backgrounds. (Katz, B162). Sometimes excessive state zeal and coercive state intervention takes place. (Burt, 108). The suggestion is made that the courts should articulate some threshold level of home deficiency justifying judicial and social welfare intervention. (Watts, 1026). Authors are deeply concerned with what they fear may be too powerful authority, arbitrary action and less than high calibre performance on the part of public and private agencies dealing with families. (Katz, B162).

JUDGES. A great need is expressed for specialized judges in juvenile and family courts. (Susman, 953). Among the articles included are some explaining the training of judges in other countries. Some authors observe that because of the nature of juvenile court proceedings, because these are held in closed sessions, the public is not aware of what occurs in the juvenile court or between the officers of the court. I have personally observed the insight and understanding of an experienced juvenile court judge when handling cases involving different cultural backgrounds, and have observed judges whose lack of sensitivity and of knowledge in juvenile and family relations represent a disservice to the community. Judges need specialized training in the use of social and psychological information, and are urged to continue their education if they wish to be capable of making well-informed disposition judgments. Perhaps judges have too powerful authority? (Katz, B162). Maybe we should have a panel of three persons as is the practice in Germany and in Great Britain. (Rowe, 824). (Overland, 726).

LABELING AND STIGMATIZATION. Various articles discuss the danger of this practice on the part of the different agencies in the juvenile justice system.

MINOR'S RIGHTS. There is an increase of the rights of youth, of children's emancipation and children's liberation. Parents' rights are declining. Some authors urge that procedures be devised to build essential personality strengths for youth. (Dunham, 267). (Loeb, B194). In some articles emphasis is placed on the difference between the "best interests" of the child and the "child's interests, i.e. his wishes." Authors also discuss the "win" or "lose" aspect of a case as opposed to morals.

PARENT-CHILD RELATIONSHIP. The parent-child relationship, although frequently referred to in quasi-sacred terminology (Katz, 544), is the least secure from outside interference. The husband-wife relations and sibling relations are much more immune from governmental intervention. What happens to individual rights when the state uses its authority to invade the parent-child relationship? Is the court, when exercising its power to separate the child from the parents, in effect, punishing both parent and child? (Dobson, 245). The child's need for the relationship is stressed. The destruction caused by judicial or agency intervention, and the myth of agency expertise is discussed. Whenever the state attempts to intervene in the parent-child relationship a conflict develops between the state's interest in promoting what the social worker or the attorney believe is the child's welfare and the parent's right to raise a family. Often an invasion of privacy and a disruption of family life may occur before judicial intervention. There should be due process rights for parents subjected to child welfare investigations. Agencies should be required to demonstrate affirmative attempts toward rehabilitative treatment for families to avoid severing the fragile parent-child relationship. (Levine, 615). Courts will have to look at the consequences of state intervention. (Foster, 336). Filial deprivation is examined (Dobson, 245), and the difficulties a mother will experience when she is expected to resume "normal patterns" after a child previously removed is returned, should be seriously considered prior to removal. (Jenkins, 505). It is of national priority that lawyers and legislators undertake to deal with the problem of the broken family and the social disintegration that it reflects. (Mathias, 663). The validity of the entire process of public intervention into the parent-child relationship, and into the procedures in the handling of neglect/abuse cases is examined also. (Katz, B163). (Weiss, 1034).

PARENTS' RIGHTS. These appear to be on the decline. (Hall, 424). Conflict arises between the parents' rights and the child's rights. Frequently, it appears, the parent/respondent is denied certain rights but is expected to live up to his/her responsibilities, and is faced with liability for his/her child's act. (Eekelaar, 288). Sometimes the state imposes its individual notion of child care and morality on parents; does it have the right? (Sullivan, 949). Authors suggest that parents' rights are disregarded by the child welfare agency. (Levine, 615). Some articles discuss the "unfit" parent. (Dobson, 245). The impact of the fourteenth amendment on substantive and procedural rights presently denied the respondent/parent in neglect proceedings is discussed. Should provision be made for counsel for parent/respondent in neglect cases? (796).

PROMISES OF THE JUVENILE COURT. This is one of the most widely discussed subjects in the articles. (Paulsen, 742).

THE POLICE AND THE CHILD. THE SCHOOLS AND THE CHILD. Authors point out that frequently children are so intimidated by police, social workers and school officials that they are not aware of their rights, and do not exercise their right to remain silent. I know personally of a youngster put under such pressure by a policeman and a school vice-principal that the words, "Well, if I have to I'll speak, but I don't want to..." were uttered, and promptly erased from the tape by the policeman who muttered something about having to protect himself from the accusation of "police brutality." Police should not be responsible for cases of neglect or child abuse unless the child is in immediate danger. (Newman, 707). Discussions on search and seizure, and on long hair and personal appearance, are included. (Thornberry, 980).

"WRONGFUL LIFE." Trends in present legal thinking now appearing in articles concern torts, children suing parents for damage for wrongful life. (Cutshaw, 214). (Tedeschi, 968).

HOW TO USE THE INDEX

The index is a sampling of the contents of the bibliography and includes only those subjects which appeared to be most prominent in the articles and books. Some are indexed under several different headings and subheadings to assist lay people since some headings are more appropriate to lawyers. Researchers should check the abstracts and articles themselves for further references. A number is assigned to each abstract, and "B" is included to indicate books. An attempt has been made to give additional breakdown by country and by state. The subjects are broken down as much as possible to assist non-law users. It is hoped that this index may inspire articles on topics which require research. Cross-references will not necessarily be found under exactly the same heading; as with all reference tools readers are encouraged to use their imagination, and to accept the fact that no bibliography can be compiled completely without errors. This one is not an exception despite the roughly 1000 hours of work invested in it. Some articles and books were easy to index, others defy a clear-cut entry. The problem of finding suitable sub-headings was the most difficult.

It is my hope that this little volume will serve as a reference tool.

Helena P. von Pfeil, B.A., B.S., M.L.S.
Assistant Law Librarian, University of Oregon
School of Law

Eugene, Oregon
May, 1974

ACKNOWLEDGMENTS

In the course of compiling this annotated bibliography, the author has accumulated a list of debts to numerous people who have given their time in various ways.

My thanks go to Senator Bette Browne for her interest in my first survey in Oregon in 1969, in connection with the impact of Gault in this state, and to Dr. James Levine, Professor of Political Science, presently at Northwestern University. Professor Levine encouraged me to read vastly in the area of juvenile rights, and to compile an extensive questionnaire which was submitted to a random sample of attorneys and judges throughout Oregon to collect the data for the survey.

Anyone who works in the field of juvenile law cannot be without debt to Dean Monrad Paulsen, University of Virginia School of Law, to Judge William Fort, and to Senator Bette Browne, editor of the Juvenile Court Digest. I am deeply honored that these three people took the time to write the kind words expressed in the foreword and in the preface. I trust that they will find the bibliography a useful tool as they continue writing in the important area of juvenile law and child/parent rights.

Very special thanks go to Dean Elizabeth Findly, School of Librarianship, University of Oregon, wonderful teacher and friend, for her tireless encouragement and for her suggestions. To thank Dr. Lucile Aly, Professor of English, dear friend, for her helpful review and corrections, and for always being ready to assist at short notice, is but a minimal expression of my gratitude.

I am indebted to Professor Donald Brodie, University of Oregon School of Law, who introduced me to the study of juvenile law in his excellent course in Domestic Relations, for the many hours he has devoted to reviewing the index several times. He was extremely helpful, and I do thank him.

I would like to mention Judge Felton, Domestic Relations Judge, Marion County, Judge Harlow Lenon and Judge Dahl, Juvenile Court, Multnomah County, and to thank also attorneys Allan Coons and Douglas McCool, of Eugene, Oregon, for their encouragement, for their quick grasp and understanding of litigants' needs, and for their sensitivity to the complexities of, and to the devastating effects on families of decisions not thoroughly thought out and envisioned in light of all possible consequences.

Much appreciation goes to my colleagues Ronald Cherry and Kay Ollerenshaw, University of Oregon Law Library faculty, and to Daveta Cooper and Virginia Manning, clerical assistants, for their support.

Without the encouragement of all the wonderful people with whom I come in daily contact in the law library, including the students who have used the bibliography in its rough form, I would not have had the stamina to finish the arduous work.

The final stage of this work was made possible by a Faculty Research Award granted me by the Office of Scientific and Scholarly Research, Graduate School, University of Oregon.

JUVENILE RIGHTS SINCE 1967

An Annotated, Indexed Bibliography of Selected Articles and Books

1 ADELSON, JOSEPH, and LYNETTE BEALL. Adolescent perspectives on law and government. Law and Society Review 4:495-504 (1970)

The research reported in this article aims at a study of the acquisition of political philosophy during the adolescent years. Youngsters were interviewed in England, Germany and the United States.

2 Admissibility of confessions obtained in violation of the juvenile code. Washington University Law Quarterly 112-120 (1967)

A discussion of State v. Arbeiter, 408 S.W.2d 26 (Mo.1966). (44 refs.)

3 ALAN, EBER. Application of the rules against search and seizure to juvenile delinquency proceedings. Buffalo Law Review 16:462-473 (1967)

A discussion of the application of rules against illegal search and seizure. (107 refs.)

4 ALERS, MIRIAM S. Transfer of jurisdiction from juvenile to criminal court. Crime and Delinquency 19:519-527 (1973)

The author believes that the transfer hearing should be treated as a criminal stage in a juvenile's case. Transfer of an accused juvenile from the jurisdiction of a juvenile court to that of a criminal court removes from the accused the rights and protections available to juveniles as a class. Lack of counsel during the transfer hearing, in the absence of a voluntary and intelligently given waiver, should be sufficient to invalidate such transfer for failure to conduct the hearing in accordance with due process. (44 refs.)

5 ALLEN, TIM. A dilemma in public high schools: school board authority v. the constitutional right of students to wear long hair. Louisiana Law Review 33:697-707 (1973)

The author submits that the "liberty" concept of the due process clause of the fourteenth amendment provides the source of a "fundamental" right to wear one's hair in the length he chooses. (63 refs.)

6 ALLENSTEIN, MORTON B. The attorney-probation officer relationship. Crime and Delinquency 16:181-184 (1970)

This article points out that the attorney working in the interests of his client, and the probation officer who must balance the rights of society against concern for the defendant, have many opportunities to meet to the advantage of client and society, and to exchange ideas.

7 ALLISON, JUNIUS L. The lawyer and his juvenile court client. Crime and Delinquency 12:165-169 (1966)

An early article on the attorney's role in juvenile court. (14 refs.)

8 ALLMAN, ROBERT L., II. Admissibility of juvenile confessions: is an intelligent and knowing waiver of constitutional rights possible without adult guidance? University of Pittsburgh Law Review 34:321-328 (1972)

A discussion of Commonwealth v. Moses, 446 Pa. 350, 287 A.2d 131 (1971). (47 refs.)

9 ALPER, BENEDICT S. The children's court at three score and ten: will it survive Gault? Albany Law Review 34:46-68 (1969)

The author argues that by reason of its unique position, by reason of the distinctive vulnerability, and because of the enormous potential represented by the young people who come within its jurisdiction, the juvenile court can yet prove to be the most important link in that chain of services for dealing with the alarming increase in delinquency. (76 refs.)

Peru

10 ALTAMIRANO, J.G. Profilaxis de la delincuencia de menores. Revista Juridica del Peru 20:73 (1969)

11 ALTMAN, MICHAEL L. The effect of the Miranda case on confessions in the juvenile court. American Criminal Law Quarterly 5:79-83 (1967)

The author argues that the Miranda decision can be applied, and should be applied, to juvenile cases. He contends that it is erroneous to state that the fifth amendment does not apply to juveniles. (25 refs.)

Virg.Is./U.S.

12 Appellate review for juveniles: a "right" to a transcript. Columbia Human Rights Law Review 4:485-496

This article considers the right to transcripts vis-a-vis due process, and examines the equal protection ramifications of the statutory silence in fourteen states and the Virgin Islands regarding transcripts of juvenile hearings. (51 refs.)

13 The applicability of the fourth amendment exclusionary rule to juveniles in delinquency proceedings. Columbia Human Rights Law Review 4:417-449 (1972)

The thesis of this article is that the fourth amendment's proscription of "unreasonable searches and seizures" and its "correlative" remedy, the exclusionary rule, should be extended to juvenile delinquency proceedings. The author states that this application should be held to be a constitutional requirement. (184 refs.)

Estonia

14 ANDERSEN, W. Jugendkriminalität in der Estnischen Sozialistischen Sowjetrepublik. Monatschrift für Kriminologie und Strafrechtsreform 54:176-192 (1971)

15 ARIESSOHN, RICHARD M. Offense vs. offender in juvenile court. Juvenile Justice 23(2):17-22 (1972)

This study indicates that the nature of the offense may have less impact on the disposition of the case by the time the matter comes before the court, than at other levels of the juvenile justice system. The philosophical differences between judge and probation officer suggest that much independent judgment exists in the juvenile justice system. (19 refs.)

California

16 ARIESSOHN, RICHARD M., and FREDERICK I. CLOSSON. Alternatives to juvenile detention. California Youth Authority Quarterly 24:17-26 (1971)
Juvenile detention in San Diego county (California) is examined, in conjunction with a Supreme Court decision. Alternatives are suggested.

17 ARMSTRONG, RALPH. Community resources in family counseling. Juvenile Court Judges' Journal 19(1):16-19 (1968)

18 ARNOLD, MARLENE. Juvenile justice in transition. UCLA Law Review 14:1144-1158 (1967)
The author raises questions as to whether the juvenile court is fulfilling its function. Included is a discussion of parens patriae, fundamental fairness, and the best interests of the juvenile. (72 refs.)

19 ARNOLD, WILLIAM R. Race and ethnicity relative to other factors in juvenile court dispositions. American Journal of Sociology 77(2):211-227 (1971)
The juvenile court records of an average city are examined, and it is concluded that there is discrimination against minorities. (18 refs.)

20 ARON, PETER S., and MARTIN L. KATZ. Corporal punishment in the public schools, Murphy v. Kerrigan. Harvard Civil Rights-Civil Liberties Law Review 6:583-594 (1971)
The question discussed is whether corporal punishment is cruel and unusual within the meaning of the eighth amendment, and whether it could be declared unconstitutional as violating the due process clause of the fourteenth amendment. (77 refs.)

New York

21 ARONSON, SIDNEY H., and CLARENCE C. SHERWOOD. Problems in social action research. Social Work 12:89-96 (1967)
The results of efforts by the research branch of an anti-delinquency project, Opportunities for Youth, Department of Sociology, New York University, to evaluate a group of demonstration programs.

22 ARTHUR, LINDSAY G. Disposition – the forgotten focus. Juvenile Court Judges' Journal 21(3):71-73 (1970)
The "crying need" is for training juvenile court judges in the dispositional process. The essence, the elemental distinction of the juvenile court is the disposition. (20 refs.)

23 ARTHUR, LINDSAY G. A revised philosophy of the juvenile court. Juvenile Court Judges' Journal 18(1):31-34 (1967)
Two recommendations of the President's Commission on Law Enforcement and the Administration of Justice are examined.

24 ARTHUR, LINDSAY G. Should children be as equal as people? North Dakota Law Review 45:204-221 (1969)

Various points are listed by the author, and explored:
I. Equal protection - A. Counsel? B. Care?
II. Equal privacy - A. Silence? B. Hearsay? C. Search? D. Arrest?
(50 refs.)

25 ARTHUR, LINDSAY G. The Uniform Juvenile Court Act. Juvenile Court Judges' Journal 19(4):153-160 (1969)

A review of the protective rights, pendente orders, court control and jurisdictions as outlined in the Uniform Juvenile Court Act are described.

26 ARTHUR, LINDSAY G., and THOMAS J. KALITOWSKI. Child vs. parent: residence, education and dates. Juvenile Justice 24(1):34-37 (1973)

However much a parent and child may love each other, once the wheels of the court are set in motion, the admonitions and commands of attorneys, examination and cross-examination, with their attendant accusations and exaggerations, take their toll and inevitably the family is driven further apart. The authors give a summary of questions raised in court, and the result of these questions. (15 refs.)

Germany

27 ASMUSSEN, H. Jugendkriminalität aus der Sicht eines Jugendrichters. Zentralblatt für Jugendrecht und Jugendwohlfahrt 59:333-338 (1972)

28 ATKINSON, KAREN L. Constitutional rights of juveniles: Gault and its application. William and Mary Law Review 9:492-508 (1967)

A brief history of the juvenile court movement is followed by an analysis of the Gault decision and its implications. (97 refs.)

29 The attorney-parent relationship in the juvenile court. St. Louis University Law Journal 12:603-630 (1968)

The attorney who is accustomed to the normal adversary situation will undoubtedly be confused by the tripartite situation in which he is involved in the juvenile court. The author discusses the parents' interests, the child's interests, and the state's interests. (77 refs.)

California

30 AUBREY, ERNEST L. The nature, scope and significance of pre-trial detention of juveniles in California. Black Law Journal 1:160-170 (1971)

The author considers questions regarding the California laws governing juveniles. Questions in connection with a minor's right to bail, due process of law, equal protection of the laws, and laws relating to the black community, are discussed. (55 refs.)

California

31 AUSTIN, KENNETH M., and FRED R. SPEIDEL. Thunder: an alternative to juvenile court appearance. California Youth Authority Quarterly 24:13-16 (1971)

The San Bernardine County (California) probation department's intensive treatment program utilizing short-term family group counseling is described as an alternative to juvenile court processes.

Oregon

32 Automobile negligence cases and the parental immunity doctrine. Willamette Law Journal 5:140-148 (1968)

Chafin v. Chafin, 239 Or. 374 (1964) is discussed. The author contends that in light of the reasoning of the Oregon court in its prior consideration of the doctrine, and of other state courts in recent decisions, that Chafin should have abolished the immunity doctrine as it is applied to automobile negligence cases. (49 refs.)

Texas

33 AYRES, JACK, Jr. Juvenile due process Texas-style: fruit of the poisonous tree resweetened. Baylor Law Review 24:71-85 (1972)

The 1967 amendments to the Juvenile Act of Texas are discussed to show that the balance sought by the act has been placed in serious jeopardy by recent decisions of the court of criminal appeals in which juvenile offenders have had jurisdiction of the juvenile court waived for trial as adults. (31 refs.)

Belgium

34 BAERT, G. Beschouwingen over de burgerrechtlijke bepalingen van de wet van 8 april 1965 op de jeugdbescherming. Rechtskundig Weekblad 31:1610-1636 (1968)

35 A balancing approach to the grant of procedural rights in the juvenile court. Northwestern University Law Review 64:87-115 (1969)

This Comment considers the reconciliation of the institution of the juvenile court and the individual rights of the juvenile. Selected procedural rights granted as a result of the Gault decision are covered. (127 refs.)

District of Columbia

36 BAMFORD, BARBARA. D.C. juvenile court: social agency or court of law? D.C. Bar Journal 35:46-57 (1968)

This article is an attempt to determine whether the due process standards specified in Gault, and other standards which that decision did not resolve, are in conflict with the claimed substantive benefits of the informal juvenile process in the District of Columbia. The present system is reviewed, and its compatability with the constitutional standards of criminal procedure is judged. (34 refs.)

37 BANKS, RUTH R., and STEPHEN B. DUNBAR, Jr. Due process and the juvenile offender: the scope of In Re Gault. Howard Law Journal 14:150-161 (1968)

A discussion of whether the state court should extend the constitutional protections provided by Gault to the pre-judicial stage of the juvenile process; or whether the juvenile will otherwise be forever victimized by the discretion permitted by the parens patriae doctrine at the pre-judicial stage. (81 refs.)

Oregon

38 BANTA, RONALD T. Divorce - the welfare and best interest of the child. Willamette Law Journal 5:82-92 (1968)

The purpose of this Note is to analyze what the court means by the "best interest of the child." Confining itself to divorce cases, this Note shows that the Oregon Supreme Court displays its use of standard in a variety of ways, each depending for its application on the factual setting of the case. Some Supreme Court opinions are discussed. (55 refs.)

39 BARD, RUTH. The now juvenile court. The Judges' Journal 10:40-41 (1971)

A detailed description of changes in juvenile court procedure since recent Supreme Court decisions.

40 BARKDULL, THOMAS H., Jr. An appeals judge looks at the juvenile court process. Juvenile Court Judges' Journal 183:96-99 (1967)

(4 refs.)

41 BARRETT, ROY L. "Delinquent child": a legal term without meaning. Baylor Law Review 21:352-371 (1969)

The difficulties in the definition of the term are discussed, and the far-reaching and adverse consequences of being adjudged a delinquent are pointed out. Various state statutes are cited, and the author includes a table indicating the results of a comparative study of the various types of conduct which constitute delinquency according to the juvenile codes of the fifty states. (68 refs.)

California

42 BARTLETT, CAROLE A. Intestate succession claims of illegitimate children in California. UCD Law Review 6:217-239 (1973)

The question of equal protection and just treatment in regard to persons of illegitimate birth and their inheritance rights is discussed. (102 refs.)

43 BASSIOUNI, M.C. The challenge of delinquency in a free society: juvenile philosophy and Gault revisited. In Illinois Institute of Continuing Legal Education, Illinois Bar Center, Vol. 6(4):97-138 (1968)

Germany

44 BAUER, G. Die Aufklärung von Triebverbrechen minderjährigen Delinquenten. Kriminalbioligische Gegenwartsfragen 9:235-262 (1969)

Germany

45 BAUER, G. Kriminalpolizei und minderjähridge Straftäter. Kriminalistik 25:527-531 (1971)

New Jersey

46 BAUMGART, ELLIOT M. Split calendar sifts out dangerous delinquents. Trial Magazine 4:13-15 (1968)

The author presumes that, since it seems that the New Jersey supreme court has minimized the administrative problem of supplying counsel by giving to the juvenile court judge power to pre-judge the gravity of his cases, only those juveniles whose cases are placed on the formal calendar will be entitled to assigned counsel since they are the only ones in jeopardy of institutional commitment.

47 BAYH, BIRCH. Juveniles v. justice. Columbia Human Rights Law Review 4:309-323 (1972)
(35 refs.)

48 BAYH, BIRCH. Toward juvenile justice. American Scholar 40:662-666 (1971)
McKeiver is discussed, and the author proposes a ten-point program which he believes can be implemented jointly by juvenile court judges and by Congress.

49 BAYH, BIRCH. Ten building blocks. Trial 7(5):13-14 (1971)
Judges are urged to investigate the administration of juvenile justice in its entirety, and to make public their findings.

50 BAYH, BIRCH. A time for improvement in the juvenile justice system. Juvenile Court Judges' Journal 22(2):30-32 (1971)
The chairman of the U.S. Senate Judiciary Committee, which is empowered to investigate juvenile delinquency, states that the McKeiver case may improve the juvenile court system, and save many children from inadequate correctional centers.

51 BAZELON, DAVID L. Beyond control of the juvenile court. Juvenile Court Judges' Journal 21(2):42-45, 50 (1970)
An address on the prevention of juvenile delinquency.

52 BAZELON, DAVID L. Justice for juveniles. New Republic 156:13-16 (April 22, 1967)
The legal justification of the juvenile court system is considered.

53 BAZELON, DAVID L. Racism, classism, and the juvenile process. Judicature 53:373-378 (1970)
The environment that breeds juvenile offenders cannot be altered by judges who must confront the gap between ideals and reality. (13 refs.)

54 BAZELON, DAVID L. The right to treatment - a symposium. The Georgetown Law Journal 57:676-679 (1969)
The author believes that a right to treatment exists under which the mentally ill, juveniles, narcotic addicts, and alcoholics involuntarily confined, may challenge their confinement against the promises of treatment by legislatures. (3 refs.)

55 BECKER, THOMAS T. Due process and child protective proceedings: state intervention in family relations on behalf of neglected children. Cumberland-Samford Law Review 2:247-265 (1971)

This article is intended to stimulate interest in legislation designed to provide due process of law for respondents in proceedings to determine child neglect, without sacrificing on the altar of due process the rights of the neglected child. (66 refs.)

Germany

56 BECKER, W. Jugendschutz und Pornographie-verbot. Film und Recht 15:318-325 (1971)

57 BEKEMEYER, DENNIS L. A child's rights against his parent: evolution of the parental immunity doctrine. University of Illinois Law Forum 805-816 (1967)

A discussion of parental immunity doctrine and cases challenging it. (84 refs.)

California

58 BEKER, JEROME, and DORIS S. HEYMAN. A critical appraisal of the California differential treatment typology of adolescent offenders. Criminology 10:3-59 (May 1972)

(34 refs.)

59 BELFATTO, HORACE S. The constitution in the juvenile court. New York Law Forum 13:1-15 (1967)

Judge Balfatto, in his address given some months before the U.S. Supreme Court delivered its opinion on the Gault case, expresses some thoughts in respect to the juvenile's right to counsel, sets forth reasons why, in some instances, the juvenile should not be represented by counsel. (76 refs.)

Colorado

60 BELL, BRIAN M., and JAMES RODE. In Re Gault and the Colorado Children's Code. Denver Law Journal 44:644-660 (1967)

This Note examines the Colorado Children's Code in depth, and points out the areas in which it has embodied the principles of due process as enunciated in Gault. (141 refs.)

61 BELZER, ROBERT A. Child v. Parent: erosion of the immunity rule. Hastings Law Journal 19:201-222 (1967)

A history of the development and the erosion of the American rule that a parent is not liable to an unemancipated minor child for torts committed by the parent against the child. In this Comment the author discusses willful or malicious torts; emancipation; persons in loco parentis; business negligence; third party liability; actions commenced when parent or child is dead; wrongful death; liability insurance; the modern trends. (143 refs.)

62 BENDER, LAURETTA. A psychiatrist looks at deviancy as a factor in juvenile delinquency. Federal Probation 32(2):35-42 (1968)

(32 refs.)

63 BERENSON, HARVEY. The lawyer in juvenile court. Journal of the Kansas Bar Association 38:15-18, 60-64 (1969)
(56 refs.)

64 BERENSON, HARVEY S., and HELEN MOUNTFORD. Waiver of jurisdiction: the last resort of the juvenile court. University of Kansas Law Review 18:55-70 (1969)
A discussion of the various factors which influence waiver of jurisdiction. (105 refs.)

65 BERKOWITZ, LOUIS, and JACOB CHWAST. Community center program for the prevention of school dropouts. Federal Probation 31(4):36-40 (1967)
(3 refs.)

Israel

66 BERMAN, YITZCHAK. Size of population and juvenile delinquency in cities in Israel. Criminology 11:105-113 (1973)
This study shows that the relationship of population size to juvenile delinquency is determined by various other factors, e.g. immigrant group, neighborhood, etc., and not by population size itself. (18 refs.)

67 BERNS, ALAN. Juvenile detention: an eyewitness account. Columbia Human Rights Law Review 4:303-308 (1972)
(6 refs.)

68 BERNSTEIN, BARRY, and I. OSSER ABE. Juries for juveniles. University of San Fernando Valley Law Review 1:73-77 (1967)
(13 refs.)

Pennsylvania

69 BERSON, LENORA. Police in the schools: politics in Philadelphia. City 32-34 (Jan/Feb. 1972)
A discussion of the police in Philadelphia public schools.

Texas

70 BERWICK, BRIAN E., and CAROL OPPENHEIMER. Marriage, pregnancy and the right to go to school. Texas Law Review 50:1196-1228 (1972)
Courts have begun to look closely at school rules that withhold educational benefits from pregnant and married students. The policies of the Texas Education Agency are discussed. (170 refs.)

71 BESHAROV, DOUGLAS J. A proposal to reorient the juvenile court process. Family Law Quarterly 7:243-249 (1973)
A discussion of the need for a family-oriented service offering out-of-court help for the child and the family, and the role of the court in relation to such a service. The author states that the juvenile court should be used with more discrimination, since inappropriate societal intervention is often worse than no help at all. The juvenile court fails to deal with the fundamental dynamics of human behavior. The goal should be family preservation. (16 refs.)

Germany

72 BEST, P. The role of the public prosecutor for juveniles in criminal proceedings. Kriminologisches Journal 3(314):167-184 (1971)

This case study in a fairly large German city deals with the interactions of the public prosecutor with juvenile court judges, police, social workers, etc.

Texas

73 BILLINGS, ROBERT B. The new juvenile delinquent law. Texas Bar Journal 31: 203-204, 242-246 (1968)

The far-reaching changes which Kent and Gault brought into the Juvenile Delinquency Act in Texas are discussed. (30 refs.)

74 BLAINE, HOWARD T., and MORRIS E. CHAFETZ. Dependency conflict and sex-role identity in drinking delinquents. Quarterly Journal of Studies on Alcohol 32: 1025-1039 (1972)

The results of a study of boys whose misbehavior was accompanied by the use of alcohol.

75 BLANK, ROBERT H. Constitutional law: the jury and the juvenile court. University of Florida Law Review 24:385-392 (1972)

The lack of a definitive standard has split lower courts on the question of a juvenile's right to trial by jury. A discussion of McKeiver v. Pennsylvania, 403 U.S. 528 (1971). (64 refs.)

76 BLINICK, MICHAEL. Delinquency and justice. The Catholic Lawyer 14:233-245 (1968)

This article explores how the system - especially its key institution, the juvenile court - tends to increase rather than lessen illegal behavior. (49 refs.)

77 BLUMBERG, ABRAHAM S. Lawyers with convictions. Transaction 4:18-24 (1967)

A poor defendant with a lawyer might not be much better off than one without a lawyer, and the recent U.S. Supreme Court decision extending the right to counsel, might have a radically different effect from that intended or anticipated.

California

78 BOCHES, RALPH E. Juvenile justice in California: a re-evaluation. Hastings Law Journal 19:47-104 (1967)

Juvenile court developments since 1961 are briefly outlined. An analysis of the juvenile court process, including a chart, is given. Double jeopardy and appellate court proceedings are discussed. A summary of recommendations is included. (303 refs.)

79 BOCK, GEORGE M. Admissibility of juvenile's statements in criminal prosecutions. Missouri Law Review 36:382-388 (1971)

A discussion of State v. Sinderson, 445 S.W.2d 486 (Mo.1970). (49 refs.)

80 BODENHEIMER, BRIGITTE M. The uniform child custody jurisdiction act. Family Law Quarterly 3:304-330 (1969)
(53 refs.)

81 BOGEN, DAVID. Drug abuse cases - their regime of care in detention: problems they pose for detention security control. Juvenile Court Judges' Journal 19(2):61-62 (1968)

82 BORCHARD, I. Unterhaltsprozesse deutscher unehelicher Kinder in der Vereinigten Staaten von Nordamerika. Zentralblatt fuer Jugendrecht und Jugendwohlfahrt 56:259-263 (1969)

Ger./Switz.

83 BOSCH, F.W. Das neue Recht des Nichtehelichen Kindes in Deutschland. Ein Vergleich mit schweizerischen Recht und schweizerischen Reformbestrebungen. Zeitschrift für das Gesamte Familienrecht 17:157-167 (1970)

84 BOSLEY, WADE R. Child support - protecting the child's interests. Family Law Quarterly 4:230-279 (1970)
The purpose of this article is to explore, and to make attorneys aware of the avenues that are open to them to make sure a child is getting the benefits of child support payments made in his behalf. (199 refs.)

85 BOTTOMS, A.E., et al. Children, young persons and the courts: a survey of the new law. Criminal Law Review 368-395 (1970)

Illinois

86 BOWLER, CLARA ANN. Child welfare reform: the impossible takes longer in Illinois. Loyola University Law Journal 3:49-70 (1972)
This article surveys the origin and effect of the new Department of Children and Family Services in the Illinois child welfare system. (80 refs.)

87 BOXER, KAREN. Juvenile defendant in federal system not entitled to counsel or hearing at time determination is made by the attorney general to proceed against him as an adult. Columbia Law Review 73:1331-1341 (1973)
A discussion of Cox v. United States, 473 F2d 334, 335 (4th Cir. 1973). (57 refs.)

88 BRADEMAS, JOHN. New directions in the control and prevention of juvenile delinquency. Juvenile Court Judges' Journal 20(3):102-104 (1969)

Colorado

89 BRAGG, DOUGLAS E. Delinquency jurisdiction in Colorado: Garcia and the children's code. University of Colorado Law Review 40:80-96 (1967)
A statuory history of the Colorado juvenile court is followed by a discussion of Garcia v. District Court, 157 Colo. 432, 403 P.2d 215 (1965), and the "Lange" case People ex.rel. Marles v. District Court, 420 P.2d 236(Colo.1966). (80 refs.)

90 BRAUN, RICHARD L. Auto theft - one thousand a day. Juvenile Court Judges' Journal 18(2):72-74 (1967)

91 BRENNAN, WILLIAM C. The probation officer's perception of the attorney's role in juvenile court. Crime and Delinquency Quarterly 16:172-180 (1970)

The Gault decision has resulted in the widespread use of attorneys in juvenile court. The purpose of this study was to examine the impact of this change on a group of 32 juvenile probation officers who had attended special institutes related to the lawyer's entrance into juvenile court. Many far-reaching inferences can be drawn from this study, particularly with regard to the nature of future professional education (both law and social work).

92 BRENNAN, WILLIAM C., and S.K. KHINDUKA. Role expectations of social workers and lawyers in the juvenile court. Crime and Delinquency Quarterly 16:191-201 (1970)

On the basis of date collected through a questionnaire from a sample of social workers and lawyers in a midwestern state, this study identifies the areas and extent of congruity and incongruity between the mutual expectations and perceptions of the two professions. (9 refs.)

93 BRENNAN, WILLIAM J., Jr. Court decisions and crime. Crime and Delinquency 15:449-458 (1969)

(27 refs.)

94 BRISCOE, O.V. The juvenile court: Judge Jeffreys of Father Christmas? Medicine, Science, and the Law 10:149-157 (1970)

95 BROWN, HOWARD G. Juvenile courts and the Gault decision: background and promise. Children 15(3):86-96 (May-June 1968)

Gault has brought children under the Bill of Rights. How this affects the social purpose of juvenile courts is discussed by two lawyers. (13 refs.)

96 BROWN, JOHN A., and ROBERT DANIELS. Some observations on abusive parents. Child Welfare 47:89-94 (1968)

A study shows that when abusive parents are viewed dynamically a clearer picture of child abuse emerges. Child abuse is invariably accompanied by other problems in the family, and the dynamics which lead to abuse parallel unresolved problems of the parent which the child, by his behavior, reactivates. These dynamics may be a configuration of psychological needs, intellectual limitations, social pressure, and economic adversities. Social workers generally show greater identification with the child, and tend to overlook some of the positive work which can be done with the parent - e.g. resolving the financial difficulties. If this tendency is not recognized, and improvements made, the social workers become punishing agents rather than helpful professionals. Supportive techniques are needed instead of separating families.

Ohio

97 BROWN, NANCY G. Bastardy proceedings - the expansion of the rights of illegitimates. Ohio State Law Journal 34:428-433 (1973)

A discussion of Franklin v. Julian, 30 Ohio St.2d 228, 283 N.E.2d 813 (1972). The author believes that this case heralds the realization of the Ohio supreme court of the import of the Supreme Court decisions expanding the rights of illegitimate children. (32 refs.)

98 BROWN, ROWLINE H., et al. Medical and legal aspects of the battered child syndrome. Chicago-Kent Law Review 50:45-84 (1973)

This article explores both the medical and legal aspects of child abuse with particular attention directed to the problems faced by the attorney involved in proceedings concerning child abuse. (176 refs.)

Oregon

99 BROWNE, ELIZABETH W. and WILLIAM S. FORT. Willamette Law Journal 5:1-27 (1968)

The authors discuss the impact of the six basic rights stressed in the Gault decision on Oregon law: notice of charges; right to counsel; right to confrontation and cross-examination; privilege against self-incrimination; right to a transcript of the proceedings; right to appellate review. Retroactivity, waiver, disposition, and the impact of Gault on mental commitment proceedings and detention are also discussed. (122 refs.)

Germany

100 BRUNNER, R. Jugendrichter und Jugendgerichtshelfner nach 20 Jahren Jugendgerichtgesetz. Zentralblatt für Jugendrecht und Jugendwohlfahrt 60:53-60 (1973)

Germany

101 BRUSTEN, M. Criminalization caused by social agencies. An analysis of child welfare office records. Neue Praxis I:174-189 (1972)

An analysis of child welfare office records shows that the definitions used by social control agencies such as the child welfare office, the court and the police, define the personality traits of juveniles in such a way that labeling results.

Oklahoma

102 BRYANT, KEITH L., Jr. The juvenile court movement: Oklahoma as a case study. Social Science Quarterly 49:368-376 (1968)

The history of the juvenile court movement in Oklahoma. (40 refs.)

103 BUICKHUISEN, W., and R.W. JONGMAN. A legalistic classification of juvenile delinquents. British Journal of Criminology 10:109-123 (1970)

A discussion of the classification of offences by juveniles. (6 refs.)

104 BURD, LEE R. Waiver of jurisdiction in the juvenile court: another Gault question still unanswered. South Dakota Law Review 15:376-385 (1970)

This paper examines the trends in present case law affecting the constitutional rights of juveniles with reference to the beclouded area of pre-adjudicative hearings, specifically the waiver of jurisdiction proceedings. (47 refs.)

105 BURDICK, EUGENE A. The uniform juvenile court act. Pennsylvania Bar Association Quarterly 40:47-56 (1968)

The following areas in the act are examined: accusatory and dispositional phases of cases; the new category of "unruly child"; conditions for transfer to adult court; the new category of "deprived child"; optional use of referees; powers and duties of probation officers; auditions for informal adjustments; custody and detention; procedural requirements; alternative disposition for different types of children; interstate cooperation; optional provisions re automobile traffic offenses; termination of parental rights; guardian Ad Litim; destruction of court records of rehabilitated child; court's contempt power; appeals; procedural rule making. (17 refs.)

Switzerland

106 BÜRGIN, D. Die Funktion des Jugendpsychiaters im Schweitzerischen Jugendstrafsrecht. Recht der Jugend 20:335-339 (1972)

107 BURLAND, J. ALEXIS, et al. Child abuse: one tree in the forest. Child Welfare 585-592 (1973)

A review of the records of 28 children who experienced parental abuse or severe neglect indicates the complexity of the parent-child relationship, and the necessity of meeting the child's needs and the parent's dependency needs, rather than focusing exclusively on the abuse itself as the major concern.

108 BURT, ROBERT A. Forcing protection on children and their parents: the impact of Wyman v. James. Michigan Law Review 69:1259-1310 (1971)

This article focuses on one of the concerns implicated in Wyman: the government's power to force assistance for the protection of children, when they or their parents are unwilling to accept that assistance. An analysis and comparison of the approaches to the rights of juveniles laid down in In Re Gault, on the one hand, and in Wyman V. James, on the other. (146 refs.)

109 BURTON, BRUCE F. Interstate placement of juveniles. Columbia Journal of Law and Social Problems 3:171-195 (1967)

Two significant trends have developed because of the need to cope with the situations arising in placement of juveniles. The horizontal expansion on the state level from the local community through cooperative arrangements is discussed. (180 refs.)

Wisconsin

110 BUSS, CHARLES A. Waiver of jurisdiction in Wisconsin juvenile courts. Wisconsin Law Review 551-555 (1968)

The results of a study of the factors considered by Wisconsin judges in contemplation of waiver, are analyzed. (23 refs.)

111 BUTLER, KENNETH D. Juvenile court waiver: the questionable validity of existing statutory standards. St. Louis University Law Journal 16:604-618 (1972)

The criteria which help to guide a juvenile court judge in his waiver determination are discussed, and the results of various studies are cited.

The author believes that by limiting a waiver determination to the suggested criteria, relevancy and uniformity would result. (72 refs.)

Wisconsin

112 BUXTON, EDWARD B. Developing guides for cooperation between the juvenile court, welfare department and schools. Child Welfare 47:226-273 (1968)
The results of a study done at the School of Social Work, University of Wisconsin, Madison, Wisconsin.

113 CADINA, CARLOS. Due process and the juvenile offender. St. Mary's Law Journal 1:23-35 (1969)
The author maintains that Gault raises more questions than it answers, and discusses these questions. (49 refs.)

114 CALLOW, WILLIAM G. Custody of the child and the uniform marriage and divorce act. South Dakota Law Review 18:551-558 (1973)
This article discusses the serious problems that today face the American family and domestic relations law in general. (31 refs.)

115 CAMERON, DALE C. Non-medical judgment of medical matters. The Georgetown Law Journal 57:716-733 (1969)
Some criteria are established for the guidance of non-medical persons in ascertaining the suitability of treatment in relation to the needs of patients. (23 refs.)

Massachusetts

116 CAMPBELL, CATHERINE E. The neglected child: his and his family's treatment under Massachusetts law and practice and their rights under the due process clause. Suffolk University Law Review 4:631-688 (1970)
The article is divided into three parts: the exercise of the parens patriae powers in Massachusetts with respect to neglected and dependent children: statutory and administrative fact; the constitutional requirements for a neglect hearing; a suggestion for meeting the neglected child's need for counsel. (224 refs.)

117 CANLIS, MICHAEL N. Tomorrow is too late. California Youth Authority Quarterly 21:9-16 (1968)

118 CANNADY, MICHAEL R. The fourth amendment and high school students. Willamette Law Journal 6:567-575 (1970)
The author comments on the three arguments relied upon by the courts when upholding the validity of warrantless high school searches. He offers counter-arguments. (42 refs.)

119 CANNON, JOE A. Federal court intervention in juvenile proceedings. Denver Law Journal 48:503-517 (1972)

The purpose of this article is to examine the viability of the tendency, since In Re Gault, to resort to federal injunctive and declaratory relief as a means of testing the constitutionality of juvenile statutes and processes. (56 refs.)

120 CANNON, JOHN J. The hearsay rule. Juvenile Court Judges' Journal 17(1):25-32 (1966)

A discussion of the common juvenile court practice of accepting hearsay evidence, and the history of this practice. Suggestions are made for limiting the reports of social workers and probation officers. (41 refs.)

Kentucky

121 CANON, BRADLEY C., and KENNETH KOLSON. Rural compliance with Gault: Kentucky, a case study. Journal of Family Law 10:300-326 (1971)

This article focuses upon the impact of the Gault decision on Kentucky juvenile court procedures with emphasis upon compliance in rural areas. (104 refs.)

122 CARKEET, R.A. This elusive thing called "due process" in the juvenile court. California Youth Authority Quarterly 20:10-19 (1967)

Oregon

123 CARMACK, MILDRED, and SHARON HAINES. A juvenile's right to bail in Oregon. Oregon Law Review 47:194-204 (1968)

A discussion of the constitutional aspects of a juvenile's right to bail, and suggestions for changes in the Oregon law. (50 refs.)

124 CARPENTER, J.W., et al. The parent-child dilemma in the courts. In Ohio State Legal Services Association Course on Law and Poverty, 1968. pp.5.01-5.18

125 CARPENTER, RONALD K. A due process dilemma - juries for juveniles. North Dakota Law Review 45:251-280 (1969)

This Note evaluates two institutions within our jurisprudential system - the juvenile court and the criminal jury. It examines: due process in juvenile proceedings; jury trial as fundamental due process requirement; merits of jury - juvenile issue. (181 refs.)

Calif./Ga.

126 CARR, W. PITTS. Juvenile court v. due process - a comparison. Georgia State Bar Journal 8:9-23 (1971)

An examination of the changes in the laws of California and Georgia that have occurred in response to Gault. These changes are compared to those constitutional rights which the Court has declared to be basic. (30 refs.)

Ga./N.C.

127 CARRINGTON, GROVER A. Torts - non-imputation of parental liability - a limitation. Wake Forest Law Review 9:288-293 (1973)

This Note analyzes a recent Georgia decision and several North Carolina cases to show how the rule of imputed negligence relates to cases where the parents' negligence is the sole proximate cause of the infant's injury. (17 refs.)

Oregon

128 CARSEL, RICHARD A. In Re Gault: juvenile justice - a proposal for reforms. Oregon Law Review 47:166-194 (1968)

The author's purpose is to identify the deficiencies within the Oregon juvenile justice system, and, with these as guides, to propose a new system. (161 refs.)

129 CARVER, LYELL H., and PAUL A. WHITE. Constitutional safeguards for the juvenile offender; implications of recent supreme court decisions. Crime and Delinquency 14:63-72 (1968)

Implications of recent Supreme Court decisions regarding juveniles are discussed: whether the Bill of Rights will apply to state action in dealing with juveniles or whether such direct application must undergo a time-consuming metamorphasis, as was the case with adult criminal procedure. (76 refs.)

130 CASHMAN, CHARLES E. Confidentiality of juvenile court proceedings: a review. Juvenile Justice 24(2):30-40 (1973)

A discussion of the nature of juvenile court proceedings, and the provisions providing for the noncriminal and confidential nature of the record. The use and abuse of juvenile court records is examined.

Canada

131 CASTEL, J.G. Custody orders: jurisdiction and recognition. Alberta Law Review 11:15-27 (1973)

Ohio

132 CATALINO, ANTHONY. A boy's committee as an instrument of communication. Crime and Delinquency 14:346-352 (1968)

A description of The Training Institution, Central Ohio's experiment with a technique of using a boy's committee to help broaden the channels of communication.

133 A cause of action for "wrongful life": (a suggested analysis). Minnesota Law Review 55:58-81 (1970)

The purpose of this Note is to analyze the damages issue involved in an action for "wrongful life", and to evaluate the duty, causation and proximate cause issues. (66 refs.)

134 CAYTON, CHARLES E. Emerging patterns in the administration of juvenile justice. Journal of Urban Law 49:377-398 (1971)

The Supreme Court's decisions have activated social forces which raise serious questions about the survival of the traditional juvenile court. The constitutionality of the juvenile court is discussed, and case studies of juvenile justice in two courts, since 1967, are examined. (21 refs.)

135 CAYTON, CHARLES E. Relationship of the probation officer and the defense attorney after Gault. Federal Probation 34:8-13 (1970)

A discussion of the three roles of the defense attorney in juvenile court: advocate; rehabilitative role; a mixture of the two roles. His relationship with the probation officer is analyzed in conjunction with the three roles. (16 refs.)

Rhode Island

136 CERILLI, BENEDATTO A., Jr. The juvenile court comes of age. Rhode Island Bar Annual 7:65-75 (1970-1971)

A discussion of decisions of the Rhode Island supreme court, the United States Supreme Court, and constitutional developments which have caused changes in the Rhode Island juvenile court system. The changing role of the attorney is also considered.

Iraq

137 CHAMBERS, CARL D., and JAMES A. INEIARDI. Deviant behavior in the Middle East: a study of delinquency in Iraq. Criminology 9:291-315 (1971)

(9 refs.)

138 CHAMBLISS, WILLIAM J., and JOHN T. LIELL. The legal process in the community setting - a study of local law enforcement. Crime and Delinquency 12:310-317 (1966)

The authors undertook a specific case in an attempt to determine some guidelines as to how police respond to "deviant" acts in the community. All aspects, including the social standing of the youth in question, the "political" impact of the prosecution or failure to prosecute such a case would have on the police in the community, or an interagency public relations, are examined. (9 refs.)

Canada

139 CHAPMAN, P.B. The lawyer in juvenile court: "a Gulliver among Lilliputians." Western Ontario Law Review 10:88-107 (1971)

This paper puts forward some of the many conflicting rationales of the differing approaches to counsel's function in the area of juvenile law. (77 refs.)

140 CHASE, EDWARD. Schemes and visions: a suggested revision of juvenile sentencing. Texas Law Review 51:673-706 (1973)

The differential sentencing of juveniles and adult offenders is discussed. (131 refs.)

141 Child neglect: due process for the parent. Columbia Law Review 70:465-485 (1970)

This note considers the impact of the fourteenth amendment on selected substantive and procedural rights presently denied to respondent-parents in neglect proceedings. (100 refs.)

142 CHILDS, MARJORIE M. 1970 White House Conference on Children - the child advocate. Women Lawyers Journal 58:v.p. (1972)

An outline of the 1970 White House Conference on Children, and some recommendations. (6 refs.)

Korea

143 CHONG, Y. Juvenile protection and Juvenile law. Sabōp haengjōng 11(12):28-32, 27-30 (1970)

New Jersey

144 CHUSED, RICHARD H. The juvenile court process: a study of three New Jersey counties. Rutgers Law Review 26:488-615 (1973)

An analysis of the case and statutory law relevant to a study, begun in 1970, of three county juvenile courts in New Jersey. The study focused primarily on the routing of cases through various procedural channels by intake personnel in the juvenile justice process. An analysis of the data obtained in included. (128 refs.)

Poland

145 CIEŚLAK, M. From the repressive measures to the protective. Palestra 17(1): 26-48 (1973)

Washington

146 Citizenship for eighteen year olds - age of majority in Washington - Ch. 292, Washington Laws of 1971. Washington Law Review 47:367-385 (1972)

The purpose of this Note is to summarize by topic the changes brought about by the 1971 Washington Statute and to identify some of the legal problems by the enactment itself. (121 refs.)

147 CLARK, BETTY J. Do juvenile courts have a duty to supervise child care agencies and juvenile detention facilities? Howard Law Journal 17:443-455 (1972)

Evidence is given that juvenile courts do indeed have a duty to supervise such agencies and facilities. Included is a discussion of cases in connection with the right to treatment, and the invasion of the privacy of a child and his parents by state social agencies. (43 refs.)

Georgia

148 CLARK, GLEN W. The new Juvenile Court Code of Georgia. Georgia State Bar Journal 7:409-429 (1971)

A discussion of the new Juvenile Court Code of Georgia. (81 refs.)

149 CLEAR, MICHAEL G. Peripheral problems of Gault. Suffolk University Law Review 81-92 (1968)

This Note considers the possible effect Gault may have upon various constitutional guarantees accorded adults in criminal proceedings but currently denied to minors in juvenile proceedings. (57 refs.)

150 CLEMENS, CAMERON L. Continuity through a lasting parentship. Public Welfare 27(4):338-343 (1969)

A discussion of foster-parent or institutional care for juveniles. (3 refs.)

151 CLEMENS, JAMES D. The Kent case: doomsday for the juvenile code. Journal of the Missouri Bar 22:408-411, 425 (1966)

Aust./N.Z.

152 CLUNIES-ROSS, J. The dilemma of the child and the law. Australian and New Zealand Journal of Criminology 1:212-224 (1968)

153 CLUTE, PENELOPE D. "Parental responsibility" ordinances - is criminalizing parents when children commit unlawful acts a solution to juvenile delinquency? Wayne Law Review 19:1551-1577 (1973)

This Comment discusses in detail a number of questions as to the legality of "parental responsibility" ordinances. A brief discussion of the efficacy of the parental responsibility ordinances in curtailing juvenile delinquency is included. (149 refs.)

154 COBURN, DANIEL R. Child-parent communications: spare the privilege and spoil the child. Dickenson Law Review 74:599-633 (1970)

The author reviews the privileges of the lawyer-client; patient-physician; priest-penitent; husband-wife; child-parent; and the basis for the privilege. (180 refs.)

155 COFFEE, JOHN C. Privacy versus parens patriae: the role of police records in sentencing and surveillance of juveniles. Cornell Law Review 57:571-620 (1972)

This article examines juvenile record systems maintained by police authorities. The author finds increasing evidence to suggest that the net effect of record keeping is to ensure that many of the subject juveniles will mature into confirmed delinquents. (187 refs.)

156 COGAN, NEIL H. Juvenile law before and after the entrance of 'parens patriae.' South Carolina Law Review 22:147-181 (1970)

This article examines juvenile law in chancery (traditionally called "infant law"), before and after parens patriae became a part of it. (178 refs.)

157 COHEN, ALBERT K. An evaluation of Gault by a sociologist. Indiana Law Journal 43:614-618 (1968)

This sociologist attempts to show that the connection between the materials he cites and the conclusions drawn by the Court in Gault, is not logically inevitable. (6 refs.)

158 COHEN, FRED. A lawyer looks at juvenile justice. Criminal Law Bulletin 7(6): 513-529 (1971)

A critical, skeptical examination is given of the stages of development of legal concern for the juvenile and judicial concern for procedural regularity in juvenile courts. (37 refs.)

159 COHEN, JAMES H. The standard of proof in juvenile proceedings: Gault beyond a reasonable doubt. Michigan Law Review 68:567-602 (1970)

The adoption of the "beyond a reasonable doubt" standard is in no way inconsistent with the rehabilitative purposes of juvenile court proceedings, states the author, and the higher standard is essential to avoid, if at all possible, the sometimes poor rehabilitation that is generally accorded juveniles, and the stigmatizing effect brought about by a finding of delinquency. (135 refs.)

160 COHILL, MAURICE B., Jr. The United States Supreme Court and the juvenile courts - an overview. Duquesne Law Review 9:573-578 (1971)
A short discussion of jury trials; standard of proof; Kent and Gault. (20 refs.)

Michigan

161 COLEMAN, MARY. Courtroom with a heart. Judicature 51:383-385 (1968)
A studied evaluation of the children's courtroom in Calhoun County, Michigan.

162 COLEMAN, RICHARD. Racial differences in runaways. Psychological Reports 22:321-322 (1968)
For the purposes of this study, male adolescents who had run away from a training school were compared in terms of race (Caucasian or negro), age, and total time as inmates. (2 refs.)

163 CONEY, MICHAEL E. Equal protection of the law: succession rights of illegitimates. Loyola Law Review 18:188-200 (1971-1972)
A discussion of various cases involving succession rights of illegitimates. (78 refs.)

164 Conference on youth and violence: a panel. Juvenile Court Judges' Journal 20(1): 2-31 (1969)

165 CONLEY, PHILIP, and PAULINE HANSON. What is the future of the juvenile court? University of West Los Angeles Law Review 1:10-20 (1969)
The need for uniformity in the areas unanswered by Gault and by Kent is discussed. (34 refs.)

166 CONNOR, RICHARD J. Constitutional law - minor's right to refuse court-ordered abortion. Suffolk University Law Review 7:1157-1173 (1973)
A discussion of In re Smith, 16 Md.App. 209, 295 A.2d 238 (1972). (93 refs.)

167 The constitution, due process and changing times - Kent and the waiver process. Juvenile Court Journal 23(1):12-17 (1972)
The following Supreme Court cases are suggested as required reading for all juvenile court judges: Kent and the waiver process; Gault and due process; and Winship and the quantum of proof. (15 refs.)

168 Constitutional law – adoption – religious matching of child and adoptive parents as required by New York Statutes held constitutional. Fordham Urban Law Journal 1:106–120 (1972)

A discussion of Dickens v. Ernesto, 30 N.Y.2d 61, 281 N.E.2d 153, 330 N.Y.S.2d 346 (1972). (94 refs.)

169 Constitutional law – due process does not require that a student be afforded the right to counsel at a public school suspension hearing. Rutgers Law Review 22:342-360 (1968)

In this Comment the following are examined: New York City suspension proceedings; the school's administration of discipline; interruption of the right to education; Madera v. Board of Education, 386 F.2d 778 (2d Cir. 1967), an evaluation of the appellate decision. (108 refs.)

170 Constitutional law – due process: no constitutional right to trial by jury for juveniles in delinquency proceedings. Minnesota Law Review 56:249–263 (1971)

A discussion of Gault, Winship, McKeiver and other cases. (82 refs.)

171 Constitutional law – equal protection of the laws – inheritance by illegitimates. Case Western Reserve Law Review 22:793–803 (1971)

While the Levy, Glona v. American Guarantee and Liability Insurance Co., 391 U.S. 73 (1968) decision sparked hopes for the extension of the rights of illegitimate children, the Supreme Court's more recent pronouncement in Labine v. Vincent, 401 U.S. 532 (1971), with its absence of sound analytical reasoning to justify the result, is likely to inhibit any further expansions of their rights. (64 refs.)

172 Constitutional law – Federal Juvenile Delinquency Act – waiver of jury trial held unconstitutional as a prerequisite to treatment as juvenile. New York University Law Review 43:769–775 (1968)

A discussion of the Federal Juvenile Delinquency Act and various court decisions. (57 refs.)

173 Constitutional law – jury trial in juvenile court – juveniles in delinquency proceedings not constitutionally guaranteed the right to a jury trial. Vanderbilt Law Review 24:1281–1288 (1971)

The author shows that, until the rights of children are delineated and enforced by the courts, juveniles must face an imperfect system without the protection of individual rights guaranteed by the constitution. (58 refs.)

New Jersey

174 Constitutional law – Miranda warnings to juveniles in New Jersey: the worst of both worlds revisited. Rutgers Law Review 26:358–382 (1973)

This Comment examines the rationale of various cases decided in New Jersey in light of the current trend of according procedural safeguards to juveniles, and attempts to clarify the "highest standards of due process and fundamental fairness" test approved by the court in two opinions. (167 refs.)

175 Constitutional law - right of a minor to fifth and sixth amendment guarantees in quasi-criminal juvenile proceedings. Brooklyn Law Review 34:110-118 (1967)
A discussion of the guarantees which the Bill of Rights affords the juvenile. (50 refs.)

176 Constitutional law - right to a jury trial and standards of proof applicable in juvenile proceedings left unresolved. Brooklyn Law Review 36:279-289 (1970)
A detailed discussion of the extension of adult criminal defendant rights to juveniles as raised in Debacker v. Brainard, 183 Neb.461, 161 N.W. 2d 508 (1968). (51 refs.)

177 Constitutional law - right to counsel - student held entitled to counsel at public school disciplinary hearing. New York University Law Review 42:961-966 (1967)
It seems that the interests of the child outweigh those of the Board of Education, states the author, who gives reasons why the presence of counsel is necessary. (35 refs.)

178 Constitutional law - standard of proof required in a delinquency adjudication. Fordham Law Review 39:121-127 (1970)
An analysis of In Re Winship. (66 refs.)

179 Constitutional law - state statute granting juvenile court proceedings to female defendants under the age of eighteen but limiting such proceedings to male defendants under the age of sixteen held violative of equal protective clause. Fordham Urban Law Journal 1:286-297 (1972)
A discussion of Lamb v. Brown, 456 F.2d 18 (10th Cir. 1972). (62 refs.)

180 Constitutional law - there is no constitutionally protected right to wear one's hair in a public high school in the length and style that suits the wearer. Houston Law Review 10:205-207 (1972)
A short discussion on the issue of hair-length regulations. (18 refs.)

Iowa

181 Contemporary studies project: juvenile delinquency in Iowa. Iowa Law Review 53: 1119-1176 (1968)
This study is based on results of questionnaires sent to district and municipal judges, probation officers, family counselors, social welfare directors, law enforcement officers, school administrators, community leaders, and mayors. (346 refs.)

Louisiana

182 COOKSEY, CHARLOTTE M. The battered child - Louisiana's response to the cry. Loyola Law Review 17:372-390 (1970-1971)
There is a certain basic procedure for handling and reporting a suspected case of child abuse in Louisiana. However, since the ultimate goal is the protection of the child as well as restoring the family structure, it must be determined whether or not existing laws are making sufficient headway in this direction. Lawmakers must learn where to draw the line between abuse and discipline. (80 refs.)

183 COOLEY, JOHN W. Constitutional law - equal protection - denial of illegitimate child's right to inheritance from father who had acknowledged but not legitimated heir does not constitute a violation of child's equal protection rights under the fourteenth amendment. Notre Dame Lawyer 47:392-403 (1972)

An analysis and comparison of the legitimation requirements of Louisiana and the other 49 states. (60 refs.)

184 COOLEY, THOMAS M. Court control over treatment of juvenile offenders. Duquesne Law Review 9:613-625 (1971)

The issue delt with is the concern (vel non) of the juvenile courts with the rehabilitative facilities to which their determinations relegate the young. (74 refs.)

185 COPELAND, GREG. Juvenile delinquency "referrals" and their effect on dispositions. American Journal of Criminal Law 1:296-317 (1972)

This article examines some of the problems in disposition, especially the use of "referrals." The term "referred" ordinarily implies that the youth was arrested and taken to a juvenile detention facility. The need for standardization of the use of referrals is emphasized. (68 refs.)

186 CORNELISON, ALBERT O., Jr. Dependency hearings: what rights for the parents? UCD Law Review 6:240-254 (1973)

This article examines the impact of a dependency hearing upon indigent parents. (94 refs.)

Texas

187 CORNETT, BILL. Juvenile legislation: time for change. Houston Law Review 10:720-731 (1973)

This article concentrates on the Texas Proposed Juvenile Code. (80 refs.)

188 Correction in the United States - a survey for the President's Commission on Law Enforcement and Administration of Justice by the National Council on Crime and Delinquency. Crime and Delinquency 13:1-281 (1967)

This survey presents a picture of correction throughout the United States: juvenile after-care; juvenile detention; juvenile institutions; juvenile probation.

Kansas

189 CORRIGAN, MICHAEL T. The juvenile court and community involvement. Osgoode Hall Law Journal 10:221-224 (1972)

A description of volunteer programs initiated in the Witchita, Kansas, juvenile court, to assist the court to live up to the expectations of the juvenile court founders. (3 refs.)

190 COUGHLIN, BERNARD J. The rights of children. Child Welfare 47:133-142 (1968)

The author discusses legislation passed in some states relating to mandatory protection of children from specific diseases, child abuse laws, and provisions for the protection of children's interests in family and domestic relations courts. (20 refs.)

191 COULSON, ROBERT. Family arbitration - an exercise in sensitivity. Family Law Quarterly 3:22-30 (1969)

The author suggests that in order to avoid the unpleasantness and anxiety that often result from litigation, the attorney should consider alternative dispute settlement techniques such as mediation, conciliation, or arbitration.

192 Counseling the counselors: legal implications of counseling minors without parental consent. Maryland Law Review 31:332-354 (1971)

This discussion centers on "counseling," "counseling relationships," and "counseling services" defined to include all services provided by social agencies to individuals between the ages of 12 and 21. (126 refs.)

Great Britain

193 COURT, J. Battering parents. Social Work (London) 26:20-24 (1969)

A discussion of the need for social workers to develop a viable relationship with the abusive parent, and to convey their concern for the parent's own suffering and deprivation, while seeking ways to remedy the family situation. Breaking up families is not the only solution.

194 COURTDALE, A. DAVID. Trial of juveniles as adults - past, present and future. Baylor Law Review 21:333-344 (1969)

The purpose of the juvenile act is discussed, and the need to achieve a proper balance between the needs of society to be protected, and the rights of the child. (24 refs.)

Texas

195 COX, CYNTHIA H. Juvenile court - waiver of jurisdiction - reaching age seventeen does not render appeal of waiver moot but only prevents a remand if the case is reversed. St. Mary's Law Journal 4:405-409 (1972)

A discussion of Hight v. State, 483 S.W.2d 256 (Tex. Sup.1972). (40 refs.)

Pennsylvania

196 COXE, SPENCER. Lawyers in juvenile court. Crime and Delinquency 13:488-493 (1967)

A study of trends in juvenile court in Philadelphia shows that the percentage of juveniles represented by counsel in that city increased from 5% to nearly 40% between 1966 and 1967. The role of counsel is also discussed. (4 refs.)

197 COYNE, THOMAS A. Who will speak for the child? Annals of the American Academy of Political and Social Science 383:34-47 (1969)

Judges have broad discretion in deciding whose ward a child should become in the case of family malfunction, e.g. in the event of death, physical and mental incapacity, disappearance of a parent, or when parental conduct conflicts with community values. The author discusses the child's need for an advocate in a custody question. (36 refs.)

198 CRAIG, MAUDE M., and LAILA A. BUDD. The juvenile offender: recidivism and companions. Crime and Delinquency 13:344-351 (1967)

A study of the "serious" and "less serious" juvenile offenders, which brings into focus various developmental factors and companionship - the mechanism by which juvenile delinquency is perpetuated and increased. (1 ref.)

199 CRESSEY, DONALD R. Organized crime and inner-city youth. Crime and Delinquency 16:129-138 (1970)

California

200 Criminal law - juveniles - minor's request to see parent made before or during custodial interrogation invokes fifth amendment privilege. (People v. Burton, 6 Cal. 3d 375, 491 P 2d 793, 99 Cal. Reptr. 1 1971). University of Illinois Law Forum 625-634 (1972)

The California practice of requiring that juveniles be given Miranda warnings is a further step toward affording juveniles the same rights as their adult counterparts. The questions arise as to whether the warnings alone are meaningful to juveniles, for example, illiterate and culturally deprived juveniles, to help them understand their rights. The author argues that the waiver of constitutional rights by juveniles should be prohibited. (47 refs.)

201 Criminal law: juveniles: prosecutor can obtain juvenile court file of youth waived to an adult court. Law and the Social Order 115-125 (1969)

A discussion of State v. Arbeiter, 408 S.W. 2d 26 (Mo.1966). (29 refs.)

202 Criminal liability of parents for failure to control their children. Valparaiso University Law Review 6:332-352 (1972)

An examination of the liability for parental ommissions in the context of constitutional standards and the criminal law. The financial responsibility of parents in tort law is discussed for comparison, and attention is focused on the liability of a parent after his child has committed a delinquent act. (138 refs.)

203 Criminal procedure - confession - juvenile may execute a valid waiver only after consultation with parents or attorney. Indiana Law Review 6(3):577-583 (1973)

A discussion of Lewis v. State, 288 N.E.2d 138 (Ind.1972). (25 refs.)

Washington

204 Criminal procedure - juvenile retroactive application of In Re Gault denied in Washington. Washington Law Review 47:183-194 (1971)

A discussion of Brumley v. Charles Denney Juvenile Center, 77 Wn.2d 702, 466 P.2d 481 (1970). On determining what due process guarantees are to be extended to juveniles, the court has consistently reasoned that only those which tend to enhance the reliability of the fact-finding process will be applied to juvenile proceedings. The author argues that this same criterion should be, and has been, the central issue in retroactivity determinations. (55 refs.)

205 Criminal procedure - juvenile delinquents: no right in delinquency proceedings to trial by jury or bail on appeal. Washington Law Review 44:481-489 (1969)

A discussion of Estes v. Hopp, 73 Wash.Dec.2d 272 (1968). The author asks just what rights other than those enumerated in Gault may be required by due process. (40 refs.)

206 Crisis in juvenile courts. U.S. News and World Report 66:62-64 (March 29, 1969)

The author examines the impact of the following on the juvenile court system: the increase in juveniles' legal rights, and lawyers in the juvenile court. He also discusses the role of parents and schools, and reforms in juvenile corrections institutions.

207 CROMER, S. KELLY. Juveniles and junkies - a step in the right direction. Hastings Law Journal 24(3):517-535 (1973)

This Note reviews the doctrine of separation of powers in People v. Navarro, 7 Cal. 3d 248 (1972). A discussion of prior judicial development of the doctrine and one possible area for further application is included. (117 refs.)

208 CROMWELL, J.C., and E.A. PERKINS. The battered child - dilemmas in management. Medical Social Work 22(5):160-168 (yr. unknown)

The authors describe an interdisciplinary conference held to encourage better understanding of the roles and interactions of medical, paramedical, social welfare, and legal personnel who deal with battered children and their families.

209 CROXTON, TOM A. The juvenile court: some current issues. Child Welfare 46:553-561 (1967)

The author discusses trends adversely affecting the juvenile court in its rehabilitative function, and legal decisions moving the court toward a more legalistic posture. The unofficial case, one in which the juvenile court personnel services a client family over which the court has no official jurisdiction, has been under heavy attack. However, with proper safeguards, most families and attorneys would prefer this process. (38 refs.)

210 CROXTON, TOM A. The Kent case and its consequences. Journal of Family Law 7:1-13 (1967)

The author sees the Kent case as a landmark decision regarding a juvenile's representation by counsel in a waiver proceeding. He proposes that the attorney become "participant decision maker" to aid the court by clarifying existing reports and requesting further investigation. (32 refs.)

Indiana

211 CULBERTSON, ROBERT G. Commitment practices in Indiana's juvenile courts. Juvenile Justice 24(3):25-30 (1973)

The results of a study undertaken in the Indiana Boy's School focusing on the offense for which each boy was committed by a county court, or returned by a parole officer. (5 refs.)

Eng./U.S.

212 CURRAN, WILLIAM J., and HARRY K. BEECHER. Experimentation in children: a re-examination of legal ethical principles. Journal of the American Medical Association 210:77-83 (1969)

Re-examination of legal and ethical principles in the U.S. and in England suggest standards for the use of children in clinical investigation. The legal consent of the minors involved is discussed also. (19 refs.)

213 The custody question and child neglect rehearings. University of Chicago Law Review 35:478-492 (1968)

This Comment is concerned with a parent's right to permanent custody, and with petitions for return of a child who has been temporarily removed from the home. The application of a general custody rule to parental petitions for return of neglected children fails to take into account the basic differences between neglect cases and other custody disputes. (68 refs.)

214 CUTSHAW, LEILA O. A survey of some recent trends in law. Social Casework 49: 541-545 (1968)

The author discusses trends in present legal thinking related to individual criminal responsibility, family law, and juvenile courts. Recent decisions are cited which reflect changed attitudes in judicial and legal minds, and a deliberate use of law as a tool of change: suits for damage for wrongful life, with the child suing his father or those responsible for the care of his insane mother for the fact of his illegitimate birth; the legitimacy of the status of a child conceived through artificial insemination by a third party with the consent of the mother's husband. (14 refs.)

215 DABROW, ALLAN M., and DANIEL M. MIGLIORE. Juvenile rights under the fourth amendment. Journal of Family Law 11:753-764 (1972)

A discussion of further "adult" constitutional protections which might be extended to the juvenile. Can the in loco parentis doctrine justify disparity in protections guaranteed to "all persons?" (73 refs.)

216 DALY, BARBARA. Willful child abuse and state reporting statutes. University of Miami Law Review 23:283-346 (1969)

In this discussion of the battered child, the solving of family problems becomes an important area. Reporting statutes are cited and recommendations for improvement of such are given. (306 refs.)

Germany

217 DAMRAN, J. Der Ausstattungsanspruch des nichtehelichen Kindes. Zeitschrift für das Gesamte Familienrecht 16:129-141 (1969)

Japan

218 DANDŌ, S. The basic problems of the juvenile law amendment. Hanrei jihō 617: 3-12 (1971)

District of Columbia

219 DARLING, STANTON G., II. Youthful offenders and neglected children under the District of Columbia Crime Act. American University Law Review 20:373-431 (1970-1971)

An analysis of the new provisions in the District of Columbia. (400 refs.)

South Africa

220 D'OLIVEIRA, J.A. v.S. Venia aetatis, emancipation and release from tutelage revisited: the Age of Majority Act, 1972. South Africa Law Journal 90:57-68 (1973)

Ohio/Argent.

221 DAVID, PEDRO R., and JOSEPH W. SCOTT. A cross-cultural comparison of juvenile offenders, offenses, due processes, and societies: the cases of Toledo, Ohio, and Rosario, Argentina. Criminology 11:183-205 (1973)

This study constitutes a comparative analysis of not only delinquency patterns but also differential due processes of law, societal life-styles, and socio-economic factors that interact with juvenile delinquency patterns in the two "somewhat comparable" cities. (10 refs.)

222 DAVIDSON, GEORGE. In Re Gault: the juvenile's Gideon. Illinois Bar Journal 56:488-503 (1968)

The author traces the struggle over the child's right to counsel in the juvenile court. (106 refs.)

Canada

223 DAVIES, CHRISTINE. Custody and adoption: some interrelated problems. University of Toronto Law Journal 23:88-110 (1973)

The author examines rules relating to custody and to dispensing with parental consent to adoption in situations where a child has not been made a crown ward. The rules of Ontario, Canada, are compared with the corresponding rules of other jurisdictions. (127 refs.)

224 DAVIS, ELAINE. Juveniles - interrogation - parens patriae v. Miranda: conflicting interests. Seton Hall Law Review 3:482-491 (1972)

A discussion of State v. In the Interest of R.W., 115 N.J. Super. 286, 279 A.2d 709 (App.Div.), cert. granted, 59 N.J. 289, 281 A.2d 802 (1971). (48 refs.)

225 DAVIS, SAMUEL M. The jurisdictional dilemma of the juvenile court. North Carolina Law Review 51:195-231 (1972)

The author establishes certain minimum standards of juvenile court jurisdiction - both as to how jurisdiction is to be defined and how it is to be exercised. (192 refs.)

226 DAVIS, SAMUEL M. Justice for the juvenile: the decision to arrest and due process. Duke Law Journal 913-937 (1971)

This article examines one crucial part of juvenile law: the power of the police to intervene in the lives and conduct of youth, to take them into custody; and the means of protecting a juvenile's rights, including a determination of what those rights are, if he is taken into custody. (111 refs.)

227 DAVIS, SAMUEL M., and SUSAN C. CHAIRES. Equal protection for juveniles: the present status of sex-based discrimination in juvenile court laws. Georgia Law Review 7(3):494-532 (1973)

The authors of this article are concerned with sex-based discrimination in juvenile court laws. They first analyze those state laws that are sexually discriminatory, and then explore the possibility of attacking these laws under the equal protection clause of the fourteenth amendment. (219 refs.)

228 DAYTON, ROBERT D. The confessions of juveniles. Willamette Law Journal 5: 66-81 (1968)

The reasoning of the Gault case was broad enough to apply the privilege against self-incrimination to the pre-judicial stage. However, if the juvenile courts interpret Gault narrowly, then the U.S. Supreme Court will probably be forced to decide the issue in the future, states the author. (77 refs.)

229 Defender survey reveals substantial juvenile representation. Juvenile Court Judges' Journal 17(4):127-128 (1967)

The results of a survey by the National Legal Aid and Defender Association are discussed.

230 DE FRANCIS, VINCENT. Child abuse - the legislative response. Denver Law Journal 44:3-41 (1967)

The subject discussed is child-abuse legislation, the so-called reporting laws. The statutory provisions of different states are compared, and criticized. (59 refs.)

California

231 DE GRAW, HAROLD. 1967 juvenile court legislation. Hastings Law Journal 19: 256-262 (1967)

A synopsis of California legislation to fulfil the requirements to realign juvenile court procedures. (21 refs.)

232 DE LA PARTE, LOUIS, Jr. A state senator looks at juvenile crime. Juvenile Court Judges' Journal 18(3):92-95 (1967)

This article was published at the time when the Juvenile Delinquency Prevention Act of 1967 was passed by the House of Representatives.

Canada

233 DEGRAVES, W.R. Damages caused by children. Law Society of Manitoba, Isaac Pitblado Lectures on Continuing Legal Education 44-48 (1970)

234 DEMBER, STUART B. New York State youthful offender procedure. New York Law Forum 17:1089-1125 (1972)

The main endeavor of this Note is to explain how the needlessly cumbersome multi-step procedure heretofore employed in youthful offender treatment has been refined and consequently attuned to the capabilities and functional mechanics of the criminal courts by a complete restructuring. (225 refs.)

235 DEMBITZ, NANETTE. Child abuse and the law - fact and fiction. Record of the Association of the Bar of the City of New York 24:613-627 (1969)
(21 refs.)

236 DEMBITZ, NANETTE. The juvenile court comes of age: the first casebook on juvenile cases - a review. The Record of the Association of the Bar of the City of New York 23:669-674 (1968)
The need for empirical data as to the effects of the juvenile justice system is emphasized. (11 refs.)

New York

237 DEMBITZ, NANETTE. Welfare home visits: child versus parent. American Bar Association Journal 57:871-874 (1971)
The Supreme Court of the United States upheld New York State's requirement that the welfare mother permit a home visit by a welfare worker. For the first time an issue of contradiction between the child's rights and the mother's rights was presented. (6 refs.)

Illinois

238 DEMSCH, BERTHOLD, et al. An advocate for intervention between the school, home and juvenile court. Juvenile Court Judges' Journal 20(4):150-153 (1969)
This paper addressed itself to some brief analyses about how an operational problem developed for the Chicago Parental School and the Illinois juvenile court, that influenced the creation of a school social work service and a role definition in the intervention process.

Indiana

239 DE ROOS, DIRK W. Dependency and neglect: Indiana's definitional confusion. Indiana Law Journal 45:606-615 (1970)
The author submits that it is time for definitional clarification of the terms "dependency" and "neglect." (78 refs.)

Tennessee

240 DERRYBERRY, GEORGE M. The Tennessee impact of the Gault decision. Tennessee Law Review 35:632-641 (1968)
This Comment attempts to evaluate the immediate effect of Gault upon certain aspects of juvenile procedure in Tennessee by comparing new requirements set out in the decision to the corresponding elements of a Tennessee proceeding. (63 refs.)

241 The dilemma of the "uniquely juvenile" offender. William and Mary Law Review 14:386-408 (1972)
This Note is predicated upon the familiar premise that present juvenile justice systems, especially as they relate to "uniquely juvenile" offenders, are far from effective in serving that purpose and, in fact, often aggravate the maladies they were designed to cure. The author suggests that such offenses be removed entirely from the purview of the courts. (107 refs.)

Oregon

242 DITTMAN, DERRYCK H. Contributing to delinquency statutes - an ounce of prevention? Willamette Law Journal 5:104-120 (1968)

The application of statutes making it a criminal offense to contribute to the delinquency of a minor with regard to their purpose and to their legal validity as criminal sanctions, is examined. Particular reference is made to Oregon statutes. The possibility of abuse in the application of a broad sanction exists, and the author explores this possibility. (105 refs.)

India

243 DIWAN, P. The welfare principle and public responsibility towards children in modern law. Lawyer (Madras) 1:147-153 (1969)

Germany

244 DOBROSHKE, E. Die Unternehmensnachfolge Minderjähriger. Betrieb 20:803-808 (1967)

245 DOBSON, MARY V. The juvenile court and parental rights. Family Law Quarterly 4:393-408 (1970)

The author fears that the juvenile court, when exercising its power to separate the child from the parents, may be, in effect, punishing both parent and child. (51 refs.)

246 DODD, CHRISTOPHER J. The adoption of Baby Lenore: two interpretations of a child's best interests. Journal of Family Law 11:285-318 (1971)

Although a great deal of attention has been given to the juvenile court system in an effort to provide greater protection for the rights of children, the area of the problem of infants and their rights in contested adoption proceedings is conspicuously absent. The author discusses the true legal and emotional difficulties involved in adoption. (25 refs.)

247 DODD, LAWRENCE R. The juvenile jury trial case - a regrettable "policy decision." Louisiana Law Review 32:133-145 (1971)

The author suggests that the decision in Duncan v. Louisiana, 395 U.S. 145 (1968) is unsatisfactory in that it ignores the possibility of a reconciliation between the rehabilitative ideal of the juvenile court system and the preservation of the individual rights of juveniles. (62 refs.)

Netherlands

248 DOEK, J.E. Mishandeling van kindern. Nederlands Juristenblad 22:639-645 (1970)

New York

249 DOHEN, DOROTHY. A new juvenile court role in an ethnically controlled community agency. Social Work 16:25-29 (1971)

This article describes the role of the court worker as developed by the New York City Juvenile Court Services Program - a project sponsored by a private, city-wide antipoverty agency run by and for Puerto Ricans. (6 refs.)

250 DOLESCHAL, EUGENE. Abstracts - law and the courts. Crime and Delinquency Literature 4(3):339-441 (1971)
Abstracts of articles on law and the courts; law enforcement and the police; juvenile delinquency and the delinquent; crime and the offender; corrections; related social issues.

New York

251 Domestic relations - appointment of counsel for the abused child - statutory schemes and the New York approach. Cornell Law Review 58:177-190 (1972)
New York's legislators, actively seeking solutions to the abuse problem, have enacted a comprehensive statutory framework affording many rights to the child. The Family Court Act of 1962, and the report of the New York State Assembly Select Committee on Child Abuse are discussed. (68 refs.)

252 Domestic relations - child custody - sufficiency of record to determine best interests of child. Iowa Law Review 52:1017-1022 (1967)
(32 refs.)

253 DONOVAN, JOHN A. The juvenile court and the mentally disordered juvenile. North Dakota Law Review 45:222-250 (1969)
This is a discussion of the need for greater uniformity and regularity in the handling of the mentally disordered juvenile. Specific problem areas which should be considered by legislators, judges and court administrators are discussed. (93 refs.)

Canada

254 DOOTJES, INEZ, et al. Defense counsel in juvenile court: a variety of roles. Canadian Journal of Criminology and Corrections 14:132-149 (1972)
This study brings data describing defense lawyers' perceptions of their function in Ontario juvenile courts. Data show that many lawyers do not believe that they have a clear enough understanding of juvenile court philosophy, and criticize court procedures and treatment facilities.

255 DORSEN, NORMAN, and DANIEL A. REZNECK. In Re Gault and the future of juvenile law. Family Law Quarterly 1:1-46 (1967)
The authors state the the Supreme Court's concern with the quality of juvenile court justice is likely to be a long-term affair. The pre-judicial and the adjudicative stages of the juvenile court process are discussed. (175 refs.)

256 Double jeopardy in juvenile justice. Washington University Law Quarterly 702-709 (1971)
An examination of the question: is the protection against double jeopardy a constitutionally required right for juveniles in the juvenile justice system? (39 refs.)

257 DOUGLAS, WILLIAM O. Juvenile courts and due process of law. Juvenile Court Judges' Journal 19(1):9-15 (1968)
The six basic rights afforded the juvenile by Gault are discussed. (34 refs.)

258 DOUGLASS, JOSEPH H. Our nation's stake in juvenile delinquency prevention: some underlying socio-economic factors. Juvenile Court Judges' Journal 20(2): 42-48 (1969)

Two papers featured at the symposium on "Youth in Crisis: Our Nation's Stake in Juvenile Delinquency Prevention," held in Washington, D.C. in February, 1969, are discussed in this article. (12 refs.)

259 DOWNS, WILLIAM T. Juvenile courts and the Gault decision: an invitation to innovation. Children 15:90-96 (1968)

The author holds that although the Supreme Court did not explicitly rule on the pre-adjudication stage, adequate notice of hearing and the privilege against self-incrimination must be granted at that stage. (13 refs.)

260 DRINAN, ROBERT F. Aftermath of apprehension: family lawyer's response. Prospectus a Journal of Law Reform 3:31-38 (1969)

This author maintains that it is the attitude of the parents towards the youth who has been apprehended by the police which is the critical factor in encouraging or deterring the youth from further delinquency.

261 DRINAN, ROBERT F. The rights of children: new frontiers. Texas Bar Journal 30:592-594 (1967)

The question of parental consent for the marriage of persons under age is examined.

New York

262 DUFFEE, DAVID, and LARRY SIEGEL. The organization man: legal counsel in the juvenile court. Criminal Law Bulletin 7:544-553 (1971)

This article appraises the effect of the Supreme Court's insistence of a juvenile's right to appointed counsel on juvenile court dispositional outcomes. The sociological perspectives are considered, and the results of a survey in a New York county are reported. (24 refs.)

263 DUFFY, JAMES E., Jr. In Re Gault and the privilege against self-incrimination in juvenile court. Marquette Law Review 51:68-88 (1967)

This article discusses the status of the juvenile court system in relation to In Re Gault and the privilege against self-incrimination. (62 refs.)

264 DUFRESNE, ELIZABETH J. "If not by birth" - the rights of foster children to financial benefits of foster parents under federal statutes. Journal of Family Law 7:613-635 (1967)

The author discusses the rights of foster children to participate in the benefits of various pieces of federal welfare legislation. (115 refs.)

Ireland

265 DUNCAN, W.R. The domicile of infants. Irish Jurist 4:36-51 (1969)

266 DUNDAS, PHILIP B. The constitutionality of excluding young people from jury service. Washington and Lee Law Review 29:131-142 (1972)

267 DUNHAM, H. WARREN. The juvenile court: contradicting orientations in processing offenders. In Cavan, Ruth. Readings in juvenile delinquency. 2d edition. New York, J.B. Lippincott, 1969. pp. 370-374.

The author analyzes the development and role of the juvenile court from five points of view. The future of the juvenile court hinges upon the capacity to analyze carefully the issues in this conflict in order that a type of institutional procedure may be devised in conformity with existing knowledge that will insure both protection for the community and essential personality strengths for the youth. (29 refs.)

268 DUNNE, A.L. The fourteenth amendment, the bill of rights, and the juvenile delinquent. The Prosecutor 3:358-363 (1967)

Illinois

269 DUNNE, ARTHUR L. 14th amendment, the bill of rights, and the juvenile delinquent - the juvenile delinquent, who is he? Chicago Bar Record 49:62-73 (1973)

A brief history of the juvenile court is followed by a discussion of the Kent and Gault decisions. The effects of the legal procedural safeguards provided by these two decisions are examined, as well as the four-step procedure regarding the operation of the court utilized in the juvenile court of Cook County.

270 DYBING, ROBERT A., and N. REED SILLIMAN. Juvenile rights under the fourth amendment. Journal of Family Law 11:753-774 (1972)

Forms of "state action" doctrine, and the difficulties and inconsistencies in applying the doctrine are discussed. The existing confusion will continue until the Court provides new guidelines for the "state action" theory. (56 refs.)

271 DYSON, ELIZABETH D., and RICHARD B. DYSON. Family courts in the United States. Parts I and II. Journal of Family Law 8:505-586 (1968) (52 refs.)

N.Y./R.I./Haw.

272 DYSON, ELIZABETH D., and RICHARD B. DYSON. Family courts in the United States. Part III. Journal of Family Law 505-586 (1968)

In Parts I and II of the published report the origin of the family court is examined, and its proposed relationship with existing court structures is described. For comparison, the author uses family courts already established in New York, Rhode Island, and Hawaii. Part III outlines procedures actually used from investigatory through post-hearing stages, with attention to the possible effect of these procedures on the litigants. (22 refs.)

California

273 EADS, WILLIAM E. Observations on the establishment of a child-protective-services system in California. Stanford Law Review 21:1129-1155 (1969) (175 refs.)

274 EAGAN, WILLIAM F., and MICHAEL P. LITKA. Due process and the juvenile court. Social Education 32:469-480 (1968)

A case study of democracy at work, as exemplified by decisions and opinions of the U.S. Supreme Court.

275 EBERHARDT, MICHAEL C. Criminal procedure – due process analysis and the right of juveniles to trial by jury: McKeiver v. Pennsylvania. North Carolina Law Review 50:128-134 (1971)

The author notes that the plurality in McKeiver substantially avoided due process analysis and attempted to support the Court's denial to juveniles of the right to jury trial. Furthermore, it deviated from the positive direction of Gault and Winship. (45 refs.)

Japan

276 EBISAWA, Y. Parent and child in Japanese conflict of laws cases. Journal of International Law and Diplomacy 68:35-109 (1969)

277 ECHOLS, ALVIN E., Jr. Deadline, vengeance and tribute – a prescription for black juvenile delinquency. Crime and Delinquency 16:357-362 (1970)

The author submits that the strategy set up by society to contain black juvenile delinquency has three elements: the deadline – keeping blacks in black neighborhoods; vengeance – a judicial and confinement system that punishes and does not rehabilitate; tribute – programs to buy off trouble temporarily. The strategy's failure to reduce crime has been placed on the black culture rather than on the society that devised the strategy and carries it out.

278 ECKHARDT, KENNETH W. Family responsibility and legal norms. Journal of Marriage and the Family 32:105-109 (1970)

The failure of common law to develop the principle of family responsibility and its subsequent statutory emergence in sixteenth century England provides the focus for examining the assumption that tensions between the family system and other institutions are unique to industrialized society. (16 refs.)

Colorado

279 EDELSON, EDWARD. It's the parent who needs help. Family Health 7:14-17 (1970)

Punishing people who beat their children is no answer, say experts at the battered child clinic in Denver, who try, instead, to repair broken lives and reunite divided families.

New York

280 EDELSTEIN, NATHAN. The law guardian in the New York family court. Juvenile Justice 24(1):14-21 (1973)

A discussion of the function of a law guardian. (22 refs.)

281 EDGE, ROBERT G. Voidability of minor's contracts: a feudal doctrine in a modern economy. Georgia Law Review 1:205-256 (1967)

The purpose of this article is to discuss the general problems of contracts made by minors. (231 refs.)

Canada

282 EDWARDS, C.H., and J. DEBIKA. Infants' liability in contract. Law Society of Manitoba, Isaac Pitblado Lectures on Continuing Legal Education 1-14 (1970)

283 EDWARDS, GEORGE. In defense of the juvenile court. Juvenile Justice 23(2):2-6 (1972)

284 EDWARDS, JAMES L. In loco parentis: definition, application and implication. South Carolina Law Review 23:114-126 (1971)

The intention of this Note is to present several of the areas in which the privilege of in loco parentis is found; to examine the law as it has developed in each area to date; and to determine the extent to which the privilege extends. (72 refs.)

285 EDWARDS, LEONARD. The rights of children. Federal Probation 37:34-41 (1973)

This article summarizes patterns and changes which are occurring today in the juvenile justice system and which should continue. New directions are also suggested.

286 EDWARDS, RALPH. Constitutional law - due process does not require a jury trial in state juvenile proceedings. Texas Tech. Law Review 3:151-158 (1971)

A discussion of McKeiver v. Pennsylvania, 403 U.S. 528 (1971). (31 refs.)

287 EDWARDS, RICHARD A. Adoption - the welfare and best interest of the child. Willamette Law Journal 5:93-103 (1968)

A discussion of what constitutes the best interests of the child, and of what factors or elements are considered by courts. (68 refs.)

Aust./Eng./Wales/Canada

288 EEKELAAR, J.M. Deprivation of parental rights: legislative contrasts in England, Wales, Australia and Canada. Family Law Quarterly 7:381-395 (1973)

This article is concerned with child welfare legislation and with state intervention against parents. The author compares the legal framework of such intervention in systems operating in Australia, England, Wales, and Canada. (46 refs.)

Great Britain

289 EEKELAAR, J.M. What are parental rights? The Law Quarterly Review 89:210-234 (1973)

An examination of parents' rights, and of their duties. (67 refs.)

290 EGER, HARVEY J., and ANTHONY J. POPECK. The abused child: problems and proposals. Duquesne Law Review 8:136-160 (1970)

The scope of the problem is examined and various studies cited. Approaches are suggested, and reasons for objections to the adversary system are given, e.g. the prosecutor's one-sided duty to bring to trial the abusing parent without any corresponding sense of obligation to keep the family intact and functioning. The authors suggest that the prosecutor's only interest is whether or not the parents "did it on purpose" or whether he has sufficient evidence to "win." Legislative solutions are proposed. (27 refs.)

291 ELLIOT, MABEL A. Trends in theories regarding juvenile delinquency and their implication for treatment programs. Federal Probation 31(3):3-11 (1967)

(26 refs.)

292 ELLISON, PATRICIA L. Juvenile law - equal protection for juveniles in the post-adjudicative process - In Re Brown (3rd Cir. 1971). San Diego Law Review 9: 345-354 (1972)

While the precise holding of Brown appears to be of direct precedential value, in few jurisdictions, the reasoning which led the Third Circuit to find a violation of equal protection of law in the area of appellate procedure might well be applied in the future to other areas of juvenile law. (40 refs.)

Oregon

293 EMBICK, MARION B. The "in blank" consent and the independent adoption: a defense. Willamette Law Journal 5:50-65 (1968)

This article is a study of the "in blank" consent as it is known and used in the practice of the law of adoption, in the independent or private placement adoption in Oregon. (76 refs.)

294 EMPEY, LAMAR T. Delinquency theory and recent research. Journal of Research on Crime and Delinquency 4(1):28-42 (1967)

The author discusses fundamental questions in an examination of empirical evidence relating to current theory on delinquency. (68 refs.)

295 EQUI, GLENN C., et al. In Re Gault: understanding the attorney's new role. Villanova Law Review 12:803-838 (1967)

The attorney properly educated in the complexities of the dispositional hearing and the tools which are employed in this phase, can insure that the child will receive the protections afforded to adults plus the solicitous care and regenerative treatment postulated for children. (295 refs.)

296 EVANS, WALTER H., Jr. The constitutional rights of juveniles - or parens patriae v. due process. Willamette Law Journal 4:152-166 (1966)

A discussion of the constitutional rights of juveniles after Kent and Miranda, but prior to Gault. (53 refs.)

297 EVERTON, A.R. The changing face of wardship. Journal of the Association of Law Teachers 2:18-26 (1968)

298 Exclusion of children from violent movies. Columbia Law Review 67:1149-1168 (1967)

The author holds that it is not clear to what extent censorship which directly attacks only expression to the young, may be given more constitutional scope than blanket censorship legislation. The cases do not reveal in what way movies may be given special treatment, treatment which would not be justified as to other media. He discusses the U.S. Court of Appeals case, Interstate circuit, Inc. v. City of Dallas, 366 F.2d 590 (5th Cir. 1966) in relation to the above. (111 refs.)

299 FABER, DIANNE M. Dependent - neglect proceedings: a case for procedural due process. Duquesne Law Review 9:651-664 (1971)

The purpose of this Comment is to set forth arguments for applying standards of due process to dependent-neglect proceedings. (58 refs.)

300 Facts and law of inter-institutional transfer of juveniles. Maine Law Review 20:93-141 (1968)

The law on juvenile transfer is often assumed to be settled. On varying theories a majority of state and federal courts have upheld the constitutionality of various transfer procedures. However, developments in other areas of the law portend a serious challenge to juvenile transfer law. (129 refs.)

301 FAIN, HARRY M. The role and responsibility of the lawyer in custody cases. Family Law Quarterly 1(3):36-47 (1967)

The need for the attorney to clarify his relationship at the outset of employment; the need to counsel the client that no one "wins" or "loses" in a custody case; the importance of discussing the fee because of the possibility of drawnout investigations; the intervention of or need for behavioral experts; and after-divorce counseling. (18 refs.)

302 FAIRLIE, CHESTER. Appellate review of juvenile court dispositions: Gault's forgotten footnote. Connecticut Law Review 5:117-142 (1972)

This paper focuses on the interaction between the legislature, correctional institutions and the trial appellate courts as these agencies grapple with the extensive and inadequately understood problem of the root causes of juvenile delinquency. The question of the degree to which the judiciary will intervene when juvenile correctional facilities are shown to be congested, understaffed or otherwise inadequate is unsettled. (105 refs.)

Connecticut

303 FAIRLIE, CHESTER. Post-commitment custody of neglected children. Connecticut Law Review 4:143-153 (1971)

An analysis of the manner in which the juvenile court in Connecticut and the Protective Services Division of the State Welfare Department handle cases involving neglected children. The author suggests that the allocation of power between these agencies may have resulted in procedures that jeopardize the interests of both parent and child. (38 refs.)

304 FANT, FRED D. Impact of the Gault decision on probation practices in juvenile court. Federal Probation 33:14-18 (1969)

The requirements of due process are not only bringing about changes in juvenile court procedure but in probation as well. There is some resistance, but further change is inevitable. There is a need for judges and probation officers to cooperate. (1 ref.)

305 FAUST, FREDERIC L. Delinquency labeling: its consequences and implications. Crime and Delinquency 19:41-48 (1973)

An assessment of the impact of intervention activities in connection with the control of juvenile delinquency. The "potential delinquent" label is virtually useless for practical application, and corrective intervention based on the assignment of that label is totally unjustified. (14 refs.)

306 FAZZONE, RICHARD A. Juvenile court procedures beyond Gault. Albany Law Review 32:126-138 (1967)

The author discusses the fourteenth amendment requirements of due process and fairness. He asks: will the assumptions made in Gault with respect to the juvenile court process be carried further when other procedural issues are decided. What will be the effect of the uniqueness of juvenile courts in determining the procedures necessary to insure due process and fairness? He concludes that there are three main operative factors in the argument for the extension and expansion of Gault. (55 refs.)

307 FELDBERG, MURRAY. Psychiatric consultation in the juvenile court. Juvenile Court Judges' Journal 20(4):130-133 (1969)

There is frequently a need for psychiatric evaluation at the dispositional stage of a juvenile court proceeding, states the author. However, the psychiatrist must be prepared to consult with the court and its staff at their level of sophistication.

Nebraska

308 FENTON, WILLIAM B. Recommended: an objective standard of care for minors in Nebraska. Nebraska Law Review 46:699-711 (1967)

This Comment is concerned with the changes that are occurring in the standard of care which is required of minors participating in certain adult activities. (47 refs.)

New York

309 FERDINAND, THEODORE N., and ELMER G. LUCHTERBAND. Inner-city youths, the police, the juvenile court, and justice. Social Problems 17:510-527 (1970)

This study done in an area of New York City shows that, in spite of the fact that black first-offender delinquents present less intensive anti-social attitudes and behavior patterns than white delinquents, they receive more severe disposition from police than do the whites. The juvenile court, however, displays little or no discrimination.

California

310 FERGUSON, A. BRUCE. Some kangaroo aspects of our juvenile courts. Journal of the State Bar of California 45:85-89 (1970)

The author points out that many aspects of the California juvenile court process continue to wear the mark of kangaroo proceedings, and that it is the present condition of the California welfare and instutions' code which fosters, albeit subtley, an irregularly operated juvenile court which condition, far too often, renders a fair trial impossible.

California

311 FERGUSON, A. BRUCE, and ALAN C. DOUGLAS. A study of juvenile waiver of rights. Juvenile Court Judges' Journal 21(1):12-22 (1970)

A study of the Miranda warning based on interviews in San Diego, California.

312 FERSTER, ELYCE Z., and THOMAS F. COURTLESS. The beginnings of juvenile justice, police practices, and the juvenile offender. Vanderbilt Law Review 22:567-608 (1969)

The purpose of this study was to gather facts on the present juvenile justice system and on proposed changes. It is concerned with the juvenile offender's initial contacts with the juvenile system, his relations with the police, and the consequences of these relations. The ambiguities and varied interpretations of the law of arrest are cited. (216 refs.)

313 FERSTER, ELYCE Z., and THOMAS F. COURTLESS. Intake process in the affluent county juvenile court. The Hastings Law Journal 22:1127-1153 (1971)

Of all juveniles arrested, less than half appear before a judge, the rest are informally handled by juvenile intake workers. The authors describe the structure of the juvenile intake process, analyze the criteria used to determine which cases will be handled informally, and propose changes in the system. (89 refs.)

314 FERSTER, ELYCE Z., and THOMAS F. COURTLESS. Juvenile detention in an affluent county. Family Law Quarterly 6:3-32 (1972)

The author examines detention practices in a particular suburban county. (115 refs.)

315 FERSTER, ELYCE Z., and THOMAS F. COURTLESS. Post-dispositional treatment and recidivism in the juvenile court: towards justice for all. Journal of Family Law 11:683-709 (1972)

A study dealing with police procedures, detention decisions, court intake, adjudication, post-dispositional treatment and dispositional alternatives. (21 refs.)

316 FERSTER, ELYCE Z., and THOMAS F. COURTLESS. Pre-dispositional data, role of counsel and decisions in a juvenile court. Law and Society Review 7:195-222 (1972)

This article is a report of a three-year research study of the juvenile justice system. The study begins with a presentation and comparative perspective on the incidence and usage both of "social study" and clinical pre-dispositional data. It is concerned also with the role of counsel in the court process. (36 refs.)

317 FERSTER, ELYCE Z., et al. Juvenile detention: protection, prevention or punishment? Fordham Law Review 38:161-196 (1969)

This article, the second in a series reporting the findings of a three year study on "The Juvenile Offenders and the Law," attempts to answer the above question. It is based on an analysis of statutes and cases, a review of the literature including statistical and field reports, and a field study. (231 refs.)

318 FERSTER, ELYCE Z., et al. The juvenile justice system: in search of the role of counsel. Fordham Law Review 39:375-412 (1971)

The role of counsel in the juvenile justice system is explored. (182 refs.)

319 FERSTER, ELYCE Z., et al. Separating official and unofficial delinquents: juvenile court intake. Iowa Law Review 55:864-893 (1970)

This article, the third in a series about the juvenile offender and the law, covers questions about "unofficial delinquency cases." The conclusions given are based on a study of pertinent statutes, court decisions, articles, and court reports. (149 refs.)

320 FINE, R.H., and J.J. FISHMAN. Institutionalized girl delinquents. Diseases of the Nervous System 29:17-27 (1968)

321 FINKLESTEIN, HARRY. Observations on the obvious. Crime and Delinquency 17:310-315 (1971)

It is generally accepted that the surface manifestations of a problem are symptomatic of a complicated psychological process. The child is done a disservice, however, if attention is focussed only on the origin of the problems while the need to do something about the behavior itself is ignored. (6 refs.)

Germany

322 FIPPINGER, F. Child protection as viewed by the younger generation. Jugendschutz 17(1):2-9 (1972)

The author reviews the results of a study of the attitudes of the younger generation in Germany towards child protection.

Ethiopia

323 FISHER, S.Z. Criminal procedure for juvenile offenders in Ethiopia. Journal of Ethiopian Law 7:115-173 (1970)

324 FLAMMANG, C.J. Reflections on the police juvenile enterprise. Juvenile Justice 24(1):22-27 (1973)

Questions are asked about the priorities and directions which affect the police role. (15 refs.)

325 FLYNN, JAMES T. After Gault. New Jersey State Bar Journal 14:8-11 (1970)

Gault still leaves juvenile court judges with many unresolved problems in the administrative attempts to live with the rationale of its jurisprudence.

326 FOGELSON, FRANKLIN B. How social workers perceive lawyers. Social Casework 51:95-101 (1970)

The author notes the results of a study of social workers in three dissimilar casework agencies. He found that most caseworkers articulated an uneasiness about their lack of legal sophistication.

327 FOLEY, TIMOTHY E. Juveniles and their right to a jury trial. Villanova Law Review 15:972-1001 (1970)

A discussion of the constitutional requirement of extending to juveniles the right to a jury trial. (168 refs.)

328 FORE, F. LARKIN, and STEPHEN H. MILLER. Juries for juveniles: a rehabilitative tool. Journal of Family Law 11:107-120 (1971)

This Comment examines the use of the jury concept in juvenile proceedings as a means of insuring this individual treatment for the juvenile who feels prejudged. The feasibility of juries in juvenile proceedings is discussed. (92 refs.)

329 FORER, LOIS G. A children and youth court: a modest proposal. Columbia Human Rights Law Review 4:338-388 (1972)

(37 refs.)

330 FORER, LOIS G. Rights of children: the legal vacuum. American Bar Association Journal 55:1151-1156 (1969)

"What are the rights of children? What is the law?" Children are at the mercy of adults with respect to obtaining medical care, and a society that does not recognize the rights of its youth will find more adults in its jails and mental institutions. (16 refs.)

331 FORT, WILLIAM S. Gault - adversity or opportunity? Judicature 51:53-57 (1967)
An examination of the status of the juvenile court in 1967 both as a legal and as a social organism. A historical background of the juvenile court and correctional practices is given in addition to the legal doctrine of parens patriae.

332 FORT, WILLIAM S. The juvenile justice system. Judicature 51:208-214 (1968)
This article concerns itself with the Task Force Report: Juvenile Delinquency and Youth Crime. The basic issue of the role of authority in the child's life is discussed also.

333 FORTAS, ABE. Equal rights - for whom? New York University Law Review 42: 401-415 (1967)
A discussion of juvenile rights immediately after Kent, and before Gault. (45 refs.)

334 FOSTER, HENRY H. Jr. Adoption and child custody: best interests of the child? Buffalo Law Review 22:1-16 (1972)
Two highly publicized cases, both wrongly decided, and then reversed by subsequent events or legislation, are discussed. (47 refs.)

335 FOSTER, HENRY H., Jr. The future of family law. Annals of the American Academy of Political and Social Science 383:129-144 (1969)
The moral sense of the community is a necessary element in family law which reflects changing social values and felt needs of people. The author hopes that legal aid and community legal services will give greater assistance to poor families with problems, and that welfare laws will eventually be changed in order to promote family stability. (50 refs.)

336 FOSTER, HENRY H., Jr., and DORIS J. FREED. A bill of rights for children. Family Law Quarterly 6:343-375 (1972)
It has been pointed out that the greatest intrusion of government into family life has been with reference to the parent-child relationship, especially in the case of the poor. Increasingly, a challenge will be made where government intervenes and courts will be forced to look at the consequences of state intervention. The authors present a bill of rights for children. (99 refs.)

337 FOSTER, HENRY H., Jr., and DORIS J. FREED. Children and the law. Family Law Quarterly 2:40-62 (1968)
The authors examine the following points at the time the Supreme Court was deliberating on the issues of In Re Gault: child custody; child support; adoption; rights of children; delinquency; dependency and neglect. (101 refs.)

Pennsylvania

338 FOSTER, ROBERT G. Proposals for change in Pennsylvania's treatment of the illegitimate. University of Pittsburgh Law Review 29:566-578 (1968)
The elimination of the status of illegitimates cannot solve the dilemma

society faces with the illegitimate. The most important effects are the social and psychological implications for the individual. Proposals for change in Pennsylvania are submitted. (87 refs.)

Canada

339 FOX, RICHARD G. and MAUREEN J. SPENCER. The Young Offenders Bill: destigmatizing juvenile delinquency? Criminal Law Quarterly 14:172-219 (1971-1972)

The four main policy objectives for introducing the Young Offenders Bill in Canada are analyzed: 1. grounds for trial in juvenile court 2. modification of the age group over which a juvenile court has jurisdiction 3. the elimination of arbitrary treatment in the trial process, and 4. social rehabilitation of juvenile offenders. (155 refs.)

340 FOX, SANFORD J. Juvenile justice reform: an historical perspective. Stanford Law Review 22:1187-1239 (1970)

A review of the juvenile justice reforms and the need, since Gault, for skillful lawyers, trained in juvenile law. (240 refs.)

341 FOX, SANFORD J. Prosecutors in the juvenile court: a statutory proposal. Harvard Journal on Legislation 8:33-53 (1970)

At issue here is the question of how much, if any, of the child welfare spirit is to survive in the juvenile court. A draft statute providing for attorneys to represent the state in juvenile courts, is added. (31 refs.)

342 FOX, SANFORD J. Responsibility in the juvenile court. William and Mary Law Review 11:695-684 (1970)

Common law defenses of infancy and insanity are reviewed as they relate to children charged with crime. The decline of these defenses in the nineteenth century is traced, and a proposal is advanced that a broadened form of those defenses now be recognized in order that grossly immature and severely ill children not be branded as delinquents. (100 refs.)

343 FOX, VERNON A. A handbook for volunteers in juvenile court. Juvenile Justice 23(4):2-31 (1973)

The entire issue of Juvenile Justice is devoted to this handbook which is arranged in four parts: the philosophy of volunteers; what volunteers can do; recruitment and assignment of volunteers; coordination of volunteer programs.

Oregon

344 FRANKLIN, JERRY, and DON C. GIBBONS. New directions for juvenile courts - probation officers' views. Crime and Delinquency 19:508-518 (1973)

Research studies on Supreme Court rulings regarding due process for juveniles are reviewed. This study examines attitudes of juvenile court counselors in Portland, Oregon, toward due process and restrictions upon the powers of the juvenile court and correctional workers. (18 refs.)

Connecticut

345 FRAUENHOFER, DAVID J., et al. Practice and procedure of the juvenile court for the state of Connecticut. Connecticut Bar Journal 41:201-261 (1967)
(261 refs.)

Yugos./U.S.

346 FREASE, D.E. The schools and juvenile delinquency in Yugoslavia and the United States. Revija za Kriminalistiko in Kriminologijo 22:11-19 (1971)

347 FREEDBERG, SHARON M. Humanizing the system. Trial 7(5):26-27 (1971)
The need for the "juvenile court clinic" as a relevant link in the juvenile justice system is examined.

Iowa

348 FREY, MARTIN A. The effect of the Gault decision on the Iowa juvenile justice system. Drake Law Review 17:53-67 (1967)
Weaknesses in the Iowa juvenile justice system occur not through direct conflict between the Iowa code and the U.S. Supreme Court's holding in Gault, but through ommissions in the code. (56 refs.)

349 FREY, MARTIN A. Intent in fact, insanity and infancy: elusory concepts in the exercise of juvenile court jurisdiction. California Western Law Review 9:273-289 (1973)
(44 refs.)

350 FREY, MARTIN A. and CHARLES P. BUBANY. Pre-adjudication review of the social record in juvenile court: a low-visibility obstacle to a fair process. Journal of Family Law 12:391-404 (1972-1973)
A discussion of the social record and its impact and effect on the juvenile court hearing, whether this may be bifurcated or non-bifurcated. (13 refs.)

Canada

351 FRIEDMAN, M.H. Infants and the corporation. Law Society of Manitoba, Isaac Pitblado Lectures on Continuing Legal Education 28-37 (1970)

North Dakota

352 FRIEDRICH, RAY R. A study and evaluation of the juvenile court - its procedure and facilities in North Dakota. North Dakota Law Review 45:183-203 (1969)
A review, in capsule form, of the major findings and recommendations of the "Study of Services for the Control and Treatment of Juvenile Delinquency in the State of North Dakota" 1968, undertaken by the U.S. Department of Health, Education and Welfare, Children's Bureau. The areas discussed are: organization and structure of services for delinquents; detention and shelter care for delinquent children; the juvenile court and probation service; aftercare supervision; staff development; legislative comment. (17 refs.)

Germany

353 FRÖHLICH, H.H. Methodologische Aspekte der Feststellung der Schuldfähigkeit Jugendlicher. Neue Justiz 25:9-14 (1971)

Japan

354 FUJIKI, H. Revision of the juvenile law. Kesei 82(2):12-19 (1971)

New York

355 GAGLIARDO, ANGELO J. Are youth bureaus the answer? Juvenile Court Judges' Journal 22(3):57-59 (1971)

A discussion of the juvenile justice system.

New York

356 GAINES, JONATHAN E., and PAUL A. SKRABUT. The youth court concept and its implementation in Tompkins County, New York. Cornell Law Quarterly 52: 942-974 (1967)

This description of the youth court, established in 1962, includes discussions of the practical means by which the youth court concept can be effectuated under existing law, the present effect of the youth court scheme on the participants, and suggested legislation. (147 refs.)

Canada

357 GALLIGAN, PATRICK. Protection of children in family disputes. Canadian Bar Journal (N.S.) 4:10-12, 21 (1973)

The interests of children involved in family disputes are discussed.

Texas

358 GALLIGAN, ROBERT L. The balance between individual rights and family preservation: the future of the parent-child immunity doctrine in Texas. St. Mary's Law Journal 4:48-63 (1972)

Indications that the Texas supreme court may be willing to abolish the parent-child immunity doctrine with respect to most acts of ordinary negligence are discussed in conjunction with the Wisconsin approach. (101 refs.)

359 GALVIN, DALE J. Olff v. East Side Union High School District: school hair regulations and the right to privacy. Willamette Law Journal 8:277-283 (1972)

The author submits that the Olff court, 445 F.2d 932 (9th Cir. 1971) failed to give proper weight to the vigilant protection of constitutional freedom. (30 refs.)

California

360 GANZFRIED, JERROLD J. Double jeopardy and the waiver of jurisdiction in California's juvenile courts. Stanford Law Review 24:874-902 (1972)

This Note examines the interplay of double jeopardy doctrines and the California scheme of waiving juvenile court jurisdiction. (139 refs.)

361 GARCIA, EDWIN C. The fallacy of the Gault case. Judicature 54:249-250 (1971)

According to the author, the assumption that procedures in criminal court and in juvenile court are fundamentally the same, and therefore, the criteria developed and meant for the one can be unconditionally applied to the other, is wrong. In Re Gault, if accepted unconditionally, will destroy the progress made in dealing with anti-social behavior of young people.

California

362 GARDNER, ROBERT. Gault and California. Hastings Law Journal 19:527-539 (1968)

An analysis of the California juvenile court law and the questions which Gault does and does not answer. (90 refs.)

California

363 GARDNER, ROBERT. Juvenile Justice. In Lee, Eugene C., and Willis D. Hawley, eds. The Challenge of California with a concise introduction to California government. Boston, Little, Brown, and Co., Inc., 1970. pp. 149-153.

The philosophy and practices of the juvenile court are examined along with the California juvenile court law of 1961, and Gault. Juvenile rights are contrasted with those of adults.

364 GARDNER, ROBERT. The Kent case and the juvenile court: a challenge to lawyers. American Bar Association Journal 52:923-925 (1966)

The author contends that the legal profession is responsible for problems existing in the juvenile court system, and that the Kent decision reflects the uneasiness of lawyers who should, in fact, be showing leadership in the reform of juvenile justice.

California

365 GARFIELD, GLENDALEE. Juvenile law - a potential for California change. Pacific Law Journal 2:737-756 (1971)

This Comment reviews and analyzes the controversy around the law in Section 601 of the California Welfare and Institutions Code which authorizes jurisdiction by the juvenile court over minors who are found to have "delinquent" tendencies. (108 refs.)

366 GARGIULO, WILLIAM C. Liability for leaving a firearm accessible to children. Cleveland-Marshall Law Review 17:472-480 (1968)

The objective of this Note is to consider whether or not the doctrine of absolute liability should be extended to hold that when a person permits a child to have a firearm, or leaves one accessible to him, he is absolutely liable for any injury or damage to real or personal property that occurs after the firearm has been discharged by the child. (50 refs.)

367 GARNER, M. CRAIG, Jr. Due process and waiver of juvenile court jurisdiction. Washington and Lee Law Review 30:591-613 (1973)

The author maintains that some method of review of the waiver decision appears necessary in order to protect the juvenile. He gives suggestions. (175 refs.)

368 GARY, HOLLAND M. Help for the retarded delinquent. Juvenile Court Judges' Journal 19(1):20-23 (1968)

(2 refs.)

Germany

369 GEISTER, E., und H. LEHMAN. Zum Ausspruch und zur Verwirklichung der Verurteilung und Bewährung und der besonderen Pflichten Jug endlicher nach §70 StGB. Neue Justiz 24:386-390 (1970)

Germany

370 GENSER-DITTMAN, U. Judicial decision making in juvenile court trials. Kriminologisches Journal 4:120-125 (1972)

A discussion of some of the variables which determine the sentence in Germany: type and severity of offense; previous convictions and record; the impression in court; social variables. The use of pre-sentence reports and court records is also examined.

371 GEORGE, B.J., Jr. The implications of Gault for welfare administration. Family Law Quarterly 2:182-199 (1968)

The author shows that pre-Gault juvenile law and the present welfare system grew out of similar backgrounds, and that both have maintained a facade of benevolence behind which an essentially punitive system functions. Gault, though it does not bear at all on the law of welfare administration, is being increasingly cited as persuasive analogy in the ever more frequent litigation seeking to bring about judicial intervention in the welfare system. (81 refs.)

372 GEORGE, B.J., Jr. Juvenile delinquency proceedings: the due process model. Colorado Law Review 40:315-337 (1968)

The Gault case is the first of a series of legal battles in which due process requirements will be expanded far beyond what has traditionally been thought their scope of application to juvenile proceedings. The author examines the application of other adult guarantees, e.g. public proceedings, jury trial, confrontation, appeal, and the recording of proceedings in considering the scope of change that Gault and similar cases dictate. (89 refs.)

Belgium

373 GERLO, J. De burgerrechtelijke bepalingen van de wet op de jeugdbeschermung. Tijdschrift voor Privaatrecht 10:113-162 (1973)

Iowa

374 GERMAN, JUDITH M. Juvenile courts - in Iowa, statutory due process requires a separate hearing on the question of transfer before a juvenile court may properly waive jurisdiction to the criminal court. Drake Law Review 22:213-221 (1972)

While rejecting the constitutional argument of double jeopardy, in State v. Halverson, 192 N.W.2d 765, 766 (Iowa, 1971), the majority of the Iowa court agreed that a denial of the juvenile's statutory right to a separate transfer hearing under Section 232.72 of the Code of Iowa is grounds for dismissal. A procedural flaw was cited by the supreme court as the basis for its ruling. (74 refs.)

Germany

375 GERNHUBER, J. Kindeswohl und Elternwille. Zeitschrift für das Gesamte Familienrecht 20:229-244 (1973)

376 GERSCH, WESLEY A. Double jeopardy and the juvenile. Journal of Family Law 11:603-614 (1972)

The following questions are examined in this Comment: 1. Should jeopardy attach in a juvenile proceeding at the same point it attaches in an adult proceeding, or does separate procedural classification between adults and juveniles justify different standards? 2. Could the rationale utilized in McKeiver be limited to a denial of a juvenile's right to a jury trial? 3. Is the protection from double jeopardy essential to the best interests of the juvenile? (67 refs.)

Germany

377 GERSON, W. Probleme im Jugendstrafvollzug, insbesondere das Problem der Anpassung. Zentralblatt fuer Jugendrecht und Jugendwohlfahrt 265-277 (1967)

378 GERWIN, S.R. And kids have rights too. In Beck, Carl., ed. Essays in honor of Robert S. Rankin. College Station, Duke University Press, 1970. pp. 121-131.

379 GIBBENS, T.C.N. Drinks, drugs, and delinquency. Medicine, Science, and the Law 12:257-265 (1972)

(1 ref.)

380 GIL, DAVID G., and JOHN H. NOBEL. Public knowledge and attitudes and opinions about physical child abuse in the United States. Child Welfare 48:395-401, 426 (1969)

The authors drew a sample chart of 1500 names from the nationwide study of child abuse conducted for the U.S. Children's Bureau, and studied these cases on a more comprehensive level. Various types of abuse are described and analyzed, for example, "mounting stress on the perpetrator because of life circumstances." This study suggests that the problem of child abuse has been greatly exaggerated, and is largely associated with the poverty syndrome.

Sweden

381 GIRSBERGER, M. Die Behandlung jugendlicher Rechtsbrecher in Schweden. Schweizerische Zeitschrift für Strafrecht 89:34-51 (1973)

382 GITCHOFF, G. THOMAS. The dilemma of the delinquent - a satirical comment on definitions and jargon. Criminology 11:115-117 (1973)

Simple definitions become ambiguous, and oftentimes fail to communicate the meaning intended, states the author, who gives some illustrations of the highly technocratic jargon that could be applied to the omnipresent problem of defining the term "delinquent," from several absurd perspectives. He includes the psychiatric view, the psychological view, the anthropological view, amongst others.

Poland

383 GIZ, J.ST. The sexual juvenile delinquent in Poland. Nowe Prawo 6:837-851 (1970)

384 GJONLIKU, L. Quelques questions concerning la criminalité des mineurs, leurs causes et l'organization de la lutte préventive. Drejtësia Popullore 25(2):65-75 (1972)

385 GLEN, JEFFREY E. Bifurcated hearing in the juvenile court. Crime and Delinquency 16:255-263 (1970)

In this paper, the nature and procedures of the juvenile court adjudication process, as distinguished from the dispositional hearings, are briefly discussed and related to the need for separate adjudicatory and dispositional hearings in the juvenile court. The problems of permitting certain dispositional functions to occur before adjudication are then considered, as well as the question of whether the dispositional hearing, or that phase of the hearing, must always take place at a later date than the adjudicatory hearing or phase. "Bifurcation," in this article, refers to the separation of the adjudicatory hearing (analogous to the criminal trial) from the dispositional hearing (analogous to the criminal sentencing hearing) by a substantial period of time, the hearings being scheduled and held on different days. (33 refs.)

386 GLEN, JEFFREY E. Developments in juvenile and family court law. Crime and Delinquency 15:295-305 (1969)

This article comments on juvenile and family court legislation enacted in 1968, and on recent cases. (13 refs.)

387 GLEN, JEFFREY E. Interrogation of children: when are their admissions admissable? Family Law Quarterly 2:280-295 (1968)

The Council of Judges of the National Council on Crime and Delinquency has proposed a rule governing the admissibility in juvenile proceedings of out-of-court statement. The author discusses the reliability of statements made in the station-house, and offers models for police investigation. (53 refs.)

388 GLEN, JEFFREY E. Juvenile court reform: procedural process and substantive stasis. Wisconsin Law Review 431-449 (1970)

The state of the law of procedure at adjudication is surveyed and evaluated. Bifurcated hearings are suggested. (73 refs.)

389 GODDARD, JEWEL, and GERALD D. JACOBSON. Volunteer services in a juvenile court. Crime and Delinquency 13:337-343 (1967)

390 GOLD, MARTIN, and JAY R. WILLIAMS. National study of the aftermath of apprehension. Prospectus, a Journal of Law Reform 3:3-12 (1969)

Two independent studies demonstrate that apprehension itself encourages rather than deters further delinquency. This article documents that conclusion. (9 refs.)

New York

391 GOLD, SARAH. Equal protection for juvenile girls in need of supervision in New York state. New York Law Forum 17:570-598 (1971)
This article examines two New York laws which treat males and females unequally. (122 refs.)

New York

392 GOLDMAN, DEBORAH G. The Gault decision and the New York Family Court Act. Syracuse Law Review 19:753-768 (1968)
A discussion of Gault, Miranda, and the New York Family Court Act. (68 refs.)

393 GOLDMAN, MIMI. Women's crime in a male society. Juvenile Court Judges' Journal 22(2):33-35 (1971)
A discussion of double standards and the female offender in juvenile court. (9 refs.)

394 GOLDMEIER, JOHN. The runaway: person, problem, or situation? Crime and Delinquency 19:539-544 (1973)
This study, conducted in a relatively affluent suburban county, compared two groups of adolescents - those who ran away once or more, and those who never ran away. The author sought explanations for runaway behavior. (27 refs.)

395 GOLMAN, SIDNEY J. The lawyer's changing role in a rapidly changing society. Denver Law Journal 44:88-101 (1967)
A thought-provoking discussion on the status of the attorney in personal injury and workmen's compensation cases.

California

396 GONION, GORDON E. Section 601 California Welfare and Institutions Code: a need for a change. San Diego Law Review 9:294-311 (1972)
Unless the public is correctly informed of the shortcomings of the criminal justice system, it cannot be expected to respond to needed changes or provide the resources necessary to deal with juveniles, whose conduct is non-criminal, but who are involved with the juvenile court system. There should be a continuation of the movement towards narrowing down the juvenile court's jurisdiction. (77 refs.)

397 GOODMAN, DONALD J. Constitutional law - parental liability statute held unconstitutional. Georgia State Bar Journal 9:129-137 (1972)
(48 refs.)

398 GOODMAN, JEROME D. New directions: child psychiatry and the juvenile court. Juvenile Court Judges' Journal 21(1):2-9, 32 (1970)
Dr. Goodman discusses the problems which beset the intimate working relationship between the child psychiatrist and the courts.

399 GOODMAN, STEPHEN M. Right to treatment: the responsibility of the courts. The Georgetown Law Journal 57:680–701 (1969)

The author compares the court's emerging willingness to scrutinize the treatment which delinquents receive, with the long-accepted right to compensation for the taking of property. He notes that the absence of treatment may "warrant the ordering of treatment or release." (88 refs.)

400 GOODSIT, SOL. The family code and the challenge of the seventies. Marquette Law Review 54:19–40 (1971)

The author draws attention to the need for legal representation for children in domestic relations cases. (33 refs.)

Germany

401 GÖPPINGER, H. Die Reform des Rechts der Unehelichen Kinder. Juristische Rundschau (4):125–129 (1967)

New York

402 GORDON, HIRAM D. Terminal placements of children and permanent termination of parental rights: the New York permanent neglect statute. St. John's Law Review 46:215–263 (1971)

This article examines the problem of those children who will neither be taken back into the homes of their natural parents nor legally freed by their parents for placement in an adoptive home. The usefulness of the three statutory schemes for resolving the problem are discussed. (237 refs.)

403 GOUGH, AIDAN R. The beyond-control child and the right to treatment: an exercise in the synthesis of paradox. St. Louis University Law Journal 16:182–200 (1971)

This essay examines the existence of the "right to treatment" as a legally-cognizable prerogative of the person affected; and the state's coercive intervention by means of the juvenile court process in cases where a child has violated no criminal law, but nevertheless engages in behavior which is thought to evidence rebellion and place his future in jeopardy. (95 refs.)

404 GOUGH, AIDAN R. Consent decrees and informal services in the juvenile court: excursions toward balance. University of Kansas Law Review 19:733–746 (1971)

The author argues against any abridgment of a juvenile's rights, and believes that too little attention has been focused on the question of consent decrees and informal processes, such as the means of diversion from court process through probation or otherwise. (79 refs.)

California

405 GOUGH, AIDAN R. Referees in California's juvenile court: a study in sub-judicial adjudication. Hastings Law Journal 19:3–28 (1967)

A study of referees and present laws relating to referees in the California juvenile court. (98 refs.)

406 GOUGH, AIDAN R., and MARY A. GRILLI. The unruly child and the law: toward a focus on the family. Juvenile Justice 23(3):9-12 (1972)

The authors believe that serious thought should be given to the feasibility of an entirely new jurisdictional concept, the Family in Need of Service (FINS) which could subsume the existing jurisdictional categories of the neglected and the beyond-control child. (15 refs.)

Poland

407 GRČAR, M. i A. WOLNY. The role of expert psychologists in obtaining and evaluating the juvenile witness' evidence. Z Zagadnień Kryminalistyki 6:30-41 (1971)

408 GREEN, MARK J. Runaways on the legal leash. Trial 7(5):28-29 (1971)

A discussion of runaway statutes and their violation of our notions of civil liberties.

New York

409 GREENBERG, WILLIAM G. The consent decree and the New York Family Court procedure in "JD" and "PINS" cases. Syracuse Law Review 23:1211-1225 (1972)

The purpose of this article is to demonstrate how the New York Family Court's pre-judicial practices might be improved: 1. examination of the family court's current procedure, 2. evaluation of the procedure's pre-judicial shortcomings, 3. alternatives and suggestions, e.g. the "consent decree." (88 refs.)

410 GREENE, NANCY B., and T.C. ESSELSTYN. The beyond-control girl. Juvenile Justice 23(3):13-19 (1972)

This discussion concerns girls who are often described as ungovernable, unmanageable, incorrigible, wayward, or predelinquent. Some conclusions on beyond-control behavior are outlined. The need for future policy decisions and noncourt services is emphasized, as the diversion of girls, without much comprehension of what this involves, may bring further problems. (12 refs.)

Canada

411 GREENLAND, C. Reporting child abuse in Ontario. Reports of Family Law 10:44-53 (1973)

412 GREENSPUN, JULIAN. Role of the attorney in juvenile court. Cleveland-Marshall Law Review/Cleveland State Law Review 18:599-609 (1969)

A review of the attorney's role in the courtroom; the attorney as an advocate and other miscellaneous vocations; the importance of presence in connection with evidence, hearsay, quantum of proof, and disposition. (51 refs.)

413 GROGAN, HIRAM J., and RUTH C. GROGAN. The criminogenic family - does chronic tension trigger delinquency? Crime and Delinquency 14:220-225 (1968)

Individual studies and background investigations of delinquents and criminals show significant and excessive tension in their family milieu. (15 refs.)

414 GROSS, SEYMOUR Z. The prehearing juvenile report: probation officers' conceptions. Journal of Research in Crime and Delinquency 4:212-217 (1967)

This study was undertaken to determine how the probation officer handling juvenile offenders conceives the importance of the various sections of the prehearing report in terms of usefulness for appropriate or accurate recommendation of disposition. (11 refs.)

Austria

415 GROSSBERGER, R. Kriminologische Aspekte des Suchtsmittel-Missbrauche Minderjähriger in Österreich. Kriminalistik 25:173-176 (1971)

Canada

416 GROSMAN, BRIAN A. Young offenders before the court. Canadian Bar Association Journal 2:6-7 (1971)

The author is afraid that the introduction of detailed rules of criminal procedure and protections will lead the juvenile courts in Canada away from their informal rehabilitative function, and towards an adversary process which might be detrimental to the juvenile's ultimate welfare.

417 GRUMET, BARBARA R. The plaintiff plaintiffs: victims of the battered child syndrome. Family Law Quarterly 4:296-317 (1970)

A discussion of child abuse. (70 refs.)

418 GRUSON, KERRY. The state's juvenile justice system is delinquent. Popular Government 36:24-29 (1970)

Once a juvenile from a poor, possibly black, possibly one-parent family, is in trouble, he is more likely to be judged delinquent by the courts.

419 GUERNSEY, CARL. The juvenile in the criminal justice system. Proceedings. In the 17th Annual Southern Conference on Corrections 17:83-88 (1972)

420 Guides to the judge in medical orders affecting children. Crime and Delinquency 14:107-120 (1968)

The following are discussed: how extreme must the danger be to justify judicial intervention? What elements must be proved to support a finding of medical neglect? What kind of evidence should be required at the hearing? Should the court have the power to order medical treatment without a hearing in some cases? Can notice to parents be dispensed with? (39 refs.)

U.S.S.R.

421 GUKOVSKAJA, N.I. Preventive measures applied to juvenile delinquents. Voprosy bor'by s prestupnost'ju 16:127-137 (1972)

A discussion of the preventive measures which are applied in Russia when: 1. there is a risk that the suspect will evade investigation and trial; 2. establishment of the facts is impeded; 3. the delinquent behavior might continue; 4. a sentence cannot be executed. Pre-trial detention is to be avoided, if possible, because even a brief period of detention can have a traumatic effect on the juvenile psyche, and unfavorable influences may be exerted by fellow prisoners.

Indiana

422 GULLICK, ROBERT. Right to jury trial: Indiana's misapplication of due process standards in delinquency hearings. Indiana Law Journal 45:578-594 (1970)
(90 refs.)

Canada

423 HAGAN, J.L. The labeling perspective, the delinquent and the police: a review of the literature. Canadian Journal of Criminology and Corrections 14(2):150-165 (1972)
A study of the policeman's response to juvenile behaviors and the application of the labeling perspective, is reviewed.

424 HALL, J.C. The waning of parental rights. Cambridge Law Journal 31:248-265 (1972)
The decline in the strength of parental rights, and the promotion of the interests of the child are discussed. (38 refs.)

425 HAMILTON, GEORGE. Some domestic relations problems connected with children. Texas Bar Journal 33:283-284, 286-288, 290 (1970)
(2 refs.)

426 HAMILTON, H. BRUCE. In re Gault and the persisting questions of procedural due process and legal ethics in juvenile courts. Nebraska Law Review 47:558-592 (1968)
The author argues that the present system fails to meet the need for an accurate determination of the facts, and that the resulting adjudication of delinquency has become as stigmatizing as being committed as a criminal. (166 refs.)

427 HAMMERGREN, DONALD R. The role of juvenile detention in a changing juvenile justice system. Juvenile Justice 24(3):46-49 (1973)

428 Handbook for new juvenile court judges. Juvenile Court Judges' Journal 23(1):1-31 (1972)
The following topics are dealth with: philosophy and theory of the juvenile court; the role of the juvenile court judge; the constitution; due process and changing times; rules of practice and procedure; role of attorney; detention and shelter use and practice; neglect, dependency, child abuse and protective services; juvenile court administration.

429 HANDLER, JOEL F. The juvenile court and the adversary system: problems of functions and form. Wisconsin Law Review 7-51 (1965)
Much of the current effort to reform the administration of juvenile justice is aimed at introducing adversary procedures to determine the statutory status and disposition of adolescents. The author analyzes the positions for and against judicializing the procedures, and concludes that neither is adequate for determining the issues. He proposes introducing adversary procedures at the administrative level of the process with provisions for judicial control and supervision. (118 refs.)

430 HANSEN, CONNOR T. Constitutional rights of juveniles: the changes wrought by Kent and Gault. Gavel 28:7-10 (1968)

(15 refs.)

431 HANSEN, RICHARD H. Suggested guidelines for child abuse laws. Journal of Family Law 7:61-65 (1967)

Child abuse laws are now in existence in forty-nine states. However, these statutes and attendant procedures do not solve the problem of child abuse. The judge should be given the power to direct studies of the child and his family to determine disposition. (8 refs.)

432 HANSEN, ROBERT W., and SIDNEY J. GOLDBERG. Casework in a family court. Social Casework 48:416-421 (1967)

The author describes the functions of the social service branch of the family court and emphasizes their diversity and philosophy. A just determination of custody of a child whose parents are litigants in a divorce action requires close collaboration of court, lawyer, and social worker. (2 refs.)

433 HARGRAVE, LEE. Fairness in juvenile court. Louisiana Law Review 27:606-624 (1967)

This comment is concerned with the delinquent child who commits a wrongful act. Although legislation clarifying and establishing the rights of a child in juvenile court is needed, better trained juvenile court judges and staff are even more urgently required. (78 refs.)

434 HARGROVE, JOHN R. Consortium - child's right to recover for negligent interference with the parent-child relationship. Indiana Legal Forum 4:552-565 (1971)

The purpose of this article is to show that a child has an enforceable right against a third party who causes the child to lose the support, guidance, assistance and maintenance of a parent - that which only a parent can provide. (66 refs.)

Australia

435 HARLAND, D.J. The contractual capacity of minors. Sydney Law Review 7:41-61 (1973)

436 HARMON, MAURICE A. Unraveling administrative organization of state juvenile services. Crime and Delinquency 13:432-438 (1967)

The trend is toward statewide consolidation of services to children and youth, including the basic programs of protection, prevention, probation, detention, diagnosed institutionalization, and aftercare. (4 refs.)

Great Britain

437 HARRIS, BRIAN. Children's act in trouble: an appreciation of the children and young persons act 1969 in operation. Criminal Law Review 670-684 (1972)

The purpose of this article is to examine, from the point of view of a practitioner in the juvenile courts, the principal legal and administrative difficulties brought about by Part I of the children and young persons act 1969, in Great Britain, and to suggest, where possible, how they can be overcome. (6 refs.)

438 HARRIS, OTEKA. Torts: responsibility of a young child for his negligent or intentional acts. Oklahoma Law Review 26:300-304 (1973)

(18 refs.)

Massachusetts

439 HARRIS, RICHARD. Annals of law - in criminal court. The New Yorker 45-88 (April 14, 1973), 44-87 (April 28, 1973)

A detailed description, in two parts, of justice melted out to young people in a Boston court. The author discusses some judges' methods of disposition/sentencing when the state's case is weak and might not hold up on appeal.

California

440 HARRIS, ROBERT L. California's predelinquency statute: a case study and suggested alternatives. California Law Review 60:1163-1195 (1972)

This Comment is a discussion of Section 601 of the California Welfare and Institutions Code in its historical context, and in the context of police action against transient juveniles in Berkeley, California. Sections 600, 601, and 602 permit broad juvenile court intrusion into the personal affairs of many minors. (175 refs.)

441 HARTMAN, MARSHALL. A constitutional challenge to the juvenile court. NLADA Briefcase 30:30-32 (1971)

A discussion of the impact of Kent, Gault, Winship, and McKeiver on juvenile courts across the United States.

Oregon

442 HATCH, JONATHAN C. Legislative opportunity for Oregon: the uniform child custody jurisdiction act. Willamette Law Journal 7:498-510 (1971)

The purpose of this paper is to advocate reassessment of the Oregon position, and to urge enactment of the Uniform Child Custody Jurisdiction Act by the legislature, as the domicile rule is no longer a useful jurisdictional determinate in these cases. (64 refs.)

California

443 HATHERLY, JOHN E. The role of the child's wishes in California custody proceedings. UCD Law Review 6:332-353 (1973)

This article discusses one aspect of the child's custody provisions - the role of the child's wishes. It examines the statutory and judicial milieu within which the expression of these wishes takes place, and concludes with a recommendation to mitigate the possible harm resulting from the traditional two-party adversary proceedings. (99 refs.)

China

444 HAUCH-WEN, W. A study of the rustication of youth on the Chinese mainland. Issues and Studies 7(4):84-95 (1971)

445 HAUSMAN, ANNE K. The administrative transfer of juveniles from juvenile to adult penal institutions. St. Louis University Law Journal 16:479-496 (1972)

In appraising the administrative transfer, questions arise as to the vitality of the juvenile court's objectives, the bases for justification of the transfer procedure, the constitutional issues litigated, the statutory response, and finally, the alternatives. (111 refs.)

Kansas

446 HAVILAND, CAMILLA K. Daddy will take care of you: the dichotomy of the juvenile court. University of Kansas Law Review 17:317-323 (1969)

The Kansas juvenile code anticipated most of the requirements of Whittington, Gault and Kent and, troublesome though its parens patriae foundation may be, the code represents a fair attempt to balance the fatherly concept with procedural safeguards. Kansas has more juvenile judges per capita than any other state. (38 refs.)

District of Columbia

447 HAWES, ALEXANDER B. Gault and the District of Columbia. American University Law Review 17:153-166 (1968)

Close examination of the majority opinion in Gault indicates that the U.S. Supreme Court has not finally decided that all of the Bill of Rights would be applicable to a juvenile court proceeding in a federal jurisdiction. By emphasizing that juvenile court proceedings are not criminal in nature, the court can avoid being forced to apply to the juvenile court of the District of Columbia all of the safeguards of adult criminal proceedings guaranteed by the Bill of Rights. (58 refs.)

Texas

448 HAWORTH, STEVEN C. Is failure to appoint a guardian ad litem fundamental error in juvenile delinquency proceedings? Baylor Law Review 24:619-630 (1972)

(38 refs.)

Japan

449 HAYASHI, Y. Analysis of juvenile traffic offenders' subjective written response to various types of treatments. Katei Saiban Geppo 22(4):131-156 (1970)

Texas

450 HAYS, J. RAY, and KENNETH S. SOLWAY. The role of psychological evaluation in certification of juveniles for trial as adults. Houston Law Review 9:709-715 (1972)

The authors feel that the present status of the psychologist as consultant to the court in Texas is adequate, but that both courts and attorneys have failed to fully understand the relevancy of psychological reports. A study of juveniles under detention in Harris County was undertaken in early 1970. (8 refs.)

Finland

451 HELASVUO, K. The treatment of juvenile delinquents within the field of child welfare. Tidskrift utgiven av Juridiska Foereningen i Finland 103:202-114 (1967)

Germany

452 HELLMER J. Hat sich das jugendstrafrecht bewährt? Zentralblatt für Jugendrecht und Jugendwohlfahrt 60:42-53 (1973)

Georgia

453 HENRITZE, LUCY S. Juvenile law and the juvenile court system. Mercer Law Review 24:187-198 (1973)

Changes in the Georgia Juvenile Court Code by the 1972 General Assembly are discussed. Evidence is noted of a laudable effort by the court of appeals, whose opinions in 1972 were full, logical, considered expositions of issues, to develop a jurisprudence of juvenile law. (42 refs.)

Georgia

454 HENRITZE, LUCY S. Juvenile law and the juvenile court system. Mercer Law Review 25(1):169-176 (1974)

A discussion of the recent amendment to the 1971 Georgia Juvenile Court Code. The author argues that the survey year indicates both a legislative and judicial retrenching from the advance marked by the passage of the 1971 juvenile court code. (39 refs.)

Georgia

455 HENRITZE, LUCY S. Persisting problems of Georgia juvenile court practice. Mercer Law Review 23:341-360 (1972)

The Georgia legislature responded to the need for reform of the basic juvenile court statute, and the new act is a progressive, vastly improved master plan for the administration of juvenile courts according to the author of this article. However, additional changes are suggested. (59 refs.)

456 HESS, ALBERT G., and FRÉ LE POOLE. Abuse of the record of arrest not leading to conviction. Crime and Delinquency 13:494-505 (1967)

This paper compares the United States with thirty-nine other countries in regard to the use of records of arrest which have not led to conviction. (48 refs.)

457 HEYNS, GARRETT. The road ahead in corrections. Federal Probation 33:11-16 (1969)

(1 ref.)

Oregon

458 HICKS, GRAHAM M. State v. McMaster: due process in termination of parental rights. Willamette Law Journal 8:284-293 (1972)

The author points out that the Oregon statute is vague and indefinite as it does not protect either the constitutional rights of the parents or the best interests of the child because there is not specific standard required of all parents. An indefinite statute does not make termination of parental rights easier; if anything it makes the termination more difficult. (36 refs.)

New York

459 HILDEBRAND, JAMES A. Reasons for runaways. Crime and Delinquency 14:42-48 (1968)

This investigation examines the runaway problem in two New York City precincts, one in a low-income and high-crime area, the other in a middle-income section. (8 refs.)

460 HILL, JAMES S. Constitutional law - schools and school districts - prohibition of long hair absent showing of actual disruption violates unspecified ninth amendment rights to govern one's personal appearance. North Dakota Law Review 49:173-179 (1972)
A discussion of Bishop v. Colaw, 450 F.2d 1069 (8th Cir.1971). (40 refs.)

Canada

461 HINES, G. In the Crown Court. Magistrate 29(1):8-9 (1973)
The author outlines critical areas in the Canadian Children and Young Person Act, 1969 pertaining to orders for care or supervision.

Texas

462 HOCKER, ELAINE A. Texas juvenile delinquency proceedings do not require proof beyond a reasonable doubt. Houston Law Review 7:400-409 (1970)
It is submitted that the problem of due process standards and the close parallel between dependency and delinquency cases should be resolved by the classification of juvenile court proceedings into three categories. (87 refs.)

463 HOFFMANN, BLAIR W. Restrictions on a parent's right to travel in child custody cases: possible constitutional questions. UCD Law Review 6:181-194 (1973)
Serving the welfare of the child, which appears to be a "constitutionally permissable state objective" is the most often stated ground for limiting the residence of the child. This article discusses whether travel restrictions are subject to constitutional limitations as an infringement of the right to travel. (79 refs.)

464 HOFFMAN, MARTIN L., and HERBERT SALTZSTEIN. Parent discipline and the child's moral development. Journal of Personality and Social Psychology 5:45-57 (1967)
In this study children were assessed on several dimensions of moral development. Discipline techniques were coded into three different categories: power assertion, in which the parent capitalizes on his power and authority over the child; love withdrawal, i.e. direct but non-physical expressions of anger, disapproval, etc.; and induction, consisting of the parents' focusing on the consequences of the child's action for other people. (19 refs.)

Texas

465 HOFFMAN, MATTHEW. The constitutionality of pre-trial juvenile proceedings in Texas - especially detention. South Texas Law Journal 14:434-457 (1973)
The purpose of this Comment is to examine pre-trial proceedings in Texas by comparing the existing statute as well as the current informal practices, with the recently enacted Texas Family Code Title III, which became effective on September 1, 1973. (122 refs.)

466 HOLDEN, JAMES S. The juvenile and the judicial function. Albany Law Review 31:197-209 (1967)

The juvenile appeal is discussed, and the difficulties which arise through the competition for dominance of the factors involved are analyzed. (57 refs.)

U.S.S.R./U.S.

467 HOLLANDER, PAUL. A converging social problem: juvenile delinquency in the Soviet Union and the United States. British Journal of Criminology 9:148-166 (1969)

Despite the growing similarity between the U.S.S.R. and the U.S. regarding juvenile delinquency, there is less violence in Russia. Juvenile delinquency is also less organized and less differentiated. These factors are discussed. (25 refs.)

468 HOLMES, ERIC M. Constitutional law - procedural due process - extention to the high school disciplinary proceeding. North Carolina Law Review 46:398-407 (1968)

The author discusses the feasibility of following appropriate due process in high school expulsions. (47 refs.)

469 HOLTON, THOMAS. Prevention of delinquency through legal counseling: a proposal for improved juvenile representation. Columbia Law Review 68:1080-1089 (1968)

Prevention of delinquency in the representation of the juvenile offender need not be limited to advocacy. In appropriate cases it should extend to counseling the youngster in the way of law and justice. It should seek out the needed services of others, but should resist any intervention which would be incompatible with the requirement of justice. (38 refs.)

Okla./N.Y.

470 HOOKS, EDWARD C. Family law - New York Family Court Section 712(b) is not void for vagueness but is unconstitutional because of sex-age discrimination - In the Matter of Patricia A., 31 N.Y.2d 83 (1972). Syracuse Law Review 4:1257-1266 (1972)

Juvenile delinquency classifications based on age and sex have recently been the subject of constitutional attack in at least two cases. These Oklahoma and New York decisions, and others, are examined. The author concludes that any finding of unconstitutionality for vagueness concerning juvenile statutes will have to come from the federal courts or perhaps the United States Supreme Court. Traditional reluctance to undo what the legislature has done by the court's refraining from acting as a "super-legislature" may be increasingly more difficult to justify in the area of sex discrimination. (81 refs.)

471 HOREJSI, CHARLES R. Attitude of parents toward juvenile court volunteers. Federal Probation 36:13-18 (1972)

This article summarizes part of a study concerned with volunteer activity in juvenile court probation, and parents' attitudes. (9 refs.)

472 HORNE, JAMES R. The vestiges of child-parent tort immunity. UCD Law Review 6:195-216 (1973)

Not until 1963 was parental immunity rejected by any court, and, although at the time exceptions to the doctrine of parental immunity were made, it now seems appropriate to consider the exceptions to see what has become, it many states, a general rule of parental liability. These exceptions, and the "reasonable and prudent parent" test are discussed. (121 refs.)

473 HOROWITZ, ALLAN H., and NANCY L. NICKERSON. McKeiver v. Pennsylvania: a retreat in juvenile justice. Brooklyn Law Review 38:650-692 (1972)
Although the Supreme Court has recently begun to apply constitutional guarantees of due process to juvenile proceedings, it denied juveniles one of the most fundamental constitutional rights - the right to trial by jury. This Note shows that these conflicting decisions cannot be reconciled, and that the McKeiver decision is unsound. (170 refs.)

474 HORWITZ, J.J. Interprofessional teamwork. Social Worker - Le Travailleur Social 38:5-10 (1970)
A San Francisco State College study, showing that recent developments require exploration of new divisions of labor and of teamwork among social workers and other professionals.

475 HOSEY, PHILIP E. Waiver in juvenile proceedings. Baylor Law Review 23:467-475 (1971)
Even the intelligent combination of parent or guardian ad litem and child poses serious constitutional questions. The trend is to presume incompetence in judicial proceedings, regardless of intellectual capacity. The author analyzes the above and makes suggestions. (48 refs.)

476 HOWLETT, FREDERICK W. Is the YSB all it's cracked up to be? Crime and Delinquency 19:485-492 (1973)
The routine and often inappropriate use of the youth service bureaus by any number of agencies fosters the illusion that something constructive is being done for the community's children and tends to perpetuate the bureau by providing it with statistical justification for its continued existence. (11 refs.)

Kent./Ohio

477 HUELSMAN, BEN R. Southern mountaineers in city juvenile courts. Federal Probation 33:49-54 (1970)
Is the Appalachian subculture inherently a crime-producing and delinquency-producing way of life, asks this anthropologist. This article is the result of a study undertaken while serving as a probation officer in Ohio. (5 refs.)

478 HUFF, FREDERICK W., and HARRY PORTER, Jr. Mental health consultation in juvenile court. Juvenile Justice 23(3):32-36 (1972)
(2 refs.)

Brazil

479 HUNGRIA, N. Delinquencia juvenil. Scientia Ivridica 21:398-407 (1972)

480 HYNES, CHRISTIAN. Principles governing intake in children's institutions. Federal Probation 36:27-29 (1972)
Some observations about intake procedures.

481 Illegitimates: definition of "children" under federal welfare legislation. Columbia Law Review 67:984-992 (1967)
In the case of an illegitimate child, no important state policies compel reference to a restrictive definition of "children" under state law. A number of federal statutes provide for the payment of benefits to the "child or children" of designated individuals and, many times, courts have had to decide whether an illegitimate child comes within this class. (44 refs.)

482 IMLAY, CARL H. The federal juvenile delinquency act and the Gault decision. Federal Probation 33:18-23 (1969)
A survey of federal procedures applicable to adults and/or juveniles, and a discussion of the rights of juveniles, and the role of the probation officer. (4 refs.)

Japan

483 INADA, F., and T. ŌKUMA. Delinquent juveniles and the regional features in Tokyo: in relation to the diseases of the city. Katei Saiban Geppo 24(1):1-32 (1972)

484 INFAUSTO, FELIX, and MILDRED A. SHANLEY. Annual review of decisions and statutory revisions affecting adoptions 1966-1967. Family Law Quarterly 2:228-247 (1968)
(77 refs.)

485 INFAUSTO, FELIX. Annual review of decisions and statutory revisions affecting adoptions (September 1, 1967 - December 31, 1968). Family Law Quarterly 3:123-143 (1969)
(81 refs.)

486 INFAUSTO, FELIX. Annual review of decisions and statutory revisions affecting adoptions (January 1 - August 1, 1969). Family Law Quarterly 4:150-166 (1970)
(42 refs.)

487 Information about defendants. Magistrate 27:115-117 (1971)
A description of the scope of social enquiries and the arrangements for the presentation of the resulting reports to magistrates' courts.

488 INKER, MONROE L. Expanding the rights of children in custody and adoption cases. Family Law Quarterly 5:417-423 (1971)
The child is the primary party in a custody proceeding, and should be represented by someone with no interest other than the child's welfare. (19 refs.)

489 INKER, MONROE L., and CHARLOTTE A. PERRETTA. A child's right to counsel in custody cases. Massachusetts Law Quarterly 55:229-241 (1970)

The thesis of this article is that the best way to realize the goal of the "best interests" of the child in custody cases, is to provide him with counsel. (41 refs.)

New York

490 INSERO, PETER P., Jr. Legislation - child protection proceedings under article 10 of the New York family court act. Buffalo Law Review 20:561-566 (1970)

The author states that the redefinition of the terms "neglected" and "abused" effectuated by the new legislation in New York, increases the circumstances under which the Family Court may intervene to aid children. The relaxed evidentiary provisions help to solve one of the primary problems found in abuse cases. (34 refs.)

491 Interstate placement of juveniles. Columbia Journal of Law and Social Problems 3:171-195 (1967)

This article focuses on the tendencies of the state to expand the placement of juveniles horizontally, at its own level, through cooperative interstate arrangements. (180 refs.)

492 IREDALE, N.L., and P.L. JOFFE. Between juvenile and adult courts: a no man's land for the youthful offender. Yale Review of Law and Social Action 1:49-54 (1971)

Kansas

493 IRMEN, J. DOUGLAS. Children's liberation - reforming juvenile justice. University of Kansas Law Review 21:177-197 (1973)

This Comment considers the present state of substantive and procedural juvenile law with particular reference to Kansas, and challenges the assumption that parens patriae is a valid justification for denying equal protection benefits to children. (100 refs.)

494 IRVING, JOHN F. Juvenile justice - one year later. Journal of Family Law 8:1-12 (1968)

The juvenile court is now involved with the implementation of the original concept of highly specialized judges, the right to competent counsel, the right to treatment, waiver, and the rights identified in Whittington. The author also discusses the need for training of juvenile court judges, and the role of the attorney. (11 refs.)

495 ISAAC, SOL M. The family lawyer and extra legal resources. Family Law Quarterly 1:13-23 (1967)

The attorney has a dual role of advocate and counselor. It is especially essential in family and juvenile law, with more complex and volatile relationships of the parties than in any other field of law, that the client's problem be understood, and to use the various resources in the community that can benefit him. The law and legal procedures do not give the lawyer, the client or the court much opportunity for analysis of the situation; and the alternatives provided by law may be harsher than necessary, especially after legal process is involved.

496 ISAACS, JACOB L. The lawyer in the juvenile court. Criminal Law Quarterly 10:222-237 (1968)

A discussion of lawyers in juvenile court, and the need for specialized training.

497 ISHMAEL, JAMES D. Jr. Juvenile right to counsel at probation revocation hearing. Journal of Family Law 11:745-752 (1972)

Can the in loco parentis doctrine justify the disparity in protections guaranteed to "all persons"? "Rights" versus "privileges" is the topic discussed in this article. (39 refs.)

Great Britain

498 JAMES, CORDELLA. Further consideration. Criminal Law Review 688-692 (1972)

The author argues that criticism of the children and young persons act 1969 has been largely misconceived, and that this is, in essence, a great act marking a positive major step forward in society's treatment of children in trouble. (1 ref.)

499 JAMES, JESSE R., and GEORGE H. SHEPARD. Police: do they belong in the schools? American Education 3(8):2-4 (1967)

Germany

500 JANS, K.W. Brauchen wir ein neues besseres Jugendwohlfahrtsgesetz? Zentralblatt fuer Jugendrecht und Jugendwohlfahrt 54:119-128 (1967)

Japan

501 JAPAN. Correction Bureau, Ministry of Justice. Outline of history of the development of correctional systems and the present situation Hoso jiho 23:579 (1971)

Poland

502 JASIŃSKI, J. Juvenile delinquency in Poland 1961-1967. Extent, structure, and the law. Archiwum Kryminologii 4:149-202 (1969)

Canada

503 JEFFERY, C.R., and J.A. JEFFERY. Delinquents and dropouts: an experimental program in behavior change. Canadian Journal of Corrections 12:47-58 (1970)

504 JENKINS, RICHARD L. The runaway reaction. American Journal of Psychiatry 128:168-173 (1971)

This psychiatrist states that delinquent behavior can usually be classified as motivation behavior, the pursuit of understandable goals by illegal means, or - as a response to frustration - maladaptive behavior without a goal. This latter group is subdivided according to the presence of the response of fight ("unsocialized aggressive reaction") or flight ("runaway reaction"). This article is concerned with characterizing the "runaway reactions." (23 refs.)

505 JENKINS, SHIRLEY. Filial deprivation in parents of children in foster care. Children 14:8-12 (1967)

The separation experiences of the parent when the child is removed have not been studied. This paper reports on a beginning research effort to explore the concept of this filial deprivation, and parents' problems. The difficulties the mother will experience when she is expected by courts and child welfare to resume "normal patterns" after such separation should be seriously considered prior to removal and placement of a child. (13 refs.)

Canada

506 JEWERS, G.O. Damages suffered by children; the standard of care owed to children. Law Society of Manitoba, Isaac Pitblado Lectures on Continuing Legal Education 49-53 (1973)

507 JOHN, ROBERT M. Constitutional law - criminal law and procedure - minor's request to see parents held to be an invocation of his fifth amendment privilege against self-incrimination. (People v. Burton, 6 Cal. 3d 375, 491 P.2d 793, 99 Cal. Rep. 1 (1971). Villanova Law Review 17:1085-1097 (1972)
(76 refs.)

California

508 JOHNSON, CHARLES W. The Family Law Act: a guide to the practitioner. Pacific Law Journal 1:147-155 (1970)
A discussion of the 1970 California Family Law Act.

509 JOHNSTON, GREG. The function of counsel in juvenile court. Osgoode Hall Law Journal 7:199-212 (1969)
The purpose of this article is to illustrate to the lawyer just how extensively he must be prepared to be involved in juvenile court proceedings, and to encourage him to assess every case thoroughly to determine to what extent he must employ his resources to truly function as "counsel." (52 refs.)

Australia

510 JOHNSTON, S.W. Strengthening the children's court in Victoria. Australian and New Zealand Journal of Criminology 5:241-249 (1972)

Nether./U.S.

511 JONKERS, W.H. Een Amerikanische Theorie en een Amerikaans experiment. Nederlands Tijdschrift voor Criminologie 9:33-49 (1967)

Montana

512 JONES, JAMES L. Montana's child neglect law - a need for revision. Montana Law Review 31:201-219 (1970)
This article provides a critical analysis of the provisions regarding dependent and neglected children in Chapter 5 of the Revised Code of Montana. (40 refs.)

Georgia

513 JORDAN, G. McGREGOR, Jr. Constitutional law - due process - parental tort liability solely on basis of parent-child relation held unconstitutional. Mercer Law Review 23:681-689 (1972)
A discussion of the due process clauses of Georgia Constitution and the federal constitution. (50 refs.)

Mississippi

514 JOYNER, BILL, and JOHN MAXEY. Juvenile offenses: a study of adjudication and disposition in Mississippi. Mississippi Law Journal 42:60-88 (1971)
(122 refs.)

Germany

515 Der Jugendamtsleiter: seine Voraussetzungen, Aufgaben, Probleme und Bestellung. Zentralblatt für Jugendrecht und Jugendwohlfahrt 58:293-301 (1971)

Oregon

516 Jurisdiction in child custody awards. Willamette Law Journal 5:171-176 (1968)
The purpose of this Note is primarily to explicate the law pertaining to child custody jurisdiction as it now stands in Oregon. (35 refs.)

517 The juvenile at waiver: is counsel required? Washington Law Review 43:639-644 (1968)
A discussion of State v. Acuna, 428 P.2d 658 (N.M. 1967) shows that the court misconstrued the critical stage analysis, and failed to give adequate consideration to the Kent-Gault rationale regarding appointment of counsel. (24 refs.)

518 Juvenile courts – juveniles in delinquency proceedings accorded same rights as adults in criminal trials. Vanderbilt Law Review 20:1161-1166 (1967)
The author of this Note states, in connection with Gault, that the introduction of the adversary system into the framework of the juvenile court poses the question of whether the parens patriae framework will be engulfed by this new element. (33 refs.)

519 Juvenile courts – juveniles in delinquency proceedings are not constitutionally entitled to the right of trial by jury – McKeiver v. Pennsylvania. Michigan Law Review 70:171-194 (1971)
The practical impact of McKeiver may be relatively insignificant, states the author, simply because it is likely that few juveniles would exercise the right to jury trial even if it were generally available. However, it is likely that the future impact of McKeiver will undermine Gault and Winship and presage a trend away from any due process analysis in juvenile delinquency cases. (138 refs.)

520 Juvenile curfews: a policy statement. Crime and Delinquency 18:132-133 (1972)
The vagueness and discriminatory applications of juvenile curfew laws are discussed. (1 ref.)

Illinois

521 Juvenile delinquency – procedural requirements in disciplinary proceedings within juvenile institutions. Boston University Law Review 52:480-493 (1967)
A discussion of In re Owens, 9 Crim.L.Rep. 2415 (Cook County, Ill., Cir. Ct. July 9, 1971). (31 refs.)

522 Juvenile due process in the lower courts. The Journal of Criminal Law, Criminology and Police Science 62:335-349 (1971)

This Comment examines some of the U.S. Supreme Court decisions since 1966, and their implications for future extensions of procedural due process standards to juvenile proceedings. (144 refs.)

523 Juvenile Justice 24(4):2-48 (1974)
This entire issue deals with articles related to computerization of juvenile records. A number of factors are explored.

524 Juvenile Justice - statutory exclusion from the juvenile process of certain alleged felons. Boston University Law Review 53:212-225 (1973)
A discussion of United States v. Bland, No. 71-1761 (D.C. Cir. Sept.6, 1972). (81 refs.)

525 Juvenile law - fourth amendment - probable cause not required to initiate formal proceedings. Rutgers Camden Law Journal 4:171-182 (1972)
A discussion of D.M.D. v. Wisconsin, 54 Wis.2d 313, 195 N.W.2d 594 (1972). (75 refs.)

526 Juvenile law - rights at probation revocation hearing - juvenile entitled to same rights as adult. Memphis State University Law Review 3:177-179 (1972)
A discussion of State ex rel. Bernal v. Hershman, 196 N.W.2d 721 (Wis.1972). (17 refs.)

527 Juvenile law - sixth amendment - due process - denial of counsel at juvenile certification hearing upheld. Rutgers Camden Law Journal 4:183-193 (1972)
A discussion of Smith v. Yeager, 459 F.2d 124 (3d Cir. 1972). (69 refs.)

New York

528 The juvenile offender's procedural rights in the New York family court. St. John's Law Review 41:386-401 (1967)
The author analyzes the principal provisions of New York State's family court act, and emphasizes those provisions which protect the minor in various circumstances. (94 refs.)

529 Juvenile police record-keeping. Columbia Human Rights Law Review 4:462-484 (1972)
The thesis of this article is that juvenile police records are not currently given proper treatment or attention and that, as a result of the inconspicuous nature of the record-keeping process, statutory assurances of confidentiality are illusory. (117 refs.)

530 Juvenile problems: minor's right to jury trial in delinquency determination based on criminal action for which adult would enjoy same privilege. University of Kansas Law Review 18:87-97 (1969)
The questions of whether or not a minor has a right to a jury trial, and whether a jury trial is desirable for a juvenile delinquent, are discussed. (69 refs.)

531 Juvenile's right to jury trial - post McKeiver. Washington University Law Quarterly 605-621 (1971)

Although the court settled most constitutional questions concerning juvenile jury trials, some equal protection or impermissible choice questions remain for the state legislatures to solve. (77 refs.)

Michigan

532 KAIMOWITZ, GABE. Legal emancipation of minors in Michigan. Wayne Law Review 19:23-48 (1972)

The author demonstrates that a minor's best interests always include the right to prosecute or defend a case and to have some access to courts and attorneys just as adults do; at the bar, therefore, a child should be the constitutional equal of any adult. (108 refs.)

Germany

533 KAISER, G. Jugendrecht und Jugendkriminalität. Recht der Jugend 18:168-175 (1970)

534 KALKER, P.R. The test case and law reform in the juvenile justice system. Yale Review of Law and Social Action 203:64-71 (1971)

Illinois

535 KALNINS, JOHN M. Right to bail for juveniles. Chicago-Kent Law Review 48:99-106 (1971)

With the failure of the juvenile court movement in its non-punitive approach and with the characterization of the juvenile process as criminal for certain purposes, a consideration of the total rights of the juvenile is needed. The eighth amendment of the federal constitution and the Illinois constitution are discussed. The author argues that under the latter there is ample ground for conferring a right to bail to juveniles. (53 refs.)

Japan

536 KAMEI, T. Answers to seven problems concerning juvenile law. Kesei 83(8):34-41 (1972)

U.S./Japan

537 KAMEYAMA, T. Due process in juvenile cases - reform trends in the United States and Japan. Juristo 480:111 (1971)

Japan

538 KANETO, Y. Treatment of juvenile traffic cases. Katei Saiban Geppo 22(4):1-30 (1970)

539 KANOWITZ, LEO. Constitutional aspects of sex-based discrimination in American law. Nebraska Law Review 48:131-182 (1968)

The purpose of this article is to describe and analyze leading decisions that have disposed of constitutional attacks upon laws that discriminate on the basis of sex; to discern current developments in this area; and to consider the desirability vel non of the proposed equal rights amendment. (195 refs.)

540 KAPNER, LEWIS. The juvenile's right to treatment - the next step. Florida Bar Journal 47:228-231 (1973)
(17 refs.)

Ohio

541 KARL, NELSON G. Banishment from the kingdom of Lake (County). Cleveland State Law Review 21:139-146 (1972)
A discussion of In re Edsall, 26 Ohio St.2d 145, 269 N.E.2d 848(1971). (41 refs.)

Japan

542 KASHIWAGI, C. On the nature of juvenile law. Keiho Zasshi 18(3/4):7-11 (1972)

New York

543 KATZ, KATHERYN D. A reappraisal of juvenile delinquency proceedings in New York. Albany Law Review 34:122-139 (1969)
A look at some of the provisions of the New York Family Court Act which may work an unintended injustice on the impoverished or minority group child and his family. Some changes are suggested. (135 refs.)

544 KATZ, SANFORD N. Children - individuals without rights. Student Lawyer 1:48-52 (1973)
The parent-child relationship, although frequently referred to in quasi-sacred terminology, is the least secure from outside interference. The husband-wife relations are much more immune from governmental intervention. When the state uses its authority to invade the parent-child relationship or usurp the parental function, what happens to individual rights?

545 KATZ, SANFORD N. Legal aspects of foster care. Family Law Quarterly 5:283-302 (1971)
The legal implications of the foster family setting are discussed. A distinction is drawn between the legal implications of the foster parent-child relationship that emerges from the common law doctrine of in loco parentis, and the foster parent-child relationship created by agencies under court authority. Agencies take inconsistent attitudes toward foster parents, and they attempt to maintain ultimate control over the foster parent-child relationship, basing their authority on the argument that the court has committed a child to them. (53 refs.)

Massachusetts

546 KATZ, SANFORD N., and WILLIAM A. SCHROEDER. Disobeying a father's voice: a comment on Commonwealth v. Brasher. Massachusetts Law Quarterly 57:43-57 (1972)
A discussion of Commonwealth v. Brasher, 1971 Mass.Adv.Sh. 907, 207 N.E.2d 389 (1971). The Massachusetts supreme judicial court recently sustained the constitutionality of the commonwealth's "stubborn" child laws against claims that the statute violated the due process, right of privacy, and equal protection provisions of the United States and Massachusetts constitutions. In this Comment the authors take issue with the court's opinion and suggest that the decision should be reversed by legislative action at the earliest possible moment. (65 refs.)

547 KATZ, SANFORD N., et al. Emancipating our children - coming of legal age in America. Family Law Quarterly 7:211-241 (1973)

A study of the legal machinery, both judicial and statutory, used presently, and in the past, to emancipate children. The law's response to the changing nature of the parent-child relationship is discussed. (164 refs.)

548 KAY, RICHARD, and DANIEL SEGAL. The role of the attorney in juvenile court proceedings: a non-polar approach. The Georgetown Law Journal 61:1401-1424 (1973)

The role of the attorney in juvenile court proceedings has become increasingly difficult to define since the Supreme Court has extended many due process requirements to those proceedings. The authors outline a new "non-polar" approach in examining several stages of the juvenile legal process. One view is that the juvenile attorney adopt a single-minded adversary stance, and do anything within ethical bounds to achieve an adjudication of not guilty, or that disposition for the client which puts the least restraint on him. The opposite pole represents the view that the attorney's role should be non-adversary, and that the lawyer should focus not so much on verdicts of not guilty or lenient dispositions as on achieving a resolution which is in a more general and less restricted sense in the "best interests of the child." (106 refs.)

Austria

549 KEISWETTER, R. Zuständigkeit und Aufgaben des Vormundschaftsgerichtes nach dem Jugendgerichtsgesetz. Österreichische Juristen-Zeitung 256-263 (1967)

Illinois

550 KEITER, ROBERT B. Criminal or delinquent? A study of juvenile cases transferred to the criminal court. Crime and Delinquency 19:528-538 (1973)

This study examines sixty-seven cases transferred in 1970 from the Cook County Juvenile Court to the criminal court, and considers the following: age, ethnic group, type of charge, past record, and gang involvement. (12 refs.)

Ohio

551 KEITH, HARRY B. Waiver of jurisdiction in juvenile courts. Ohio State Law Journal 30:132-143 (1969)

The object of this article is to investigate the theoretical conception of the juvenile court judge as he actually functions, unburdened in many areas by procedural requirements. An analysis of the Ohio juvenile court system is included. (27 refs.)

552 KELLY, DELOS H., and WILLIAM T. PINK. School commitment, youth rebellion and delinquency. Criminology 10:473-486 (1973)

(19 refs.)

553 KETCHAM, ORMAN W. Can Gault's guidelines protect public interest? Trial Magazine 4:15-18 (1968)

A discussion of whether Gault marks new legal ground (and deserves commentary as such), or merely confirms and formalizes policy and procedure generally accepted by the juvenile court system.

554 KETCHAM, ORMAN W. Changing philosophy of the juvenile justice system. Juvenile Court Judges' Journal 20(2):59-63 (1969)
(12 refs.)

555 KETCHAM, ORMAN W. Commentary: what happened to Whittington? The George Washington Law Review 37:324-340 (1968)
The chronology of the Whittington case and the legal issues involved. The Whittington and Gault cases are compared. (65 refs.)

556 KETCHAM, ORMAN W. Guidelines from Gault: revolutionary requirements and reappraisal. Virginia Law Review 53:1700-1718 (1967)
A description of both the immediate and the long-range changes which can be expected to arise from Gault. (45 refs.)

557 KETCHAM, ORMAN W. The legal renaissance in the juvenile court. Kaitei Saiban Geppo 20:1-21 (1968)

558 KETCHAM, ORMAN W. McKeiver v. Pennsylvania: the last word on juvenile court adjudications? Cornell Law Review 57:561-570 (1972)
A discussion of the rational of McKeiver, the Court's attitude towards jury trials, and the impact on the juvenile justice system. (46 refs.)

559 KETCHAM, ORMAN W. The need for law and order in the juvenile court: some unanswered questions. Family Law Quarterly 1(2):78-87 (1967)
Judge Ketcham discusses the need to bring together law and behavioral science in an effort to solve the many problems of the juvenile court. (9 refs.)

Austria

560 KIESSWETTER, R. Die Altersgrenzen im Straf-und Pflegeschaftsrecht in praktischer Sicht. Österreichische Juristen-Zeitung 26:169-175 (1971)

Japan

561 KIKUCHI, N. Problems of the outline of the juvenile law amendment. Juristo 465: 59-68 (1970)

Texas

562 KIMBLE, WILLIAM K. Application of Gault: its effect on juvenile delinquency proceedings in Texas. Baylor Law Review 20:113-121 (1967)
The author outlines the holdings of the court on each point, and explores the effect of each holding on juvenile delinquency proceedings in Texas. He points out areas where he believes the Texas law is defective and suggests measures to improve. (36 refs.)

Japan

563 KIMURA, E. Correctional treatment in the general plan of the revision of juvenile law. Keisei 81(11):12-19 (1970)

Mississippi

564 KING, DONALD B. Training in juvenile delinquency law: the St. Louis University Law School Forum Clinic. St. Louis University Law Journal 12:597-602 (1968)

A description of the St. Louis University Law School Forum Clinic - a special training project. (8 refs.)

565 KITTRIE, NICHOLAS N. Can the right to treatment remedy the ills of the juvenile process? The Georgetown Law Journal 57:848-885 (1969)

This article assesses the possible utility of the newly formulated "right to treatment" as a tool for the overhaul of the juvenile system. (168 refs.)

566 KLABER, JANE K. Person in need of supervision: is there a constitutional right to treatment? Brooklyn Law Review 39:624-657 (1973)

The author of this Note submits that the concept of treatment, drawn from the writings of early reformers, has been used as rhetoric in a smokescreen attempt to enable the courts to continue to "warehouse" undesirable members of the community. A need for court supervision is demonstrated. (192 refs.)

567 KLAPMUTZ, NORA. Children's rights - the legal rights of minors in conflict with law or social custom. Crime and Delinquency Literature 4(3):449-477 (1972)

A discussion of legal rights, procedural rights, the right to be left alone, and the children's right movement. (111 refs.)

Illinois

568 KLECZEK, ANDREW J. Procedure in the Illinois juvenile system. John Marshall Journal of Practice and Procedure 6:48-76 (1972)

This article explains the present procedure in the Illinois juvenile court system. (121 refs.)

569 KLEINFELD, ANDREW J. The balance of power among infants, their parents and the state. Part I. Family Law Quarterly 4:320-350 (1970)

This essay criticizes and surveys a few of the most fundamental devices and concepts in the structure of infants' law. (133 refs.)

570 KLEINFELD, ANDREW J. The balance of power among infants, their parents and the state. Part II. Family Law Quarterly 4:409-443 (1970)

In this second part of a three part series, the author discusses parental power. (110 refs.)

571 KLEINFELD, ANDREW J. The balance of power among infants, their parents and the state. Family Law Quarterly 5:63-107 (1971)

Part III. The infant's relation to the state is discussed. (215 refs.)

Connecticut

572 KNAG, PAUL E. The Connecticut eighteen-year-old emancipation act: problems of construction and application encountered by the estates and trust practitioner. Connecticut Bar Journal 47:147-166 (1973)

The change in the age of majority in Connecticut poses many questions for the estates practitioner. The following are the areas of concern: interpretation of documents referring to "minors," etc.; capacity and necessity for guardianship; Uniform Act custodianships and trusts; duty of support; rule against perpetuities. (67 refs.)

573 KNOWLES, LAURENCE W. High schools, marriage and the fourteenth amendment. Journal of Family Law 11:711-736 (1972)
The questions discussed are: does the law protect married students from arbitrarily based regulations? What is the law regarding married students and the schools? The author concludes that it is up to the community and the schools to clarify attitudes towards the domestically involved student. (55 refs.)

574 KOBETZ, RICHARD W. Police and juveniles and discretion. Justice Magazine 1: 14-15 (1972)
A discussion of police and the juvenile justice system.

District of Columbia

575 KOLKER, PETER R. The test case and law reform in the juvenile justice system. Yale Review of Law and Social Action 1:64-71 (1970)
This article explores the reaction of the juvenile justice system in the District of Columbia to efforts at procedural reform on three frontiers: establishing minimum standards for the treatment accorded to pretrial detainees; defining specific criteria governing the pretrial release of juveniles charged with delinquency; and winning the right to probable cause hearings for juveniles charged with serious crimes. (43 refs.)

Great Britain

576 KOLVIN, ISRAEL, and CHRISTOPHER OUNSTED. Remand delinquents; the court and the psychiatrist. Medicine, Science, and the Law 8:109-118 (1968)
This article considers the agreement between medical recommendation and court disposal of delinquents in Great Britain; and the association between specific court decisions and the behavior and social background of 234 boys involved in a survey. (19 refs.)

577 KRAFT, CARLAN J. A right to a jury trial for juveniles? - the implications of McKeiver. North Dakota Law Review 49:625-642 (1973)
It is pointed out that the thrusts of the decisions in Gault and McKeiver differ in one important aspect. The author asks how much formality would actually be added to the juvenile proceedings by the presence of a jury, since the juvenile's right to counsel has already injected many elements of the adversary system into the process. (128 refs.)

Australia

578 KRAUS, J. Children's court policy in New South Wales. Australian Law Journal 47:197-202 (1973)
This study is concerned with the relationship of long-term trends in the sentencing policy of the Children's Court to rates of offences committed by male juveniles in New South Wales. (22 refs.)

Austral./N.Z.

579 KRAUS, J. Some factors related to orders made by children's courts. The Australian and New Zealand Journal of Criminology 3:76-82 (1970)

580 KRAUSE, HARRY D. The bastard finds his father. Family Law Quarterly 3:100-111 (1969)

The author discusses the question of whether, and to what extent, the manifold discriminations still imposed by state and federal law between the father and the illegitimate child are subject to constitutional attack. Several state supreme court decisions are included. (25 refs.)

581 KRAUSE, HARRY D. Child welfare, parental responsibility and the state. Family Law Quarterly 6:377-403 (1972)

This paper focuses on child welfare and deals with parental nonsupport and neglect. What is done, or not done, in child welfare now will determine the quality of life a generation hence. (83 refs.)

582 KRAUSE, HARRY D. "Why bastard, wherefore base"? Annals of the American Academy of Political and Social Science 383:58-70 (1969)

The 1968 U.S. Supreme Court decision should bring substantial legal equality to the illegitimate child as a matter of constitutional law. This article discusses the prospect of such a development as well as its specific meaning for the person of illegitimate birth. Present law is presented in some detail in order to provide a frame of reference. (20 refs.)

Ohio

583 KRAVITZ, MAX. Due process in Ohio for the delinquent and unruly child. Capital University Law Review 2:53-85 (1973)

The purpose of this article is to outline some of the more dramatic changes in the procedural requisites now afforded to juveniles, to examine the recent case law affecting these revisions, and to identify some of the problem areas that must be dealt with in the future. (170 refs.)

584 KULIKOWSKI, JOHN M. Waiver - right to counsel - certification of juvenile to criminal proceedings. Natural Resources Journal 9:310-318 (1969)

The author discusses the question of what effect the presence of counsel has when the right of an accused is allegedly waived. (52 refs.)

India

585 KUMAR, N.V. The jurisdiction of the high court under section 12 of the Hindu minority and guardianship act. Lawyer (Madras) 1:96-102 (1969)

Germany

586 KUNTZE, J. Anmerkungen zum neuen Sorgenrechtsentwurf. Juristischen Rundschau (7):273-277 (1973)

587 LAMAR, CHARLES W. III. Sentencing under the federal youth corrections act: the need for an explicit finding and a statement of reasons. Boston University Law Review 53:1071-1086 (1973)

588 LAMBERT, RICHARD D., et al. The future of corrections. The Annals of the American Academy of Political Science 381:1-158 (1969)

589 LANGFORD, JOHN S., Jr. America' most discriminatory laws and courts. Mercer Law Review 20:400-413 (1969)

An examination of the present state of the law concerning a juvenile's affairs; military obligations; voting privileges; driving rights; property rights; civil rights and the liability for his acts. (37 refs.)

Tennessee

590 LANGLEY, MICHAEL H. The juvenile court: the making of a delinquent. Law and Society Review 7:273-298 (1972)

In this study the author provides evidence of the procedural laxities and prostitution of the juvenile court philosophy in a specific juvenile court in Tennessee. (7 refs.)

591 LANGLEY, MICHAEL H., et al. Juvenile court and individualized treatment. Crime and Delinquency 18:79-92 (1972)

This study considers the extent to which both the national statistics on delinquency and data from one metropolitan juvenile court support the objective of individualized treatment. Data concerning the legal and social treatment provided are presented. (9 refs.)

592 LARSON, JOHN F. Identifying court needs, programs to meet them. Juvenile Court Judges' Journal 20(3):91-95 (1969)

Great Britain

592a LASOK, DOMINIK. Custody - judicial or administrative decision? The New Law Journal 120(5449):817-818 (1970)

The author discusses some controversial issues of law and social policy on parental rights, the foster parents' claims, the child's welfare and the role of the courts and agencies in resolving conflicts over custody. A great need for the establishment of guidelines and standards for the practical application of the child's welfare doctrine is demonstrated. (2 refs.)

593 Lawyer-Social Worker Relationships in the Family Court Intake Process. In National Conference of Lawyers and Social Workers, Publication No. 4, 1967. pp. 1-7

Because of the unique development of the family court as a socio-legal institution, some of the functions of social workers and lawyers within them differ from those in other courts. The role of the social worker is more significant, and that of the lawyer is modified because of greater informality and flexibility in procedure and disposition. The careful definition of concepts basic to working relationships is therefore essential.

District of Columbia

594 LAWTON, MARY C. Juvenile proceedings - the new look. American University Law Review 20:342-372 (1970-1971)

An analysis of the District of Columbia Court Reform and Criminal Procedure Act of 1970 which was specifically designed to bring the juvenile code up to date and to forestall a great deal of litigation in the juvenile area. (62 refs.)

Yugoslavia

595 LAZAREVIĆ, L. Criminal legislation on juvenile delinquency after the promulgation of the amendments to the constitution. Jugoslovenska Revija za Kriminologiju i Krivično Pravo 10:423-431 (1972)

596 LEFSTEIN, NORMAN. In Re Gault, juvenile court and lawyers. American Bar Association Journal 53:811-814 (1967)

Many questions on the impact of the case remain unanswered. Much depends on the extent of attorney representation. (19 refs.)

597 LEFSTEIN, N. In the wake of Gault. In Ohio State Legal Services on Law and Poverty: the minor, 1968. pp.8.01-8.12

598 LEFSTEIN, NORMAN, et al. In search of juvenile justice: Gault and its implementation. Law and Society Review 3:491-562 (1969)

A description of the response of three urban juvenile courts to In Re Gault. (191 refs.)

599 LEGER, RICHARD R. A jury of peers. Juvenile Court Judges' Journal 17(4):150-152

This article considers the use of juvenile jurors.

600 Legislative and judicial recognition of the distinction between custody and termination orders in child neglect cases. Journal of Family Law 7:66-80 (1967)

The recent trend toward enactment of termination statutes is some evidence that legislatures are becoming increasingly aware of the distinction between temporary and permanent custody. (51 refs.)

601 LEHMAN, PAUL S. A juvenile's right to counsel in a delinquency hearing. Pennsylvania Bar Association Quarterly 38:65-73 (1966)

A discussion of the right to counsel before the Gault ruling. (17 refs.)

California

602 LEMERT, EDWIN M. Legislating change in the juvenile court. Wisconsin Law Review 421-448 (1967)

This article studies a comprehensive change in the California juvenile court law that was enacted in 1961, and it inquires into the possibility of changing behavior patterns by legislation. (37 refs.)

603 LENG, ANN, and K.S. WALSCH BRENNAN. A study in delinquency. The

Criminologist 8:31-38 (1973)

604 LENON, HARLOW F. On re-examining Gault - again and again. Family Law Quarterly 4:387-392 (1970)

In this article Judge Lenon analyzes the article by Frank J. Parker in Family Law Quarterly 4:113-129, June 1970. The judge hopes that among the articles written interpreting Gault, there will be one writer who has been adversely critical, and who will have expressed a small, mild, shy doubt about the Court's sociology, its notion of child psychology, its view of the plight of urban adolescents, its statistics, its practical grasp of the juvenile court process, the intimacy of its acquaintance with the low income family, its sense of the incompetence of social workers, its view of the contribution which the Miranda device may make to the child's proud acceptance of the trial process, and a host of other issues it may be considered to have stirred up...

Wisconsin

605 LENTZ, WILLIAM P. Police attitudes to delinquency control. Law and the Social Order 17(6):42-44 (1969)

The author gives the results of a survey undertaken in Wisconsin to compare the views of the general public, and those of juvenile law officers.

606 LEONARD, JERRIS W. LEAA and federal delinquency control programs. Juvenile Justice 23(2):7-11 (1972)

A discussion of the Law Enforcement Assistance Administration programs and funding.

607 LERNER, SAMUEL. Treatment of children: whose responsibility? Journal of Jewish Communal Service 43:335-345 (1967)

The author states that the problem of responsibility for the treatment of children is systematically avoided on an operational and administrative level by the agency involved. There is a need for a change of focus in staff training, consultation, and supervision so as to readjust thinking and attitudes.

California

608 LETTUNICH, MARTIN N. Does parental liability for legal fees infringe upon a juvenile's constitutional rights? Santa Clara Lawyer 10:347-359 (1970)

This Comment discusses various factors which, considered together, throw deep suspicion on the constitutional validity of sections 634 and 903.1 of the Welfare and Institutions Code of California. (81 refs.)

609 LEVIDOW, BEATRICE. Overdue process for juveniles: for the retroactive restoration of constitutional rights. Howard Law Journal 17:402-434 (1972)

An analysis of earlier juvenile court challenges, and recent decisions, attempts to reconcile the intended purpose of the twentieth century reform movement in juvenile justice with the real abridgment of constitutional rights of the juvenile. (167 refs.)

610 LEVIN, IRA S. Long hair and the equal protection clause: King v. Saddleback Junior College District. UCLA-Alaska Law Review 1:134-153 (1972)
The author discusses the "long hair controversy" and the applicability of fundamental rights and the equal protection clause to such cases. (142 refs.)

Great Britain

611 LEVIN, JENNIFER. Children and young persons act 1969. The Solicitor's Journal 114:179-181, 200-201, 218-219 (1970)
An analysis of the children and young persons act 1969, in Great Britain.

612 LEVIN, NORMAN L. The role of the lawyer in juvenile proceedings. Pennsylvania Bar Association Quarterly 39:427-437 (1968)
An examination of the sources of a conflict to which the lawyer is exposed. The lack of training in juvenile law is also discussed.

Iowa

613 LEVINE, DAVID N. Child custody: Iowa corn and the avant garde. Family Law Quarterly 1:3-9 (1967)
(19 refs.)

New York

614 LEVINE, HOWARD A. The youthful offender under the New York Criminal Procedure Law. Albany Law Review 36:241-256 (1972)
This paper discusses the operation of the statutory framework embodying the basic approach of the youthful offender provisions of New York's former Code of Criminal Procedure under the old law; other reasonable alternatives the revisions could have adopted, and the changes effected under the youthful offender provisions which were finally enacted by the new Criminal Procedure Law. (64 refs.)

615 LEVINE, RICHARD S. Caveat parens: a demystification of the child protection system. University of Pittsburgh Law Review 35:1-52 (1973)
The author traces the history and vehicle through which states have sought to protect children from neglect and abuse. By examining the operation of child welfare agencies and the interests of parents suspected of neglecting their children, the author shows why intervention by the child protection system lacks procedural safeguards for the parents. Greater review of agency decisions is advocated. (296 refs.)

Texas

616 LEWIS, TRYON D. Parental immunity doctrine in Texas in light of the Felderhoff case. Baylor Law Review 25:156-162 (1973)
A discussion of Felderhoff v. Felderhoff, 470 S.W.2d 301 (Tex.1971). (36 refs.)

617 LINCOLN, JAMES H. Remember the good as well as the bad. Juvenile Court Judges' Journal 22(2):26-29, 45-48 (1971)
A discussion of some of the U.S. Supreme Court decisions with particular reference to the reports and documents used and misused by the Court as a basis for its decisions. Proposals by the National Council of Juvenile Court Judges for the improvement of juvenile justice, are

included. (27 refs.)

618 LINDE, LLEWELLYN H. Ceremonial litigant. Juvenile Court Judges' Journal 19(4):141-143 (1969)
(5 refs.)

619 LIPSITT, PAUL D. Due process as a gateway to rehabilitation in the juvenile justice system. Boston University Law Review 49:62-78 (1969)
The author maintains that the future of the juvenile justice system will be determined by two factors to insure its effectiveness and fairness. He discusses these. (76 refs.)

620 LIPSITT, PAUL D. The juvenile offender's perceptions. Crime and Delinquency 14:49-62 (1968)
A study of the perceptions of the juvenile offender in court. (6 refs.)

Canada

621 LITSKY, HERMAN. The cult of the juvenile court in Canada - justice with mercy. Juvenile Court Judges' Journal 20(4):134-137 (1969)
This attorney discusses alternatives to the traditional cult of the juvenile court in Canada.

Oklahoma

622 LITTLE, PRUDENCE. Courts: due process and the Oklahoma juvenile courts. Oklahoma Law Review 22:71-81 (1969)
This Note discusses the requirements of due process as applied to a procedure in which a determination of delinquency is made and an incarceration may result, and also the new Oklahoma Juvenile Code. (52 refs.)

Canada

623 LITTLE, WILLIAM T. The need for reform in the juvenile courts. Osgood Hall Law Journal 10:225-228 (1972)
Judge Little describes the steps which the Canadians have taken to improve their juvenile court system. The most important points in the Juvenile Court Act are discussed. (7 refs.)

624 LOCKWOOD, ROBERT W. The role of the attorney in the treatment phase of the juvenile court process. St. Louis University Law Journal 12:659-678 (1968)
Examined are certain elements of the attorney's function, including both his legal and non-legal roles. (61 refs.)

625 LOFTQUIST, WILLIAM A. The framework and experience of juvenile probation. Social Casework 48:17-21 (1967)
The author views probation as a structural process through which probationer and probation officer move, each responsible for his own part. The process takes place within a framework determined by legal and procedural considerations: the probationer experiences firmness and understanding from the probation officer, and faces clearly defined choices that he must make for himself. It also places responsibility for social work function squarely on the officer. (3 refs.)

626 LOURIE, R., and M.N. ROUR. The new faces of advocacy. Journal of the American Academy of Child Psychology 11(3):401-414 (1972)

The authors discuss the need for an effective advocacy system in behalf of children's needs as proposed by the Joint Commission on the Mental Health of Children. The many aspects of this concept include political, legislative, social and operational forms of advocacy. These are discussed.

Illinois

627 LUEDKE, GAIL. Illinois tort remedies available to juvenile victims of residential lead poisoning. Chicago-Kent Law Review 49:212-220 (1972)

(37 refs.)

628 LUNDEN, WALTER A. The orphaned juvenile court. Trial 7:20, 22 (1971)

East Germany

629 LUNGWITZ, I. Einige Probleme aus der Arbeit der geselschaftlichen Gerichte im Jugendsachen. Schöffe 20:20-26 (1973)

630 LYSAGHT, BRIAN C. Children in transit: child custody and the conflict of laws. UCD Law Review 6:160-180 (1973)

The present state of the law with respect to the dilemma of the interstate child is frequently at odds with the best interests of the child. The latter's interests do not lie in a judicial free-for-all in custody litigation. Jurisdiction and authority to alter a given custodial arrangement will attach in a court elsewhere simply by the presence of the child in a new forum. The thesis of this article is that the child's interests lie not in the continuation or expansion of this authority, but in its restriction. (117 refs.)

North Carolina

631 McCARTER, CHARLES T. Constitutional rights of juveniles in criminal cases - Gault and beyond in North Carolina. Wake Forest Law Review 7:440-450 (1971)

This Comment examines the impact of In Re Gault and subsequent decisions dealing with the constitutional rights of juveniles at the adjudicative phase of the North Carolina juvenile court system. (67 refs.)

Ireland

632 McCARTHY, P.W. Children, the courts, and the child psychiatrist. Dublin University Law Review 1:74-77 (1968)

633 McCARTY, WILLIAM M. Juvenile justice: the economics of ineptitude. San Diego Law Review 10:250-265 (1973)

The author argues that while the average annual cost to the taxpayer of an institutionalized child is more than $5,000, plus costs of juvenile courts, juvenile probation systems and law enforcement, this money is being spent without substantial direction and without adherence to the most basic of business principles. It is time leadership is exerted before the current federal appropriation of $75 million for juvenile crime prevention is lost. (37 refs.)

634 McCONNELL, EDWARD B. The national center for state courts and the juvenile courts. Juvenile Justice 24(3):50-56 (1973)

The author makes the point that he thinks the time is overdue when juvenile court judges should seriously re-assess their status and role, reassess their relation to the judicial structure and the judicial process, so as to assist the juvenile court to achieve full stature.

635 McDONALD, PATRICK. Juvenile law - standard of proof required in criminal prosecution of juveniles. Journal of Urban Law 48:1008-1014 (1971)

A discussion of In Re Winship, 396 U.S. 885 (1970). (23 refs.)

636 McDONALD, WILLIAM E. A case for independent counsel to represent children in custody proceedings. New England Law Review 7:351-360 (1972)

A study of the child's rights in custody proceedings. (42 refs.)

Arkansas

637 McDONOUGH, T. JAMES. The juvenile court and judicial reform in Arkansas. Arkansas Law Review 22:17-42 (1968)

This article examines and makes recommendations regarding the judicial process into which society throws the juvenile problem. This is most specifically the concern of lawyers as lawyers. (89 refs.)

638 McFADEN, WILLIAM E. Changing concepts of juvenile justice. Crime and Delinquency 17:131-141 (1971)

The Gault decision and the report of the President's Commission on Law Enforcement and Administration of Justice have called attention to the long-standing failure of the juvenile court to carry out its stated purpose and make major changes. These changes, and the roles and responsibilities of those involved in the juvenile court process are discussed in this article. (3 refs.)

639 McGUIRE, JOAN M. Discovery rights in juvenile proceedings. University of San Francisco Law Review 7:333-347 (1973)

This Comment discusses discovery rights in juvenile proceedings. Some suggestions are made for expanding these in all juvenile proceedings. (56 refs.)

640 McHARDY, LOUIS W. Assessment of juvenile probation services. Juvenile Justice 24(2):41-46 (1973)

Juvenile probation services and alternatives to the juvenile court are examined. (10 refs.)

641 McHARDY, LOUIS W. The court, the police and the school. Federal Probation 32(1):47-50 (1968)

(9 refs.)

642 McKAY, JAMES A., Jr. Juvenile law, 1969 A.D.,2A.G. Texas Bar Journal 32: 291-292, 322-326 (1969)

A discussion of the most serious threat which Gault poses - the interpretation and, per se, the extension by innuendo of its essence and its application by state appellate courts. (8 refs.)

643 McKINNIS, MICHAEL B. Juvenile social records and criminal discovery. Missouri Law Review 35:113-118 (1970)

A discussion of State ex rel. Arbeiter v. Reagan, 427 S.W.2d 371, 377-378 (Mo. En Banc 1968), rehearing denied May 13, 1968. (54 refs.)

644 McLEAN, DANIELS W. An answer to the challenge of Kent. American Bar Association Journal 53:456-457 (1967)

The problem of due process procedures under the parens patriae doctrine is discussed in relation to the Kent decision, and to the rehabilitation of juveniles.

Great Britain

645 McLEAN, J.D. Another view. Criminal Law Review 684-687 (1972)

A discussion of the difficulties of the children and young persons act 1969, and its unpopularity with juvenile court magistrates in Great Britain since its implementation. (13 refs.)

646 McMILLIAN, THEODORE, and DOROTHY L. McMURTRY. The role of the defense lawyer in the juvenile court - advocate or social worker? St. Louis University Law Journal 14:561-603 (1970)

The authors review the role of the lawyer from pre-trial through post-trial. Questions and problems are set forth which the new, and perhaps even the experienced attorney, may face in the post-Gault juvenile court. (203 refs.)

647 McNAUGHTON-SMITH, P. The second code toward (or away from) a theory of crime and delinquency. Criminologica 7:15-24 (1969)

The subject of this study is the definition of crime and of delinquency, and the significance of the individual's first labeling by means of a court's finding of guilt. (15 refs.)

648 McNULTY, JILL K. The right to be left alone. Journal of Family Law 12:229-255 (1972-1973)

This article focuses on questioning the wisdom of the juvenile court's involvement with children engaged in antisocial but non-criminal activity, for these may be the most abused by formal processing through the juvenile court system. (86 refs.)

649 McSHANE, JOHN Q. The federal government's role in the treatment of youth offenders: two approaches. St. Louis University Law Journal 16:459-478 (1972)

The impact of the Federal Juvenile Delinquency Act, and the Federal Youth Corrections Act, and the Juvenile Delinquency Prevention and Control Act, with amendments, is discussed. Modifications to make them applicable are suggested. (56 refs.)

650 MAGUIRE, MIKE. Illegitimacy and equal protection. New England Law Review 7: 361-370 (1972)

An inquiry into the constitutionality of laws which classify persons according to their legitimate or illegitimate birth - is such classification suspect? (45 refs.)

651 MALMQUIST, C.P. The delinquent and the insane: right and adequacy of treatment. American Journal of Orthopsychiatry 40:388-396 (1970)

652 MALMQUIST, C.P. Dilemmas of the juvenile court. Journal of the American Academy of Child Psychiatry 6:723-748 (1967)

653 MALMQUIST, CARL P. Juvenile detention: right and adequacy of treatment issues. Law and Society Review 7:159-193 (1972)

The thesis of this paper is that the accomplishment of legal safeguards for juveniles at the trial level will still leave vast numbers who are remanded to various institutions for confinement. This fact raises several questions about juvenile rehabilitation, which the author discusses. (16 refs.)

Canada

654 MARCOTTE, GUY. Les cour familiales dans le Quebec/family courts in the province of Quebec. Revue des services de bien-etre a l'enfance et la jeunesse 7:137-140 (1968)

The author stresses the need for specialized courts to deal with the multiple legal problems of the family in Canada as emphasis has shifted to the family as the basic unit of society. These would differ from other courts in their legal function, their specialized procedure, their sponsorship of psychological and social study and treatment (this would be conducted by persons who are not part of the judiciary), and their integration with the general social and family policy. These specialized family courts would be on the borderline between the social welfare and judicial agencies.

655 MARCOVSKY, GERALD. Commonwealth v. Johnson, right to jury trial in juvenile proceedings. University of Pittsburgh Law Review 29:330-341 (1967)

Arguments are submitted to show the role of the jury in protecting the guarantees of essential fairness and due process for juveniles in a situation where the actual guilt of the juvenile is put in question. (53 refs.)

656 MARCOVSKY, GERALD B. Double jeopardy and due process in the juvenile courts. University of Pittsburgh Law Review 29:756-766 (1968)

The object of this Note is to explore three constitutional issues arising out of two basic factual situations which are related to Gault and its consequences: the incarceration of a juvenile twice for an identical act, and the occurrence of a single criminal act which entails several offenses. (49 refs.)

657 MARCOVSKY, GERALD B. Right to jury trial in juvenile proceedings. University of Pittsburgh Law Review 29:330-341 (1967)

A discussion of Commonwealth v. Johnson, 211 Pa.Super.62, 234 A2d 9 (1967). (53 refs.)

N.Y./Calif.

658 MARCUS, STEPHEN H. Equal protection: the custody of the illegitimate child. Journal of Family Law 11:1-48 (1971)

An examination of the law of child custody as it is applied to children born out of wedlock. (244 refs.)

659 MARING, DAVID S. Torts - parent and child - unemancipated minor entitled to bring action against parent to recover for personal injuries sustained in motor vehicle accident. North Dakota Law Review 49:179-185 (1972)

A discussion of Smith v. Kaufmann, 212 Va. 181, 183 S.E.2d 190 (1971). (44 refs.)

California

660 MARSH, RICHARD M. Breaking the juvenile crime cycle: what the court can do. Judicature 56:336-338 (1973)

(5 refs.)

661 MARTIN, ROBERT B. Constitutional law - stop and frisk - an informant's tip by itself can provide the requisite amount of probable cause to justify stop and frisk. Journal of Urban Law 50:790-794 (1973)

The author maintains that tampering with the delicate balance between the rights of American citizens to be free from government intrusion, and the government's need to intrude can have onerous results. (20 refs.)

France

662 MASSIP, J. Das neue französische Kindschaftsrecht: Gesetz vom 3.1.1972. Standesamt 26:105-117 (1973)

663 MATHIAS, CHARLES M., Jr. Despite what we say in America, "children and families come last." Student Lawyer 1:14-17, 68 (1972)

For lawyers and legislators, the problem of juvenile delinquency and child crime, the broken family and the social disintegration that it reflects, poses a very special challenge. It is of the most urgent national priority that lawyers and legislators undertake to reform the system. The role that law plays in helping to deal with the problem may well determine the degree to which the rule of law continues to reign supreme in our society.

664 MATSUO, K. Recent trend of juvenile procedure in U.S.A. Katei Saiban Geppo 5:1-102 (1968)

Germany

665 MATZLER, A. Minderjähriger Mörder. Kriminalistik 26:227-233, 273-277 (1972)

666 MAZUR, LLOYD D., and CHARLES P. ROSE, Jr. The "adversary" process in child custody proceedings. Western Reserve Law Review 18:1731-1752 (1967)

The authors suggest that, because child custody proceedings are nonadversary, the courts must be willing to recognize that certain requirements of due process should not restrict the use of outside investigations, and that this can be accomplished by a revision of the state statutes to stress the necessity for investigatory reports. It is necessary for social workers to become better educated as to the nature and function of the judicial process so as to make their reports more consistent with the traditional notions of justice. (114 refs.)

Utah

667 MECHAM, GARTH D. Proceed with caution - which penalties slow down with the juvenile traffic violator? Crime and Delinquency 14:142-150 (1968)

This study of juvenile courts in Utah which regularly use punitive and educational dispositions for traffic violations, attempts to determine which kind of disposition is most effective. (11 refs.)

668 MENNEL, ROBERT M. Origins of the juvenile court: changing perspectives on the legal rights of juvenile delinquents. Crime and Delinquency 18:68-78 (1972)

The founding of juvenile courts may be seen as both the culmination of distrust in custodial institutions, and an attempt to recast the parental authority of the state in a different mold. In 1972, as in 1872, interest in providing delinquent children with legal safeguards is based upon belief that the state has not fulfilled its parental duties. Gault, and O'Connell of nearly a century ago, are compared. (43 refs.)

669 MERZ, CHARLES L. Representing the juvenile defendant in waiver proceedings. St. Louis University Law Journal 12:424-465 (1968)

This article provides a basic discussion of the waiver proceeding, with emphasis on the role of counsel in relation thereto. (144 refs.)

Italy

670 MEUCCI, G. Suggestions for selection of juvenile court judges. Esperienze di Rieducazione 18:24-29 (1971)

The juvenile court judge, whose decisions can assume the nature and effects of laws, is expected to make far-reaching decisions which demand considerable knowledge and insight as regards civil measures concerning the parents, the rehabilitation and sentencing of the juvenile offender. The author makes suggestions for the improvements in the training of these specialized judges in Italy.

Belgium

671 MEULDERS-KLEIN, M.T. Zum belgischen Jugendschutzesetz. Zeitschrift für das Gesamte Familienrecht. 14:199-204 (1967)

672 MICHAEL, GREGORY E. Criminal law and procedure - youthful offender's right to a trial by jury. Suffolk University Law Review 6:196-201 (1971)

A discussion of McKeiver et al. v. Pennsylvania, 403 U.S. 528 (1971). (35 refs.)

673 MICHAEL, RICHARD A., and WILLIAM C. CUNNINGHAM. From Gault to Urbasek: for the young – the best of both worlds. Chicago Bar Record 49:162-168 (1968)
Two basic questions unanswered by Gault are discussed. (21 refs.)

Texas

674 MILLER, CLARK J., et al. A study of mentally retarded juvenile offenders in Corpus Christi, Texas. Federal Probation 37(2):54-61 (1973)
The two most important aspects needed in treatment of the retarded offender are constant supervision and repetition of expectations. The author discusses data available about retarded offenders who appear in juvenile courts, and lists considerations for therapy. (10 refs.)

675 MILLER, JEROME G. The dilemma of the post-Gault juvenile court. Family Law Quarterly 3:229-239 (1969)
A discussion of George H. Meads' article, "The psychology of punitive justice," in the American Journal of Sociology, volume 23, 1918, pp. 577-602. Meads' ideas have immediate relevance to the post-Gault juvenile court system. (15 refs.)

676 MILTON, MURRAY M. Post-Gault: a new prospectus for the juvenile court. New York Law Forum 16:57-92 (1970)
(161 refs.)

Minnesota

677 Minnesota juvenile court rules symposium. Minnesota Law Review 54:301-484 (1969)
An analysis of recently adopted Minnesota juvenile court rules. (refs.)

678 MITCHELL, LYNN T. Child welfare workers in court. Crime and Delinquency 1: 59-62 (1965)
This article is divided into three sections the first of which deals with court organization, child welfare workers' roles and responsibilities towards the juvenile court and the circuit court. Secondly, the author deals with the "mock trial technique" to prepare the workers for testifying as witnesses in court hearings. The third section deals with the different roles of lawyers and social workers, and the feelings of each group toward the other.

Germany

679 MIYAZAWA, K. The development of the juvenile justice system and Freudenthal's contributions to it in West Germany. Katei Saibab Geppó 24(7):1-52 (1972)

Japan

680 MIYAZAWA, K. A general criticism on the outline of the juvenile law amendment. Horitsu jiho 42(13):1-15 (1970)

Japan

681 MIYAZAWA, K. Um den Jugendarrest. Hogaku Kenkyu 40(6):1-21 (1967)

Germany

682 MIYAZAWA, K., und H. MOROSAWA. Betrachtungen zur geschichtlichen Entwicklung der Jugendgerichtshilfe in Deutschland. Hogaku Kenkyu 43(5):31-66 (1970)

683 A model act providing for consent of minors for health services. Pediatrics 51: 293-296 (1973)

This Model Act is drafted with the purpose of stimulating all states of the Union to review their statutes in regard to minors' consent for health services. The goal of this Model Act is to insure that all minors have quality health services by granting the minors self-consent in conditions and instances that prevent them from seeking services if parental consent is required, and by encouraging health professionals to deliver quality services to minors without incurring legal liability.

684 MORA, STEVEN H. Juvenile detention: a constitutional problem affecting local government. Urban Lawyer 1:189-216 (1969)

The author attacks the unjustifiable nature of present practice and of statutory provisions regarding detention and release for juveniles on constitutional grounds. (128 refs.)

Japan

685 MORIJA, K. Disposal of cases outside of family courts, and due process of law in juvenile cases. Katei Saiban Geppo 24(9):95-142 (1972)

France

686 MORISHITA, T. Treatment of criminal and dangerous juveniles in France. Katei Saiban Geppo 19(1):1-30 (1967)

687 MORREALE, GERALD. Parental right to inspect school records. Buffalo Law Review 20:255-271 (1970)

The nature of the parent's relationship to school authorities, and the fact that records are required to be maintained by law are important elements in the common law right to inspect records. (79 refs.)

Great Britain

688 MORRIS, ALLISON M. Children's hearings in Scotland. Criminal Law Review 693-701 (1972)

A discussion of Part III of the social work (Scotland) act 1969, the purpose of which was to remove juvenile delinquents from the courts, and to deal with them in a social welfare context. (13 refs.)

Oregon

689 MOSHOFSKY, WILLIAM J. A proposal to improve court services to families and children in Oregon. Oregon Law Review 46:77-87 (1966)

A critical analysis of a report by the National Council on Crime and Delinquency on Oregon's court machinery to handle family and other related matters. (20 refs.)

690 MOSK, STANLEY. Coping with change: can youth do it? Juvenile Court Judges' Journal 20(3):108-115 (1969)

691 MOUNTFORD, HELEN, and HARVEY S. BERENSON. Waiver of jurisdiction: the last resort of the juvenile court. University of Kansas Law Review 18:55-70 (1969)

The factors involved in the waiver of jurisdiction by the juvenile court are examined. (105 refs.)

692 MUDD, JOSEPH E. The constitution and juvenile delinquents. Montana Law Review 32:307-321 (1971)

This Note reviews the constitutional safeguards that must be provided in juvenile delinquency proceedings in light of the trend observed in the law of the recent Supreme Court opinions. (95 refs.)

Montana

693 MUDD, JOSEPH E. Indian juveniles and legislative delinquency in Montana. Montana Law Review 33:233-254 (1972)

This Comment interrelates the results of research, both legal and empirical, in order to make a complete delineation of Indian juvenile procedures. (114 refs.)

694 MURPHY, PATRICK T. Defending a juvenile court proceeding. Practical Lawyer 15:31-40 (1969)

This article describes the role of the defense lawyer in representing delinquest and dependent children in juvenile courts operating within the constitutional framework laid down by the Supreme Court in In Re Gault.

Illinois

695 MURPHY, PATRICK T. NLDA juvenile court project. The Legal Aid Briefcase 27:224-233 (1969)

The author maintains that lawyers, if tenacious enough, are well suited to push bureaucracies into recognizing the individual. The results of a study conducted in the Illinois juvenile court in Cook County relating to the role of the lawyer representing individuals in the dependent and neglected child area are discussed. Based on this study, it is concluded that an aggressive attorney is uniquely situated to prod agencies to follow the law and, upon their refusal, to employ tactics such as mandamus, taxpayer injunction suits, civil rights action, and many other methods to force the agencies to live up to their responsibilities.

Canada

696 MURPHY, W. Family relations act and its application. Provincial Judges' Association of British Columbia. Conference Proceedings 1:49-60 (1972)

697 MYERS, PHYLLIS. Police in the schools: two troubled institutions meet. City 27-31 (Jan/Feb 1972)

The increasing use of police in city schools raises many questions. The results of a survey are reviewed.

698 NAHUM, A.M., and A.W. SIEGEL. Injuries to children in automobile collisions. International Society of Barristers Quarterly 4:36-80 (1969)

Japan

699 NAKAGAWA, M. A view of the history of juvenile law practice. Haurei taimuza 256:2-9 (1971)

700 NAVIN, WALTER D., Jr. The contracts of minors viewed from the perspective of fair exchange. North Carolina Law Review 50:517-547 (1972)

The purpose of this article is to explore the ramifications of contractual liability. The hypothesis is that possibly the time has come to treat the incapacity of minors in a manner similar to the incapacity of the mentally ill so as to redress the severe consequences visited upon the adult who has entered into a contractual relationship with a minor. (139 refs.)

701 NEAL, JAMES R. Constitutional law - equal protection - necessity of standards in statute allowing probate court to waive jurisdiction of a minor to circuit court. Journal of Urban Law 50:782-789 (1973)

A discussion of People v. Fields, 199 N.W.2d 217 (1972). (26 refs.)

702 NEIGHER, ALAN. The Gault decision: due process and the juvenile courts. In Cavan, Ruth. Readings in juvenile delinquency. 2d edition. New York, J.B. Lippincott, 1969.

The Gault decision does not accord to juveniles all of the protections of the Bill of Rights, states the author, as all juvenile courts, with the exception of the District of Columbia, are, in fact, state courts. (9 refs.)

703 NEITHERCUTT, M.G. Consequences of "guilty." Crime and Delinquency 15:459-462 (1969)

This article discusses examples of two categories of the sanctions imposed on offenders: those delineated in criminal law, and those imposed by civil law and the numerous hardships imposed by "unofficial" authority. (31 refs.)

704 NEJELSKI, PAUL. The missing links. Trial 7(5):17,19 (1971)

The need for national standards for the equitable administration of justice is discussed, and seven specific areas which would provide the basis for model codes and administrative guidelines are stressed.

705 NELSEN, R. OWEN. The clinical psychologist in juvenile court. Juvenile Justice 23(3):26-31 (1972)

The role of the psychologist and his "expert" advice within the juvenile court is examined. (2 refs.)

Wyoming

706 NELSON, KENNARD F. The Wyoming juvenile court act of 1971. Land and Water Review 8:237-269 (1973)

The purpose of this Comment is to explore some of the provisions of Wyoming's Juvenile Court Act of 1971 in light of recent decisions by the Supreme Court of the United States, various appellate courts, and the provisions of several model juvenile codes with a view to revealing the various strengths and weaknesses in the Act. (207 refs.)

707 NEWMAN, CHARLES L. The constructive use of police authority with youth and families in crisis. Police 12:18-23 (1968)

The author points out that police must be careful not to allow their personal assessments to become the basis for decision-making. Police should not be responsible for cases of neglect or child abuse unless the child is in immediate danger.

708 NICOL, A.R., et al. The quantitative assessment of violence in adult and young offenders. Medicine, Science, and the Law 12:275-282 (1972)

The reliability and validity of a method of estimating violent behavior at an interview is explored and discussed. (6 refs.)

New York

709 Nondelinquent children in New York: the need for alternatives to institutional treatment. Columbia Journal of Law and Social Problems 8:251-284 (1972)

This article investigates one aspect of the juvenile legal system: the status and treatment of nondelinquent children under the laws and practices of the City and the State of New York. The conditions of the institutions where these children are placed are examined. An appraisal of viable alternatives to the present system is offered. (228 refs.)

Pennsylvania

710 NOVAK, RAYMOND A. The incorrigible child under the new Pennsylvania juvenile act: an unsound, unsupportable, and unfortunate policy choice. University of Pittsburgh Law Review 35:73-92 (1973)

The thesis of this article is that the drafters of the new Pennsylvania juvenile act of 1972 made an unsound policy choice when they decided to classify the incorrigible child as "delinquent." (72 refs.)

Pennsylvania

711 NOVAK, RAYMOND A. S439, the proposed Pennsylvania juvenile act: a two-edged sword. University of Pittsburgh Law Review 34:221-241 (1972)

(78 refs.)

712 NOVOVICH, SERGE. Constitutional law: due process requires proof beyond a reasonable doubt for juveniles. Tulsa Law Journal 7:63-67 (1971)

A discussion of juvenile rights afforded by In Re Gault and In Re Winship. (26 refs.)

713 NOYES, ALFRED D. Has Gault changed the juvenile court concept? Crime and Delinquency 16:158-162 (1970)

The Gault decision, which extended certain constitutional rights to children appearing in juvenile courts for alleged delinquency, has influenced some courts to adopt criminal court procedures, with prosecutors appearing in behalf of the state. The Supreme Court appears to have rejected the principle that the right of a child is not to liberty but to custody. Due process of law for a child does not require a criminal proceeding in the juvenile court. A child is entitled to more than the bare legal rights afforded an adult. The Gault decision has given aid and comfort to those who would weaken the juvenile court concept of a non-adversary judicial proceeding in which the judge administers the precept of parens patriae.

Georgia

714 O'CONNOR, JOHN V. Torts: the constitutional validity of parental liability statutes. Marquette Law Review 55:584-590 (1972)

A discussion of Corley v. Lewless, 227 Ga. 745, 182 S.E.2d 766 (1971). (26 refs.)

715 O'DONNELL, KEVIN M. Inferential impeachment: the presence of parole officers

at subsequent juvenile adjudications. Marquette Law Review 55:349-368 (1972)

Until the dispositional phase, the parole officer is merely a non-participating observer - a spectator who, although passive by his very status or presence, serves to impeach, contrary to statute, the credibility of the child. (93 refs.)

Japan

716 OGALA, K.A. A study of the attitudes of juvenile traffic offenders through the use of the sentence completion test. Katei Saiban Geppo 22(4):157-194 (1970)

Ireland

717 O'MAHONEY, MICHAEL V. Legal aspects of residential child care. The Irish Jurist 6:217-236 (1971)

A discussion of juvenile rights in Ireland. (64 refs.)

718 O'NEIL, CARLE F., and ANTHONY P. TRAVISONO. Understanding the family of the delinquent child. Juvenile Court Judges' Journal 19(4):147-152 (1969)

(19 refs.)

Oregon

719 Oregon's child abuse legislation: some additional proposals. Willamette Law Journal 5:131-139 (1968)

This Note discusses what brought about the interest in producing legislative solutions regarding child abuse. The Oregon law is examined and modifications in the existing statute are suggested. (43 refs.)

Argentina

720 ORELLE, J.M.R. La capacidad del menor em emancipado luego de la reforma del código civil. Revista del Notariado 71:777-844 (1968)

721 ORLANDO, FRANK A. The judge's angle. Trial 7(5):21,23 (1971)

The author suggests that the juvenile courts must become full family courts, dealing with the entire problem of the family and not with the problems of the children only, and to have the jurisdiction and the authority to require governmental agencies to meet their legislated responsibilities.

Connecticut

722 O'ROURKE, THOMAS P., and RICHARD G. SALEM. A comparative analysis of pretrial release procedures. Crime and Delinquency 14:367-373 (1968)

This study of release on own recognizance pretrial practices confirms that alleged offenders are indeed returning to court for trial, and it also indicates that a specially administered program is substantially more effective than the police in actually releasing those arrested. (11 refs.)

723 ORTBALS, MARY B. Appellate review of juvenile court proceedings and the role of the attorney. St. Louis University Law Journal 13:90-105 (1968)

This discussion examines and reviews the various aspects of the appeal of a juvenile case and the role of the attorney in relation thereto. Much of the study is directed toward providing information concerning juvenile appeals. (65 refs.)

Canada

724 O'SULLIVAN, J.F. Infants and contributory negligence. Law Society of Manitoba, Isaac Pitblado Lectures on Continuing Legal Education 38-43 (1970)

Austria

725 OVENDORF, R. Erfahrungen des Richters mit der Bewährungshilfe. Österrichische Notoriats-Zeitung 102:129-135 (1970)

Ger./Engl.

726 OVERLAND, MARK, and JAMES NEWHOUSE. Juvenile criminal law in the Federal Republic of Germany and in England. California Western Law Review 4:35-64 (1968)

This comparative analysis treats the jurisdiction over juvenile offenders, the structure of the courts, and required qualifications for participants in juvenile hearings. Differences are discussed. The comparison of West German and English juvenile court structure and procedure is followed by a description and critique of radical proposals to reform the English system. (122 refs.)

Florida

727 PADGETT, JAMES L. Negligence: minor held to adult standard of care while operating a motor vehicle. University of Florida Law Review 20:107-110 (1967)

A discussion of Medina v. McAllister, 196 So.2d 773 (3d D.C.A. Fla. 1967). (18 refs.)

East Germany

728 PAERSCH, G. Schlussfolgerungen für die weitere Bekämpfung der Jugendkriminalität in der DDR. Staat und Recht 20:72-92 (1971)

729 PALMIER, JOSEPH P. Juvenile court intake: form and function. Willamette Law Journal 5:121-130 (1968)

This article confines itself to the functions of the juvenile intake process and the role of the juvenile officer, i.e. the probation officer, police officer, and social welfare officer. (26 refs.)

730 Parens patriae and statutory vagueness in the juvenile court. Yale Law Review 82:745-771 (1973)

(159 refs.)

Wisconsin

731 PARINS, ROBERT J. Habeas corpus review (what the juvenile court record should include to stand the test of habeas corpus). Wisconsin Bar Bulletin 42(5):20-26 (1969)

The functions and purpose of the writ are outlined and discussed in relation to the Wisconsin statute. (15 refs.)

732 PARKER, FRANK J. Instant maturation for the post-Gault "hood." Family Law Quarterly 4:113-129 (1970)

Gault and Arizona was such a fundamental departure from traditional American juvenile delinquency law that three years after the decision, the reaction is still settling. It is the purpose of this article to extend the conclusions of Gault in the hope of achieving a more successful approach than presently exists. Thus, even though the need for Gault is admitted and its conclusions heartily endorsed, there still remains a need for further modification and refinement. (13 refs.)

Canada

733 PARKER, GRAHAM. The appellate court view of the juvenile court. Osgood Hall Law Journal 7:155-197 (1969)

An examination of the Canadian juvenile court through the eyes of the appellate courts in this country. The author concludes that the courts have little conception of or only slight regard for the concept of the juvenile court, and the potential importance of its work. (51 refs.)

Canada

734 PARKER, GRAHAM. Juvenile delinquency - transfer of juvenile cases to adult courts - factors to be considered under the Juvenile Delinquents Act. Canadian Bar Review 48:336-346 (1970)

A comparison of some Canadian cases. (41 refs.)

Gr.Br./Austral./Scand./Calif.

735 PARKER, GRAHAM E. Some historical observations on the juvenile court. The Criminal Law Quarterly 9:467-502 (1967)

A history of the concept of the juvenile court, and historial background of the juvenile court laws. Reference is made to Scandinavia, Great Britain, Australia, and California. Australian statistics are included. (90 refs.)

736 PARRISH, SHEILA M. Due process in juvenile proceedings. North Carolina Central Law Journal 3:255-259 (1972)

Juvenile court records need to be impounded, states the author in this discussion of due process. (9 refs.)

737 PAULSEN, MONRAD G. The child, the court and the commission. Juvenile Court Judges' Journal 18(3):79-83 (1967)

A discussion of the juvenile court as characterized by the President's Commission of Law Enforcement and the Administration of Justice.

738 PAULSEN, MONRAD G. Children's court - gateway or last resort. Case and Comment 72:3-9 (1967)

The court, the legislatures, and the President's Commission all point to a new juvenile court that will be quite different from the one proposed by the reformers. The new court is to be a court of last resort, not a gateway to rehabilitation and re-education. To put this into effect, more than law is required, states the author.

739 PAULSEN, MONRAD G. The constitutional domestication of the juvenile court. Supreme Court Review 233-266 (1967)

A detailed discussion of In Re Gault, and the six basic rights allegedly denied the respondent. A number of constitutional issues are raised. The role of the "law guardian" is examined, and the place of the adversary process in juvenile court. (89 refs.)

740 PAULSEN, MONRAD G. Child abuse reporting laws: the shape of the legislation. Columbia Law Review 67:1-49 (1967)

This article analyzes the child abuse statutes existing in 1967. The statutory texts themselves do not always offer a reliable guide to the way in which cases are actually handled, and obviously cannot ensure an effective program for child protection and family treatment. Caseworkers need caseloads limited in size to permit case work, not merely case carrying. (159 refs.)

741 PAULSEN, MONRAD G. Juvenile courts and the legacy of 1967. Indiana Law Journal 43:527-557 (1968)

This study includes sections on notice: a complete record, the privilege against self-incrimination, retroactivity, and the burden of proof in juvenile court proceedings. (123 refs.)

742 PAULSEN, MONRAD G. Juvenile courts, family courts and the poor man. California Law Review 54:694-716 (1966)

Juveniles who come under the delinquency jurisdiction of the Family Court are an unrepresentative sample of our youth. The poor and the black appear in disproportionate numbers. This phenomenon "transforms the court into a class institution, a fact which may inhibit its development and, indeed, may have an impact on all sorts of legislative changes." The problems of communication between court officials and lower-class defendants are discussed, and the types of delinquents, and jurisdiction of juvenile and family courts delineated. Also discussed are: judges with no specialized training in the use of social and psychological information, careless and slipshod procedures, ill-formed dispositional judgments together with inadequate facilities for care and treatment, and the problems raised by the issue of morals vs. conciliation in the family court. (72 refs.)

743 PAULSEN, MONRAD G. Legal protections against child abuse. Children 13(2): 42-48 (1967)

The author reviews the legal framework in which the problem of child abuse was being dealt with in this country in 1967. (12 refs.)

744 PAULSEN, MONRAD G. New horizons for juvenile court legislation. Pennsylvania Bar Association Quarterly 40:26-36 (1969)

The author states that the Gault case did not address itself to the issues of law surrounding police action or questioning, nor to any of the juvenile court proceedings before a fact-finding hearing. It said nothing about a dispositional hearing, the right to an appeal, or the right to have a transcript made as an aid in pursuing appeal. In order to provide guidelines for judges, a range of possible dispositions should be developed. (3 refs.)

745 PAULSEN, MONRAD G. The role of juvenile courts. Current History 53:70-75 (1967)

A brief description of the creation and development of the juvenile court is followed by a discussion of the impact of legislation and court decisions. (12 refs.)

New York

746 PEDIGO, ELIZABETH S. Standard of proof in delinquency adjudications: New York takes the narrow view. Journal of Family Law 9:316-324 (1969)

A discussion of the problem of whether a finding by "fair preponderance of the evidence" is sufficient to adjudge a twelve year old juvenile delinquent for stealing $112 from a pocket book. (30 refs.)

747 PENDLETON, BRIAN. Waiver of constitutional rights by minors: a question of law or fact? Hastings Law Journal 19:223-255 (1967)

In this Note the author treats the competence of a child to waive his constitutional rights, for the purposes of juvenile court as well as for criminal proceedings. (100 refs.)

748 PETERSON, R. THOMAS. Juvenile justice and pre-adjudication detention. UCLA-Alaska Law Review 1:154-171 (1972)

This article focuses upon the rights, remedies, and rationale behind juvenile pre-adjudication detention. (110 refs.)

Czechoslavakia

749 PETRULÁKOVÁ, J. On the system of legal regulations concerning the parent-child relationship as adopted by the family law codes of European socialist countries. Právnické Stúdie 17:403-426 (1969)

Virginia

750 PHILPOTT, JAMES A., Jr. Jury trials for juvenile delinquents in Virginia. Washington and Lee Law Review 28:135-146 (1971)

A discussion of juvenile trial rights under the Virginia constitutions. (75 refs.)

751 PILIAVIN, IRVING M., et al. Delinquency, personal costs and parental treatment a test of a reward-cost model of juvenile criminality. The Journal of Criminal Law, Criminology and Police Science 60:165-172 (1969)

An analysis of a questionnaire survey that was conducted to determine the effect of selected elements of the environment on deterring delinquency. (23 refs.)

752 PILPEL, HARRIET F. Minors' rights to medical care. Albany Law Review 36: 462:487 (1972)

Problems regarding medical care for minors and possible legislative solutions are discussed. (31 refs.)

France

753 PIRET, J.M. Le juge de la jeunesse vu par cinquante mineurs. Revue de Droit et de Criminologie 49:884-913 (1969)

754 PIRSIG, MAYNARD E. The constitutional validity of confining disruptive delinquents in penal institutions. Minnesota Law Review 54:101-145 (1969)

There is a genuine need for separate facilities, specially designed for difficult juveniles, and provided with measures of security not needed or desirable for the remainder of those committed by juvenile courts. (178 refs.)

Illinois

755 PLATT, ANTHONY, and RUTH FRIEDMAN. The limits of advocacy: occupational hazards in juvenile court. University of Pennsylvania Law Review 116:1156-1184 (1968)

This study in legal sociology examines the role played by private attorneys defending youthful offenders in Chicago's juvenile court. (98 refs.)

756 PLATT, ANTHONY, et al. In defense of youth: a case of the public defender in juvenile court. Indiana Law Journal 43:619-640 (1968)

The purpose of this article is to analyze one major consequence of In Re Gault in which the United States Supreme Court held, inter alia, that juveniles are entitled to: timely notice of the specific charges against them; notification of the right to be represented by counsel in proceedings which "may result in commitment to an institution in which the juvenile's freedom is curtailed;" the right to confront and cross-examine complainants and other witnesses; adequate warning of the privilege against self-incrimination, and the right to remain silent. (75 refs.)

Czechoslovakia

757 POHANKA, M. The concept, development and assessment of child crime. Pravnik 109:1003-1008 (1970)

758 POLIER, JUSTINE W. The Gault case: its practical impact on the philosophy and objectives of the juvenile court. Family Law Quarterly 1:47-54 (1967)

Two troubling questions for juvenile court judges are raised by the Gault decision: how much further would, or should, safeguards established in criminal cases be extended to juvenile court proceedings, and how should the jurisdiction of the courts be narrowed in the light of their actual capacity to secure the services needed for care, treatment, and rehabilitation? "Distributive justice" - individual justice - has been prevented by the failure to provide necessary personnel facilities and techniques. The judicial system must concern itself with substantive justice. (9 refs.)

Texas

759 POLOW, BERTRAM. The impact of Gault on the juvenile process. Juvenile Court Judges' Journal 20(4):159 (1969)

(2 refs.)

New Jersey

760 POLOW, BERTRAM. Reducing juvenile and domestic relations caseloads. Juvenile Justice 24(2):55-59 (1973)

This article describes the organization, the working procedures, and the goals of the State Law Enforcement Planning Agency which was established in Morris County, New Jersey, as a more effective system for initial handling of all juvenile and family-oriented complaints. (6 refs.)

761 POPKIN, ALICE, and FREDA LIPPERT. Is there a constitutional right to the insanity defense in the juvenile court. Journal of Family Law 10:421-442 (1971)

The authors state reasons why it is crucial that the insanity defense be utilized to protect the mentally ill juvenile from punishment, and to guarantee him needed treatment in the available facilities. (82 refs.)

762 POPKIN, ALICE B., et al. Another look at the role of due process in juvenile court. Family Law Quarterly 6:233-278 (1972)

The authors consider major supreme court decisions insofar as they concern the constitutional requirements for juvenile proceedings. They also discuss lower court decisions since Gault, concerning the application of due process requirements, and they attempt to draw some conclusions regarding the role of due process in future juvenile proceedings. (229 refs.)

Great Britain

763 POWER, M.J., et al. Neighborhood, school and juveniles before the courts. The British Journal of Criminology 12:111-132 (1972)

The results of a study of children before the courts in the London Borough of Tower Hamlets. The study concentrates on the major influences on boys before the courts: the neighborhood, the family and the schools. (31 refs.)

764 PRAGER, BARBARA, and STANLEY A. ROTHSTEIN. The adoptee's right to know his natural heritage. New York Law Forum 19:137-156 (1973)

(104 refs.)

Arizona

765 Pre-interrogation waiver of constitutional rights by juveniles. Arizona Law Review 14:487-497 (1972)

A discussion of State v. Hardy, 107 Ariz. 583, 491 P.2d 17 (1971), a decision which radically changes Arizona's system of juvenile justice, as the child confronted by police is no longer assured of adult aid in deciding whether to waive constitutional rights. (61 refs.)

Illinois

766 PRITCHETT, L. BOW. Comparative negligence contribution, collateral source - an Illinois appraisal. Illinois Bar Journal 468-478 (1968)

Examination of the above principles of negligence law is particularly relevant at this time. This article examines their relationship in a modern loss distribution system. (62 refs.)

767 Prosecutorial discretion and the decision to waive juvenile court jurisdiction. Washington University Law Quarterly 436-444 (1973)

An analysis of United States v. Bland No. 71-1761 (D.C.Cir., Sept. 6, 1972). (36 refs.)

North Carolina

768 PURCELL, JOHN. North Carolina: corrections and juvenile justice in a rural state. Columbia Human Rights Law Review 5:187-206 (1973)

This report focuses on the effect of federal Law Enforcement Assistance Administration findings in the area of juvenile services, both pre-delinquent and delinquent, and in the area of juvenile corrections. (108 refs.)

Texas

769 PURDOM, THOMAS J. Juvenile court proceedings from the standpoint of the attorney for the state. Texas Tech Law Review 1:269-322 (1970)
This article concerns juvenile proceedings in Texas from the standpoint of the attorneys for that state. (123 refs.)

Illinois

770 PUSATERI, LAWRENCE X., and ROBERT K. SCOTT. Illinois' new unified code of corrections. Illinois Bar Journal 61:62-75 (1972)
(117 refs.)

Oklahoma

771 PUTNAM, GARY L. Children - dependent and delinquent - definitions: Okla. Sess. Laws 1972, Ch. 122. Tulsa Law Journal 8:265-267 (1972)
The discriminatory nature of previous definitions and recent statutory amendments in Oklahoma are discussed. (20 refs.)

Oklahoma

772 PUTNAM, GARY L. Minors and adults - rights, and obligations: Okla. Sess. Laws 1972, Ch. 221. Tulsa Law Journal 8:268-269 (1972)
Recent statutory amendments in Oklahoma regarding the terms "minor" and "majority" are discussed. (13 refs.)

773 PYFER, JOHN F., Jr. The juvenile's right to receive treatment. Family Law Quarterly 6:279-320 (1972)
Until the administrative problems of providing adequate treatment are solved, clearly establishing the constitutional right to treatment remains the surest way of protecting the liberty and interest of all civil commitants. (220 refs.)

774 Quantum of proof in delinquency hearings. Willamette Law Journal 5:149-156 (1968)
This Note discusses the quantum of proof which must be met before a juvenile may be adjudged delinquent on the basis of having commited an act which, if done by an adult, would constitute a crime. (54 refs.)

Germany

775 QUENSEL, S. Wie wird man Kriminell? Kritische Justiz 4:375-382 (1970)

New Mexico

776 QUINN, STEPHEN K. The freedom of the press vs. the confidentiality provisions in the New Mexico's children's code. New Mexico Law Review 4:119-126 (1973)

Netherlands

777 RAFFALLI, H.C. Medische, jurische en sociale aspecten van kindermishandling. Documentatiblad 3:105-113 (1971)

778 RAILSBACK, THOMAS F. 'Less than the sum of its parts.' Trial 7(5):15,24 (1971)
The increase of crime and lawlessness among juveniles is discussed, and the need for the establishment of an Institute for Continuing Studies of Juvenile Justice is emphasized.

779 RALSTON, WILLIAM H. Jr. Intake: informal disposition or adversary proceeding? Crime and Delinquency 17:160-167 (1971)

The Gault decision has provoked extended discussion and debate because of its revolutionary impact on juvenile justice. This article discusses the application of the decision to the preadjudication stage of the juvenile court proceeding. (3 refs.)

780 RANKIN, HAYWOOD. Criminal procedure - juries in the juvenile system? North Carolina Law Review 48:666-677 (1970)

This Note shows why each of the arguments given against juries for juveniles fails. (50 refs.)

781 RAY, MONTFORT S. Student's right to control his personal appearance is protected by a constitutional right to privacy. Journal of Public Law 17:165-174 (1968)

The issue of individual freedom is discussed. (116 refs.)

782 REAGAN, PAUL V. Constitutional law - juvenile proceedings - jury trials - a jury trial is not required in a state juvenile delinquency adjudicative hearing under the due process clause of the fourteenth amendment. Notre Dame Lawyer 47:655-668 (1972)

(121 refs.)

783 REASONS, CHARLES E. Gault: procedural change and substantive effect. Crime and Delinquency 16:163-171 (1970)

To gauge the effects of the Gault decision, this study analyzed a juvenile court's records for a two-year period. Both quantitative and qualitative changes were discovered, even though no statutory changes occurred. A doubling in the percentage of cases with counsel and a reduction in the total number of cases reflect an increased emphasis upon legal fact-finding. This change of normative emphasis was brought about primarily by changes in the attitudes of court personnel and law enforcement agencies. (23 refs.)

Ohio

784 REBER, ROBERT D., Jr. Right of an indigent juvenile in Ohio to a transcript at state expense. Akron Law Review 5:117-127 (1972)

An analysis of existing case law in Ohio and throughout the nation, as well as statutory language and its interpretation by Ohio courts of the right of an indigent juvenile to a free transcript. (48 refs.)

California

785 Recent trends in the California law concerning the best interests of the child. Pepperdine Law Review 1(1):89-100 (1973)

(35 refs.)

786 REDDICK, W.H., and J.G. BOUZEK. Forensic social workers and social service lawyers as team public defenders for juveniles in new court. Police 11(2):22-27 (1966)

These authors feel that forensic social workers, acting as case-finders for juvenile public defenders, can perform certain specialized functions.

787 REED, AMOS E. Gault and the juvenile training school. Indiana Law Review 43: 641-654 (1968)

The author states that training schools and courts must evoke respect and cooperation between professional agency staffs and attorneys in order to preserve the individualization of treatment without sacrificing or ignoring basic rights. (41 refs.)

Switzerland

788 REHBERG, J. Die Sanktionen in revidierten schweizerischen Jugendstrafsrecht. Strafvollzug in der Schweiz 7:6-23 (1970)

Israel

789 REIFEN, DAVID. Family situations in an Israeli juvenile court. Journal of Jewish Communal Service 47:316-322 (1971)

Special aspects of the juvenile court system are discussed and examples are cited. Special training for juvenile court judges is also discussed. (11 refs.)

Israel

790 REIFEN, DAVID. Juvenile judicial procedure in Israel. Revue de Troit Penal et de Criminologie (Brussels) 48:771-783 (1968)

Three stages of juvenile judicial procedure exist in Israel: establishment of facts; application of laws; decision on the type of legal treatment/punishment. Whereas the first two stages are purely legal, in the third, the juvenile court uses wide discretionary authority -- increased emphasis is placed upon the function of the court as a social service agency rather than merely as a part of the judiciary. The atmosphere in the court should promote closer interpersonal relations between the juvenile officers, the juvenile and the parents, thus enabling the judge to arrive at decisions conforming to the ideal of the individualization of sentence.

New York

791 REINGOLD, MARK S. Abortion law reform in New York: a study of religious, moral, medical, and legal conflict. Albany Law Review 31:290-309 (1967)

This study presents a concise, objective statement of the relevant legal, religious, moral, and medical arguments involved in the quest for abortion law reform in New York. (95 refs.)

792 REINHARD, WALTER G. Retroactive application of the jury trial requirement. Dickinson Law Review 74:556-561 (1970)

Do juveniles have the right to trial by jury in state juvenile court proceedings, and should this right be applied retroactively? (54 refs.)

793 REINHOLD, ROBERT J. The role of the attorney in juvenile court intake processes. St. Louis University Law Journal 13:69-89 (1968)

This Comment is concerned only with the role of the attorney in the intake process of the court, and not with his involvement in the court hearing itself. Intake in the court includes all of the processes of the court from the time of the arrest and referral to the court until the petition for formal court action is filed. (107 refs.)

794 RENDLEMAN, DOUGLAS R. Parens patriae: from chancery to the juvenile court. South Carolina Law Review 23:205-259 (1971)

The author traces through the nineteenth century the progress and manner of what cases came to the juvenile court. (279 refs.)

795 RENN, DONNA E. The right to treatment and the juvenile. Crime and Delinquency 19:477-484 (1973)

The right to treatment has been suggested as a legal tool to assure the therapeutic ideal premised by juvenile law. This article examines the theoretical basis of the right to treatment, its foundation in law, and its application to the juvenile. (40 refs.)

New York

796 Representation in child-neglect cases: are parents neglected? Columbia Journal of Law and Social Problems 4:230-254 (1968)

In its 1962 Family Court Act, New York recognized its duty to provide minors with legal assistance compensated by the state. Despite this concentration on fairness, the Act failed to assure effective legal representation for parents in neglect cases, although under the new Act the parent (respondent) must be notified of his right to counsel. This study of records in Kings County (Brooklyn) Family Court, indicates the extent and effect of parent's lack of representation, and the constitutionality of the present system. According to the various statistics and tables, the presence of an attorney may have a great effect on the final disposition. Inadequate provision for counsel for respondents in neglect cases leaves a parent without assistance in a proceeding which may seriously affect him and his family. A solution is proposed. (166 refs.)

Michigan

797 RESTEINER, HAROLD E. Delinquent or criminal: the problems of transfers of jurisdiction. Juvenile Justice 24(1):2-13 (1973)

A discussion of the area of transfer of jurisdiction. (28 refs.)

U.S.S.R.

798 REUTER, L. Experience derived from the activities and practices of the Soviet courts in combating and preventing juvenile delinquency. Neue Justiz 26:204-208 (1972)

Some aspects of criminal procedure against juveniles and the task of the courts in the USSR are discussed: public prosecutors and judges; co-operation between courts and commissions involving minors; detection and elimination of detrimental influences of adults.

799 REUTERMANN, NICHOLAS A., et al. Juvenile detention facilities: summary report of a national survey. Criminology 9:3-26 (1971)

(12 refs.)

800 REUTERMANN, NICHOLAS A., et al. A partial evaluation of Bloch and Niederhoffer's theory of gang delinquency. Criminology 10:415-425 (1972)

(15 refs.)

801 REYNOLDS, JIMMIE B., Jr. Constitutional law - application of basic constitutional guarantees to juveniles. Mississippi Law Journal 39:121-131 (1967)

This Note analyzes the trends leading to the Gault decision, explains how it compares with present law, and what impact it will have on the juvenile system. (104 refs.)

802 RIBACK, LINDA. Juvenile delinquency laws: juvenile women and the double standard of morality. UCLA Law Review 19:313-342 (1971)

This Comment demonstrates, amongst other things, that juvenile morals statutes are unconstitutionally vague, that they punish a status, and encourage selective enforcement against female juveniles based on a double standard of sexual morality. (141 refs.)

803 RICKNER, GARY J. Wrongful death - prenatal injuries - claim allowed where fetus viable at time of injury and child born alive. Cumberland-Sanford Law Review 4:200-206 (1973)

A discussion of Husky v. Smith, 265 So.2d 596 (1972). (35 refs.)

Germany

804 RIEDEL, H. Sozialsrecht und Jugendwohlfahrtsrecht. Deutscher Rechtspfleger 75:335-341 (1967)

805 RIEFF, JONATHAN D. Relational interest: a minor child's action against a third party who alienates the affections of a parent. Journal of Family Law 7:14-30 (1967)

A discussion of the substantive value of the particular relational interest that the child has in his home when faced with an intentional enticement of a parent, and the fact that this is becoming more apparent and more susceptible to judicial protection. (82 refs.)

Great Britain

806 RIEGE, MARY G. Parental affection and juvenile delinquency in girls. British Journal of Criminology 12:55-73 (1972)

The author discusses the results of a study of the roles of both parents of a group of 25 delinquent girls, and a matched sample of non-delinquent girls.

Virginia

807 Right to counsel in Virginia juvenile proceedings. University of Richmond Law Review 3:316-321 (1969)

This Comment considers the effect of the Gault guarantee of counsel upon the administration of juvenile justice in Virginia. (32 refs.)

808 The right to treatment - a symposium. The Georgetown Law Journal 57:673-890 (1969)

The authors believe that a right to treatment exists under which the mentally ill juveniles, the narcotic addicts, and the alcoholics involuntarily confined may challenge their confinement against the promises of treatment extended by legislatures.

809 A right to treatment for juveniles? Washington University Law Quarterly 157:196 (1973)

This Note examines the question of whether the constitution requires the judiciary to recognize a medically and psychiatrically oriented juvenile right to treatment. (178 refs.)

810 Rights and rehabilitation in the juvenile courts. Columbia Law Review 67:281-341 (1967)

The author of this Note demonstrates the ways in which rehabilitative considerations enter into the actual process of adjudication in the juvenile courts. An attempt is made to determine the degree to which procedures founded upon a desire to rehabilitate may survive the extension of constitutional safeguards. (310 refs.)

District of Columbia

811 RILEY, DAVID. Runaways: and then there were thousands. Delinquency Prevention Reporter 3-11 (Feb., 1972)

A description of the philosophy of Runaway House in Washington, D.C.

812 RITTER, ROBERT F. The role of the lawyer in preparation for a delinquency hearing in juvenile court. St. Louis University Law Journal 12:631-643 (1968)

This writing is directed to the role of the lawyer in one phase of a delinquency proceeding, to wit, the preparation for the delinquency hearing. (54 refs.)

California

813 ROBERTS, DAVID E. The California juvenile: his rights and remedies. Pacific Law Journal 1:350-363 (1970)

A discussion of the California juvenile system. (97 refs.)

814 ROBEY, A. The runaway girl. In O. Pollak and A. Friedman, eds., Family dynamics and female sexual delinquency, Palo Alto, Science and Behavior Books, 1969. pp. 127-137

815 Roe v. Doe: child's right to a college education v. parent's right of control. St. John's Law Review 46:139-146 (1971)

A discussion of Mary L. Doe v. John Doe, 29 N.Y.2d 188, 272 N.E.2d 567, 324 N.Y.S.2d 71 (1971). (48 refs.)

Germany

816 ROESTEL, G. Drug-dependent youngsters in the juvenile court. Jugendschutz 17:106-108 (1972)

In the German Federal Republic both traffic in and the use of drugs are punishable. Three categories of youngsters are seen in juvenile court in this context: pushers who obtain their wares from the international market or by stealing from pharmacies; addicts who steal their drugs in distress; occasional thieves and curious incidental users.

Connecticut

817 ROGERS, KRISTINE O. "For her own protection...": conditions of incarceration for female juvenile offenders in the state of Connecticut. Law and Society Review 7:223-246 (1972)

A study of differential treatment for young male and female offenders. (14 refs.)

818 ROOS, ROBERT A. How to change the law, or the lawyer as a marriage, family and child counselor: a case study. Los Angeles Bar Bulletin 47:481-488 (1972) (6 refs.)

Great Britain

819 ROSE, G.N.G. The artificial delinquent generation. Journal of Criminal Law, Criminology and Police Science 59:370-385 (1968)

The author discusses the results of trends in Great Britain in criminal statistics, and considers the validity of these statistics. (11 refs.)

820 ROSE, ROBERT G. Juvenile statutes and non-criminal delinquents: applying the void-for-vagueness doctrine. Seton Hall Law Review 4:184-209 (1972)

The successful application of the void for vagueness doctrine to non-criminal conduct statutes is a further affirmation by the federal courts that the constitutional domestication of the juvenile court system is still in progress, states the author, who analyzes two opinions which, he maintains, throw considerable doubt on the constitutional validity of most of the nation's juvenile court statutes. (187 refs.)

821 ROSENBERG, CHAIM M., and HERBERT J. PAINE. Female juvenile delinquency: a nineteenth century follow-up. Crime and Delinquency 19:72-78 (1973)

This study provides a perspective on the present crisis in the management of young delinquents. The authors point out the disturbing lack of research on female juvenile offenders. (5 refs.)

822 ROSENWALD, RICHARD J., and JOSEPH MAYER. Runaway girls from suburbia. American Journal of Orthopsychiatry 37:402-403 (1967)

This is the third in a series of studies examining aspects of juvenile delinquency in a group of largely suburban adolescent females.

Australia

823 ROULSTON, R.P. Sentencing a juvenile for manslaughter. Australian and New Zealand Journal of Criminology 1:147-156 (1968)

Great Britain

824 ROWE, A.J.B. Children's hearings. New Society 19:444-446 (1972)

A discussion of the Scottish Social Work Act of 1968 which provides for non-criminal hearings for any child up to the age of sixteen, by a three-member panel selected by the Children's Panel Advisory Committee. All panel members have to be trained in child development, delinquency, and family counseling. The three-member panels are used whenever circumstances present a case for compulsory intervention, and the powers of these hearings are considerable.

Connecticut

825 ROWE, DANIEL S., et al. A hospital program for the detention and registration of abused and neglected children. The New England Journal of Medicine 282:950-952 (1970)

A description of the program at Yale University Medical Center, and the results after a year. (9 refs.)

826 ROYBAL, EDWARD R. Void for vagueness: state statutes proscribing conduct only for a juvenile. Pepperdine Law Review 1:1-20 (1973)

(42 refs.)

Belgium

827 ROZIE, M. De bevoegdheid van de Jeugdrechter brokkelt af! Of de wet van 9 Mei 1972. Rechtskundig Weekblad 36:1505-1512 (1973)

828 RUBIN, JOSEPH L. Constitutional rights in juvenile court. Cleveland-Marshall Law Review 16:477-486 (1967)

The purpose of this article is to provide adequate understanding of the law prior to the U.S. Supreme Court decision, In Re Gault. (47 refs.)

829 RUBIN, SOL. The juvenile court system in evolution. Valparaiso University Law Review 2:1-20 (1967)

This article deals with court cases concerning juvenile court procedure both in the U.S. Supreme Court and the state supreme court. The author also discusses the punitive school of thought and suggests changes. (56 refs.)

830 RUBIN, SOL, and JEFFREY E. GLEN. Developments in correctional law. Crime and Delinquency 14:155-170 (1968)

This article, one of a series appearing annually in the April issue of Crime and Delinquency, covers court decisions of general interest, and also covers key legislation enacted in 1967. (10 refs.)

831 RUBIN, TED. How to make the criminal courts more like the juvenile courts. Santa Clara Lawyer 13:104-120 (1972)

After briefly describing what the juvenile courts have learned from the adult criminal courts, this article examines five major dimensions of practice unique to the juvenile court. The author shows why such dimensions should be incorporated into the adult criminal justice system and suggests that judges and probation officers should take a long hard look at the progressive trends that have taken form in the juvenile system. (57 refs.)

832 RUBIN, TED, and RICHARD S. SHAFFER. Constitutional protection for the juvenile. Denver Law Journal 44:66-87 (1967)

The authors examine the historical development of the juvenile court system, the current practices within the system, and the necessity for completing this transformation now in progress. (62 refs.)

833 RUDSTEIN, DAVID S. Double jeopardy in juvenile proceedings. William and Mary Law Review 14:266-311 (1972)

This article focuses on the fifth amendment protection against double jeopardy and its relation to delinquency proceedings. (168 refs.)

834 Runaway children - a problem for more and more cities. U.S. News and World Report 72:38-42 (1972)

Another article on the runaway phenomenon in the United States.

835 RUNKEL, ROSS R., and WADE P. BETTIS, Jr. Public schools and personal appearance. Willamette Law Journal 7:419-434 (1971)

This article examines some of the theories which courts have applied to rules imposing certain standards of personal appearance, especially in those cases in which a rule is applied by a public school against a student. (71 refs.)

836 RUPPERT, ERNEST R. Juvenile criminal proceedings in federal courts. Loyola Law Review 18:133-149 (1971-1972)

In this Comment an effort is made to present an overview of the federal approach to juvenile criminal conduct. The author summarizes the standards required of all juvenile courts and articulated in Supreme Court decisions. Included is a discussion of the existing statutes, the Federal Juvenile Delinquency Act, 18 U.S.C. Sect. 5031-5037 (1948, and the Federal Youth Correction Act, 18 U.S.C. Sect. 5005-5026 (1950). An evaluation is given of the existing statutory approach in light of current constitutional standards, and the proposed Section 50 of the Final Report. (64 refs.)

837 RUSSELL, D.H. Children in court: obligations for legal psychiatry. Newsletter 3:1-15 (1972)

The author states that more attention should be given to the needs of children in the legal proceedings of divorce, child custody, neglect, etc., and he believes that legal psychiatry has a special obligation in this area.

838 RUSSO, RONALD G. When is a criminal trial not a criminal trial? - the case against jury trials in juvenile court. The Catholic Lawyer 18:148-159 (1972)

The issue presented by McKeiver and its companion cases. (74 refs.)

Ohio

839 SACCUZZO, DENNIS P., and JOHN R. MILLIGAN. Mass truancy hearings: a follow-up study. Juvenile Justice 24(3):31-40 (1973)

This article provides an evaluation of an experimental project in group court hearings. Complaints of school truancy are received by the court, and a single mass hearing is set with appropriate legal notice to all parties.

Australia

840 SACKVILLE, R., and A. LANTERI. The disabilities of illegitimate children in Australia: a preliminary analysis. Australian Law Journal 44:5-13, 51-64 (1970)

Germany

841 SAITO, T. The development of the law of juvenile court in Germany. Hogakuronso 84(4):36-84 (1969)

Maryland

842 SALISBURY, SUZANNE B. The young offenders - a study of the juvenile justice system in Baltimore City. The University of Maryland Law Forum 3:100-107 (1973)

843 SAMFORD, FRANK P., III. State discrimination against dependent children. Alabama Law Review 24:45-85 (1971)

This article describes the methods of, and some of the reasons for the singling out by many states of actual and potential recipients of Aid to Families with Dependent Children for discriminatory treatment. It describes the theoretical bases for and the results of attempts to combat such discrimination by litigation. (234 refs.)

Germany

844 SAMTLEBEN, J. Die Staatsangehörigkeit des ehelichen Kindes und der Grundsatz der Gleichberechtigung. Zeitschrift für das Gesamte Familienrecht 20:1-4 (1973)

Great Britain

845 SAMUELS, ALEC. Children and the young persons act 1969. The New Law Journal 1084-1086 (1969)

846 SAROSIEK, PETER A. Constitutional law - due process - revocation of a juvenile's parole. Wisconsin Law Review 3:954-962 (1973)

A discussion of State ex rel. Bernal v. Hershman, 54 Wisc. 2d 626, 196 N.W.2d 721 (1972). (81 refs.)

847 SARRI, ROSEMARY C. The rehabilitation failure. Trial 7(5):18-19 (1971)

Japan

848 SATO, T. On the parent-child contract. Journal of the Faculty of Laws and Politics 7(3):41-66 (1970)

East Africa

849 SAWYER, G.F.A. Contractual capacity of minors and the conflict of laws in East Africa: a study in conflicts method. Eastern Africa Law Review 1:1-32 (1968)

850 SAYLOR, CHARLES H. Interrogation of juveniles: the right to a parent's presence. Dickinson Law Review 77:543-560 (1973)

This Comment analyzes the approaches taken by various courts when dealing with the problems of juvenile interrogation, the protection a right to a parent's presence may provide, the arguments against the existence of this right, and the constitutional basis of the right. (134 refs.)

851 SCARPITT, FRANK R., and RICHARD M. STEPHENSON. Juvenile court dispositions - factors in the decision-making process. Crime and Delinquency 17:142-151 (1971)

This article discusses the decision-making process of juvenile court judges and, more specifically, the factors associated with judicial decisions. Data were gathered over a three-year period on 1,210 adjudicative delinquents, and included social background and delinquency history information as well as scores on a standard personality inventory. (9 refs.)

Germany

852 SCHAFFSTEIN, F. Die Bemessung der Jugendstrafe. Zentralblatt fuer Jugendrecht und Jugendwohlfahrt. 54:129-139 (1967)

Germany

853 SCHAFFSTEIN, F. Zur Prolematik des Jugendarrests. Zeitschrift für die Gesamte Strafrechtwissenschaft 82:853-895 (1970)

854 SCHECTER, MARTHA. Juvenile case law after Gault. Journal of Family Law 8:416-433 (1968)

Two points are discussed in evaluating the trend of juvenile courts to broaden the scope of juvenile rights in the name of liberty and equal protection. (77 refs.)

855 SCHEPPNER, HAROLD E., Jr. You have a juvenile matter today. Journal of the Missouri Bar 29:386-390 (1973)

856 SCHEPSES, ERWIN. Delinquent children and wayward children. Federal Probation 32(2):42-46 (1968)

Recent court decisions and legislative enactments appear to undermine traditional juvenile court procedures in the U.S. The trend is what to do to a child rather than what to do for a child, and may lead to a quasi-criminal procedure in dealing with delinquent children, states the author. (16 refs.)

857 SCHETTER, CARL F. Gerald Gault - what really occurred? Gavel 29:12-13 (1968)

Austria

858 SCHINDLER, S. Familienbeziehungen und Bewährungschilfe. Österreichische Notariats-Zeitung 102:135-139 (1970)

Oregon

859 SCHLEGEL, JENA V. The role of counsel in the juvenile proceeding. Willamette Law Journal 5:28-49 (1968)

A discussion of the attorney-client relationship; the role of the attorney; the function of the lawyer in delinquency; and dependency cases and appeal cases. (55 refs.)

Germany

860 SCHLOTTHEIM, H.H. Empfiehlt es sich, die Gerichtsorganisation im Hinblick auf die Jugend- und Vormundschaftsgerechtsbarkeit zu ändern? Recht der Jugend 18:245-250 (1970)

East Germany

861 SCHMIDT, H.T. Entwicklung und Gestaltung des Jugendstrafsrechts in der DDR. Zeitschrift für die Gesamte Strafrechtswissenschaft 84:353-379 (1972)

862 SCHOENFELD, EUGENE, and HOWARD TETEN. Class and delinquency: an action approach. Georgia Journal of Corrections 1:44-53 (1972)

The findings of a questionnaire administered to a random sample of high school seniors from a mid-South city are discussed.

863 SCHORNHORST, F. THOMAS. The waiver of juvenile court jurisdiction: Kent revisited. Indiana Law Journal 43:583-613 (1968)

The message of Kent and Gault, with respect to waiver, is that no longer is the presumed "expertise" of the juvenile judge to be relied upon without proof of the proper employment of that knowledge. (167 refs.)

864 SCHOTTLAND, CHARLES I. Social work and the law - some curriculum approaches. Buffalo Law Review 17:719-731 (1968)

The current interest in co-operation between social workers and the legal profession is a constructive one. However, there are psychological attitudes that must be overcome if social workers are going to develop the right point of view. There are many ways in which a course on law and social work can be taught, but there are several points that social workers, at the conclusion of the course, should know, e.g. that the social policy of the law and the basic social work principles may be in conflict. (43 refs.)

865 SCHULTZ, J. LAWRENCE. The cycle of juvenile court history. Crime and Delinquency 19:457-476 (1973)

The author points out that understanding the significance of the basic elements and intellectual tendencies of the juvenile courts can help put present controversies about juvenile court reform in perspective. (68 refs.)

866 SCHULTZ, LEROY G. The adversary process, the juvenile court and the social worker. UMKC Law Review 36:288-302 (1968)

Because of the Kent and Gault decisions the role of the social worker in the adversary process has changed. Given the right to counsel and cross-examination, amongst other rights, the juvenile defendant has the opportunity to present a report by a social worker in his behalf. This report may challenge that of the court social worker, but the confrontation will produce a more objective view of the situation for the judge and the jury. (61 refs.)

867 SCHULTZ, LEROY G. The pre-sentence investigation and victimology. UMKC Law Review 35:247-260 (1967)

A study of the degree and type of participation of the victim in the generation of an offense, and an evaluation of what should be a just part of every pre-sentence investigation. (58 refs.)

868 SCHUM, RANDY. Juvenile law - an important step towards recognition of the constitutional right to treatment. St. Louis University Law Journal 16:340-354 (1971)

An examination of cases involved in the development of the right to treatment. The author believes that the eighth amendment has the greatest potential for establishing a new constitutional right. (100 refs.)

869 SCHWARZENBERGER, SUSAN. Juvenile probation: restrictions, rights and rehabilitation. St. Louis University Law Journal 16:276-293 (1971)

The concept of probation as an act of grace has now largely given way to the new concept that probationary conditions are subject to certain limitations. It has been well documented that juvenile probation workers and child welfare workers are lacking in professional training. There is every reason to require close scrutiny of conditions placed on the probationer, and these should be clearly spelled out. (89 refs.)

Germany

870 SCHWERDTNER, E. Kindeswohl oder Elternrecht? Archiv für die Civilistische Praxis 173:227-249 (1973)

Washington

871 SCHWERIN, LAWRENCE R. The juvenile court revolution in Washington. Washington Law Review 44:421-447 (1969)

This Comment analyzes Kent and Gault and explores some of the ramifications of the "revolution" for Washington law. (173 refs.)

872 SCOTT, JOSEPH W., and JERRY B. HISSONG. Changing the delinquent subculture: a sociological approach. Crime and Delinquency 15:499-509 (1969)

The authors demonstrate that the very nature of institutional living produces a delinquent subculture which militates against traditional treatment and, in effect, becomes the antithesis of treatment. They advocate guided group interaction which dissolves the subculture and develops a milieu in which the treatment objectives of the children are aligned with those of the administration and staff. (12 refs.)

Kansas

873 SEATON, RICHARD H. Amending the Kansas juvenile code. University of Kansas Law Review 16:277-284 (1968)

The author suggests adjustments in the Kansas juvenile code to meet the requirements of Gault. (42 refs.)

Israel

874 SEBBA, L. Youth bill, 1969. Mishpatim 2:388 (1970)

875 SEIDELSON, DAVID E. The right to counsel: from passive to active voice. The George Washington Law Review 38:849-872 (1970)

(88 refs.)

Japan

876 SEKI, T. Present efficiency of the probation and parole supervision office, and the unexpected revision of the juvenile law. Katei Saiban Geppo 19:61-70 (1967)

877 Selected bibliography of the juvenile court. Hastings Law Journal 19:263-265 (1968)
Articles on the following are included in this bibliography: the present juvenile court system; criticism of the juvenile court system; practice in the juvenile court; problems the juvenile court faces.

Yugoslavia

878 SELIH, A. Participation of social welfare authorities in the pre-dispositional procedure in connection with juveniles. Revija za Kriminal istiko in Kriminologijo 20: 150-158 (1969)

Canada

879 SESSAR, K. Beispiel einer totalstrategie in der Behandlung jugendlicher Straftäter: die Anstalt Boscoville in Quebec Kanada. Zeitschrift für die gesamte Strafrechtswissenschaft 84:353-379 (1972)

880 SEWINSKY, HENRY E., Jr. Infants - state must prove defendant to be a delinquent beyond a reasonable doubt - proof by preponderance of evidence insufficient. Dickinson Law Review 72:547-552 (1968)
Since the consequences of a finding of delinquency are essentially no different than a finding of guilty in an adult criminal case, the reasonable doubt test is the better standard. (37 refs.)

881 SEYMOUR, J.A. Youth services bureaus. Law and Society Review 7:247-272 (1972)
This paper examines the Crime Commission's proposals for the establishment of youth service bureaus. (13 refs.)

882 SHAFFER, THOMAS L. Abortion, the law and human life. Valparaiso University Law Review 2:94-106 (1967)
The issue in abortion "reform" is whether existing criminal sanctions against doctors and pregnant women should be abolished or liberalized. The author of this article believes that the proponents of reform fail to make a case. (77 refs.)

Great Britain

883 SHARP, W.T. The juvenile court and civil rights. Criminologist 7:37-50 (1972)
A history of the juvenile court in Great Britain and the United States. The effect of special treatment of juvenile cases in the following areas is described: cautioning and statements; notification of proceedings, etc., to parents; aid to the defendant to present his case; jury trial. (51 refs.)

Louisiana

884 SHAVER, EILEEN G. Louisiana constitutional reforms: a new juvenile court article. Loyola Law Review 19:273-294 (1972-1973)
The author of this Comment compares the content of the Louisiana constitution with similar provisions in other state constitutions. A new section on the juvenile court is suggested. (29 refs.)

885 SHAW, W. IRVING. The attorney-parent relationship in the juvenile court. St. Louis University Law Journal 12:603-630 (1968)

The attorney who is accustomed to the normal adversary situation will undoubtedly be confused by the tripartite situation in which he is involved. The author discusses: the parent's interests; the child's interests; and the state's interests. (77 refs.)

886 SHEAHAN, ROBERT M. Constitutional law - due process - juvenile court hearings. Case Western Reserve Law Review 19:394-402 (1968)

(49 refs.)

887 SHEEHAN, JOHN T., Jr. Custody awards of minors. New England Law Review 6: 201-211 (1971)

A discussion of the need for the adoption, by all states, of the Uniform Child Custody Jurisdiction Act. (44 refs.)

888 SHERMAN, PETER R. "...Nor cruel and unusual punishments inflicted" - the eighth amendment and the juvenile court. Crime and Delinquency 14:73-84 (1968)

This author endeavors to understand and assess the last clause of the eighth amendment to the constitution of the United States. A review and an analysis of the major case development, and some of the major problem areas are included. (76 refs.)

889 SHERIDAN, WILLIAM H. The Gault decision and the probation services. Indiana Law Journal 43:655-660 (1968)

This article discusses Gault with reference to its impact upon probation services. The primary and appropriate functions of probation officers at various stages of juvenile court proceedings are set forth: intake; pre-dispositional study; court appearance; rehabilitation. The six basic issues of Gault are presented. (19 refs.)

890 SHERIDAN, WILLIAM H. Juveniles who commit noncriminal acts: why treat them in a correctional system? Federal Probation 31(1):26-30 (1967)

(17 refs.)

891 SHERIDAN, WILLIAM H. New directions for the juvenile court. Federal Probation 31(2):15-20 (1967)

(31 refs.)

892 SHERIDAN, WILLIAM H. Structuring services for delinquent children and youth. Federal Probation 31(3):51-56 (1967)

(16 refs.)

893 SHERMAN, EDNA S. The role of a juvenile court citizens' advisory committee. Crime and Delinquency 14:151-154 (1968)

The author discusses the importance of a citizen's advisory committee in providing support to the juvenile court judge in selling the court and its program to the public.

Pennsylvania

894 SHIBLA, R. STEPHEN. Education: the right of retarded children to receive an education suited to their needs. Dickinson Law Review 77:577-584 (1973) (70 refs.)

Ohio

895 SHIERING, G. DAVID. A proposal for the more effective treatment of the "unruly" child in Ohio: the youth services bureau. University of Cincinnati Law Review 39: 275-290 (1970)

This Note demonstrates the applicability of the Youth Services Bureau concept to Ohio, together with the practical need for such a service. (102 refs.)

California

896 SHOBEN, ELAINE W. The interrogated juvenile: caveat confessor? Hastings Law Journal 24:413-430 (1973)

The author submits that the right of the juvenile suspect in California to receive Miranda warnings, and the accompanying right of refusing to waive these constitutional rights, are not effective as safeguards against coercion, since a juvenile may be less sophisticated than an adult in an expression of his desire to assert his fifth amendment right against self-incrimination. (81 refs.)

897 SHOCKLEY, WILLIAM I. Wyman v. James, 400 U.S. 309, 91 S.Ct. 381, 27 L. Ed.2d 408 (1971). Connecticut Law Review 4:154-179 (1971)

A discussion of the above case. (84 refs.)

Israel

898 SHOHAM, S., et al. Immigration, ethnicity, and ecology as related to juvenile delinquency in Israel. In Tel Aviv University Institute of Criminology and Criminal Law. Israel studies in criminology. Vol. 1, 1970. pp. 77-96

Japan

899 SHOJI, K. Juvenile law and the idea of parens patriae. Keiho Zasshi 18(3/4):37-49 (1972)

900 SHONG, ELLENMARIE. The legal responsibility of parents for their children's delinquency. Family Law Quarterly 6:145-178 (1972)

An examination of the legal implications of the parent-child relationship. Included in the discussion are: psycho-sociological theories; the role of the parent during the arrest, the adjudication and dispositional phases of the judicial proceeding; family treatment; and an examination of how parents may be legally affected by their child's delinquencies and subsequent punishment. (57 refs.)

Massachusetts

901 SIDMAN, LAWRENCE R. Massachusetts stuborn child law: law and order in the home. Family Law Quarterly 6:33-58 (1972)

The question raised is whether the juvenile court is a fitting forum for entertaining parent-child disputes. The time has come for new and widely differing structures which offer a range of distinctive treatments. Court clinics and community treatment facilities represent the first tentative steps in that direction - possibly as adjuncts to new child-care units instead of to courts. Lawyers, physicians, social workers, psychologists, educators and recreation specialists might be brought together to serve as a clearing house for juvenile/family problems. The courts should be the last rather than the first resort. (124 refs.)

New York

902 SILVER, MARTIN T. The New York family court: a law guardian's overview. Crime and Delinquency 18:93-98 (1972)

The author contends that law guardians are incorrect in their wholesale adoption of criminal defense tactics in juvenile matters.

903 SIMMS, LARRY L. Courts, the constitution and juvenile institutional reform. Boston University Law Review 52:33-63 (1972)

This Note demonstrates that the identification and application of constitutional and other rights to the detention and incarceration stages of the juvenile process will serve to stimulate and force reform. (228 refs.)

Germany

904 SIMONSOHN, B. Der Beitrag der Psychoanalyze zum Problem der Jugendkriminalität und des Jugendstrafrechts. Zentralblatt für Jugendrecht und Jugendwohlfahrt 60:65-72 (1973)

Georgia

905 SIPPLE, DAVID F. Juvenile courts - Georgia code section 24A-2304 - a return to the "woodshed" theory. Mercer Law Review 23:393-398 (1972)

Children subject to juvenile court jurisdiction in Georgia are classified by the new code of 1971 in three core categories: delinquent juveniles, unruly juveniles, deprived juveniles. This section forms the subject matter of this article. (30 refs.)

Great Britain

906 SKEGG, P.D.G. Consent to medical procedures on minors. Modern Law Review 36:370-381 (1973)

This paper examines the capacity of minors to consent to the performance of medical procedures on themselves, and the capacity of parents and others to consent to the performance of medical procedures on minors. (69 refs.)

907 SKOLER, DANIEL J. Counsel in juvenile court proceedings - a total criminal justice perspective. Journal of Family Law 8:243-277 (1968)

Mr. Skoler, using the Gault decision as his base point, has attempted to determine the future role of counsel in juvenile court proceedings. (114 refs.)

908 SKOLER, DAVID L. The right to counsel and the role of counsel in juvenile court. Indiana Law Journal 43:558-582 (1968)

The purpose of this article is to assess the impact of the Gault decision on the right to counsel and the role of counsel in the American juvenile court. (105 refs.)

Netherlands

909 SLAGTER, S. Op zoek naar andere structuren voor kinderbescherming. Nederlands Juristenblad (32):989-997 (1973)

910 SLOANE, HOMER W. Relationship of law and social work. Social Work 12:86-93 (1967)

The author discusses the results of a study drawn from twenty-two interviews, of the attitudes of lawyers and social workers toward each other. An unmistakable and severe mutual antagonism is uncovered. This hostility compels attention since law and social work have already been drafted as partners in basic socio-legal institutions such as juvenile and family courts. The adversary system of the law etches the mutual misunderstanding in high relief. Social workers fear confrontation and cross-examination, whereas lawyers prize the right to confront as essential to the concepts of due process and a free society. Recommended remedial measures center mainly on revised educational approaches in law schools and schools of social work. (12 refs.)

911 SMALL, JAMES M. Criminal procedure - due process in juvenile delinquency proceedings. Louisiana Law Review 28:492-498 (1968)

Gault's importance lies in the court's recognition that due process requires more safeguards in juvenile courts than have previously been provided. (29 refs.)

912 SMITH, A.D. The social worker in the legal aid setting: a study of interprofessional relationships. Social Service Review 44:155-168 (1970)

In this study the professional relationships between lawyers and social workers employed by a legal service agency were explored. The results show that while social workers often seemed to forget, or were frustrated by, the fact that the organization was primarily providing legal services, many lawyers failed to recognize the secondary service. Suggestions are made for incorporating and maximizing the value of social service within a legal setting. (5 refs.)

913 SMITH, CHESTERFIELD. The challenge of law in a changing society. Juvenile Justice 23(2):12-16 (1972)

A discussion of what a National Institute of Justice would be designed to do, and what it would not do.

Kentucky

914 SMITH, JAMES H. Juvenile right to bail. Journal of Family Law 11:81-105 (1971)

In-depth analysis by leading scholars indicate that areas of juvenile law with which Gault did not deal, are far more numerous than those with which it did deal and often equally important. (118 refs.)

California

915 SMITH, SHERMAN W. The juvenile court in transition. Los Angeles Bar Bulletin 43:319-323 (1968)
(15 refs.)

916 SNAVELY, JOHN T. In Re Gault - Supreme Court formalizes juvenile court procedures. Tulsa Law Journal 5:43-61 (1968)
Discussed are: notice of charges; right to counsel; appellate review and transcript of proceedings. Particular emphasis is given to the question as to whether a child must have an attorney in juvenile proceedings. (77 refs.)

917 SNYDER, ELOISE C. Impact of the juvenile court hearing on the child. Crime and Delinquency 17:180-190 (1971)
This study shows that the juvenile court hearing has a significant impact on the child involved rendering at least some children, more capable of change during this phase in the delinquency pattern than during any later phase. This change capability seems to decrease markedly with the passage of time. (8 refs.)

918 SOMERVILLE, JAMES G. A study of the preventive aspect of police work with juveniles. Criminal Law Review 407-414, 472-484 (1969)
This survey explores the variations in police cautioning, and considers the factors and attitudes which influence the decision whether to prosecute. (24 refs.)

China

919 SOONG, I.-k. A comparative study of juvenile delinquency. Chengchi Law Review 4:13-48 (1971)

South Africa

920 SORNARAJAH, M. Parental custody: the recent trends. South African Law Journal 90:131-149 (1973)

921 SPECA, JOHN M., and FLOYD A. WHITE, Jr. Variations and trends in proposed legislation on juvenile courts. University of Missouri at Kansas City Law Review 40:129-169 (1971-1972)
Proposed legislation is a manifestation of current thought on our juvenile courts. Three overriding trends in the proposals of various states are discernible, and are commented upon. (280 refs.)

Pennsylvania

922 SPECK, NANCY L. Parental responsibility laws reviewed. Juvenile Court Judges' Journal 19(3):90-97 (1968)
This article refers to the Pennsylvania statute imposing liability on parents for the willful, tortious acts of their children. Implications of such a statute are discussed. (26 refs.)

Pennsylvania

923 SPECK, NANCY L. The Pennsylvania parental liability statute. University of Pittsburgh Law Review 29:578-597 (1968)

The purpose of this Note is to consider the constitutionality and wisdom of the above enactment, particularly as it affects the operation of juvenile courts in Pennsylvania. (73 refs.)

South Africa

924 SPIRO, E. The age of majority act 1972. South African Law Journal 90:48-56 (1973)

California

925 SPRAGG, DONNA. Admission and use of evidence in the California juvenile courts. The Hastings Law Journal 18:668-677 (1967)

A discussion of the California juvenile court procedure, the protection of constitutional rights of juveniles, and the admission of evidence to court. (82 refs.)

Kentucky

926 STAMM, MORTIMER J. Child advocacy and legislative reform in Kentucky. Juvenile Justice 24(2):3-16 (1973)

A review of the progressive steps Kentucky has been taking towards reassuming its obligations under the mutual compact theory of juvenile justice which it seeks to honor. (10 refs.)

Texas

927 The standard of proof in juvenile trials in Texas in the absence of George Santana. Texas Southern University Law Review 3:58-67 (1973)

A discussion of State v. Santana, 444 S.W. 2d 614, Tex. Sup.Ct. 1969, reh. denied, 397 U.S. 596 1970, vacated and remanded, 457 S.W.2d 275, Tex. Sup.Ct. 1970.

928 STANSBY, JANET F. In Re Gault: children are people. California Law Review 55:1204-1218 (1967)

The problems in the juvenile court before Gault, and the specific rights claimed in the Gault case, are discussed. (86 refs.)

929 STANTON, NILE. McKeiver v. Pennsylvania: juries and juveniles - parens patriae revived. Indiana Legal Forum 5:197-207 (1971)

In McKeiver the U.S. Supreme Court ruled that trial by jury is not constitutionally required in state juvenile delinquency proceedings, and thus halted, at least temporarily, the liberal trend established in Kent and Gault. Thus, the scope of due process guarantees for juveniles was delimited and new force was given to the rubric of parens patriae. An analysis of the nature of the proceedings is presented, and alternatives are discussed. (69 refs.)

930 STAPLETON, VAUGHN. A social scientist's view of Gault and a plea for the experimenting society. Yale Review of Law and Social Action 1:72-81 (1970) (33 refs.)

931 STARRS, JAMES E. A sense of irony in southern juvenile courts. Portia Law Journal 1:107-130 (1966) (82 refs.)

932 STARRS, JAMES E. Southern juvenile courts - a study of irony, civil rights, and judicial practice. Crime and Delinquency 13:289-306 (1967)

Discussed in this article are: detention, bail, release procedures, jurisdiction, hearings, and appeal. (82 refs.)

Oregon

933 State of Oregon v. Dwain Lee Little: disposition from the juvenile court. Willamette Law Journal 5:157-170 (1968)

This Note considers the effect of statutes which vest juvenile court jurisdiction by the age of the individual at the time of the offense; those which vest jurisdiction by the age at the time of the proceedings; and those which allow the juvenile court to waive its jurisdiction by remanding the individual to adult court. Abuses inherent in these statutes may lead to disposition of juveniles as adults, or allow criminal prosecution of adults for wrongful juvenile acts. (71 refs.)

934 STATSKY, WILLIAM P. The training of community judges: rehabilitative adjudication. Columbia Human Rights Law Review 4:401-416 (1972)

This article examines the genesis and execution of a training curriculum for "community judges". (20 refs.)

Connecticut

935 Statutory vagueness in juvenile law: the Supreme Court and Mattiello v. Connecticut. University of Pennsylvania Law Review 118:143-153 (1969)

Vague delinquency provisions based on subjective determinations of "immorality" and unsupported predictions of future criminal conduct have not legal or practical justification. (60 refs.)

Ohio

936 STEINER, RUSSEL A. The viable infant - the "but for" person. Capital University Law Review 1:216-231 (1972)

A discussion of State v. Dickenson, 28 Ohio St.2d 65, 275 N.E.2d 599 (1971). (116 refs.)

Texas

937 STEINFELDT, RUTH, et al. The impact of the Gault decision in Texas. Juvenile Court Judges' Journal 20(4):154-158 (1969)

The results of a survey in Texas.

938 STEKETEE, JOHN P. Aftermath of apprehension: juvenile court judge's response. Prospectus a Journal of Law Reform 3:25-30 (1969)

This article is concerned with the question of how the findings of a study of juvenile apprehension relate to the juvenile court. (3 refs.)

939 STERN, J.B. Medical treatment and the teenager: the need for parental consent. Clearinghouse Review 7:1-5 (1973)

American Samoa

940 STEWART, WILLIAM J. Treatment of delinquency in American Samoa. Juvenile Justice 23(2):23-26 (1972)

(19 refs.)

Germany

941 STRASBERG, W. Die Aufgaben der Gerichte zur Erhaltung und Festigung von Ehe und Familie. Neue Justiz 24:445-449 (1970)

942 STRAUSS, PETER L., et al. The relationship between promise and performance in state intervention in family life. Columbia Journal of Law and Social Problems 9:28-62 (1972)
(39 refs.)

943 STRIEKER, GARY G. Waiver of constitutional rights by minors: a question of law or fact? Hastings Law Journal 19:223-231 (1967)
This Note considers the competence of a child to waive his constitutional rights for the purposes of the juvenile court as well as for the criminal court proceedings. (63 refs.)

944 STUART, RICHARD B. Aftermath of apprehension: social scientist's response. Prospectus a Journal of Law Reform 3:13-23 (1969)
The intent of this article is to suggest avenues available for reforms in social institutions dealing with youth, and in the juvenile justice system. (33 refs.)

945 STUBBS, ROBERT S., II. The juvenile court act of 1968. Georgia State Bar Journal 5:219-228 (1968)
A discussion of the Juvenile Court Act of 1968, including disposition and pre-disposition procedure; court structure; probation; trial by jury. (78 refs.)

Canada

946 STUBBS, ROY S. The young offender. Manitoba Law Journal 5:19-39 (1972)
The author stresses the need for the public to know what the juvenile court is trying to achieve. (41 refs.)

Can./Gr.Br./US

947 SUDDICK, DAVID E. Runaways: a review of the literature. Justice 24(2):47-54 (1973)
A review of British, Canadian, and American literature on runaways. (71 refs.)

Arizona

948 SULLIVAN, DANIEL F. Juvenile law - standard of proof required for revocation of probation. Law and the Social Order 551-556 (1973)
A discussion of In Re Anonymous, 16 Ariz.App. 597, 494 P.2d 1342 (1972). (30 refs.)

949 SULLIVAN, MICHAEL F. Child neglect: the environmental aspects. Ohio State Law Journal 29:85-115 (1968)

The author criticizes the vague statutes governing child neglect trials, and the simultaneous delegation of power to the judiciary which allows the courts to impose their individual notions of child care and morality on parents. An alternative approach is suggested, which focuses on the causal relationship between parental behavior and harm to the child, and gives weight to the rights of parents. (91 refs.)

950 SULZER, E.S. Individual freedom, law and social welfare. Community Health Journal 3(1):49-52 (1967)

The author states that two simultaneous but divergent philosophies are operating within the social welfare movement: the principle of individual choice with the worker operating to "help" the client to fulfil his goal; and the assumption that the professional is endowed with superior wisdom that empowers him to dictate the modes and goals of living of those he presumably serves. A dramatic case history is cited to point up the injustice an individual can suffer under present legal and social welfare authority, making deprivation of freedom possible under the guise of welfare legislation. It is possible to become the victim of a system of mental illness and incompetence. Social welfare must choose a system that maximizes individual choice and provides for increased opportunity, not one that minimizes freedom by penalizing idiosyncratic behavior.

California

951 SUMNER, HELEN. Locking them up. Crime and Delinquency 17:168-179 (1971)

This article summarizes the findings of a study of juvenile detention practices in eleven California counties. Evidence is given of contradictory procedures, and of those of dubious legality. Recommendations are made. (7 refs.)

952 Supreme Court review (1971). The Journal of Criminal Law, Criminology and Police Science 62:463-530 (1971)

A review of important court decisions in the following areas: jury trial in juvenile court; involuntary confessions; confrontation; contempt; search and seizure; fifth amendment. (50 refs.)

District of Columbia

953 SUSMAN, JACKWELL. Juvenile justice: even-handed or many-handed? An empirical investigation of decision processes in disposition hearings. Crime and Delinquency 19:493-507 (1973)

The results of a study undertaken in the District of Columbia to assess the impact of court reorganization on juvenile justice. An effort was made to measure judicial attitudes and severity in sentencing. It was found that the experienced judges were in conflict with probation officers and defense attorneys; that probation officers were more successful in getting their recommendations accepted by judges; and that experienced judges sentenced juveniles more severely than the inexperienced judges did. (27 refs.)

New York

954 SUSSMAN, ALAN. The confidentiality of family court records. Social Service Review 45:455-81 (1971)

Ten recommendations are made for insuring the confidentiality of juvenile court records. (25 refs.)

Japan

955 SUZUKI, S. Due process in juvenile proceedings. Keiho Zasshi 18(3/4):30-36 (1972)

956 SWANSON, DALE T. Constitutional law - In Re Winship a new standard of proof for juveniles. New England Law Review 6:130-137 (1970) (37 refs.)

Florida

957 SYLVESTER, WALTER W. The bar's role in preventing juvenile delinquency. Florida Bar Journal 42:381-386 (1968)
The author feels that our court system should be concerned and working in concert with an approach which will educate our youth about what the laws of our society expect of him as a responsible citizen. Teenagers need to be given a clear understanding of what acts are illegal, and to be given a clear picture of the penalties awaiting when the law is broken. Mandatory courses in high school are recommended.

958 Symposium: juvenile delinquency. Criminal Law Bulletin 7:489-572 (1971)
This issue explores the several dimensions of juvenile delinquency through the varied perspectives of law, sociology and psychology.

959 Symposium on child abuse. Pediatrics 51 Suppl.4. (1973)

960 SZASZ, THOMAS S. The right to health. The Georgetown Law Journal 57:734-751 (1969)
The author disagrees with the premise that a legal right to treatment is an effective way to determine those governmental policies best suited to securing good medical care for the maximum number of people. (31 refs.)

Poland

961 SZPUNAR, A. For der Geburt des Kindes verursachter Schaden. Studia Cywilistyczne 13-14:369-383 (1969)

Canada

962 TADMAN, MARTIN. Critical analysis of bill C-192: the young offenders act. Manitoba Law Journal 4:371-380 (1971)
An analysis of the Canadian Young Offenders Act. (32 refs.)

963 TAIT, C. DOWNING, Jr., and EMORY F. HODGES, Jr. Follow-up study of predicted delinquents. Crime and Delinquency 17:202-212 (1971)
The authors of the study come to the conclusion that the basic issue is an absence of a satisfying and useful place in the school society for the child. Measures to promote child development should be instituted. (18 refs.)

964 TAKSIN, AARON. Torts - guest statute - the "minors of tender years" exception now court-made law in Illinois. DePaul Law Review 20:559-573 (1971)
This Note traces the origin, construction, application, and interpretation of guest statutes, as well as the court-formulated exceptions which have resulted in the preferred status of certain classes. (98 refs.)

965 TAMILIA, PATRICK R. Neglect proceedings and the conflict between law and social work. Duquesne Law Review 9:579-589 (1971)
The author states that although the conflict of lawyers and social workers in the arena of social welfare may be an irritant to all who must function therein, it will eventually mean a better deal for the many unfortunate people who must look to these services. (24 refs.)

Japan

966 TANAKA, M. The traffic ticket system and its application to juvenile cases. Horitsu jīho 43(8):110 (1971)

967 TAYLOR, RICHARD. Law and morality. New York University Law Review 43: 611-647 (1968)
(41 refs.)

968 TEDESCHI, G. Tort liability for "wrongful life." Journal of Family Law 7:465-495 (1967)
The author suggests that children have a right to recover damages from their parents for physical and social hardships caused by the parents before the birth of the children, and that this right has been neglected. (60 refs.)

969 TEITELBAUM, LEE. The use of social reports in juvenile court adjudications. Journal of Family Law 7:425-441 (1967)
The pros and cons of social reports prepared for use by the court in adjudication of juveniles are discussed in relation to the recent Gault decision and its emphasis on the constitutional safeguards of juveniles: inherent weaknesses of social reports; hearsay evidence; possibility of constitutional barring of social reports. (65 refs.)

970 TEITELBAUM, LEE F. Gault and the "experimenting society": a response to Mr. Stapleton. Yale Review of Law and Social Action 1:86-92 (1970)
(30 refs.)

971 TENNEY, CHARLES W., Jr. The new dilemma in the juvenile court. Nebraska Law Review 47:67-81 (1968)
A discussion of different points of view regarding the administration of juvenile courts, and juvenile court hearings. (38 refs.)

972 TENNEY, CHARLES W. The utopian world of the juvenile courts. Annals of the American Academy of Political and Social Science 383:101-118 (1969)
The author gives a history of the juvenile court, and states that examinations

of the actual nature of the court and its procedures have revealed that as a "social agency" the court and its procedures remain largely an idea and an ideal. The court's traditionally informal procedures, designed to reflect its non-criminal nature, have been criticized in recent Supreme Court cases. The resulting return to a more legalized approach may signal, therefore, a retrenchment or reassessment in the work of the juvenile courts. (51 refs.)

973 TERRY, R.M. Discrimination in the handling of juvenile offenders by social-control agencies. Journal of Research in Crime and Delinquency 4:218-230 (1967)
This study examines the question of whether social-control agencies base decisions concerning the handling of offenders upon sex, ethnic background, and socio-economic status. (21 refs.)

974 TERRY, ROBERT M. The screening of juvenile offenders. Journal of Criminal Law, Criminology and Police Science 58:173-181 (1967)
This study is an attempt to specify the criteria utilized by control agencies, i.e. by the police, the probation departments, and the juvenile court, in the sanctioning of juvenile offenders. The author states that his findings have relevance for assessing the functioning of control agencies. (33 refs.)

Germany

975 THIESMEYER, H. Jugendgerichtsgesetz und Strafrechtsreform. Recht der Jugend 18:33-40 (1970)

Germany

976 THIESMEYER, H. Die voraussichtliche Weiterentwicklung des Jugendstrafsrechts. Recht der Jugend 20:339-343 (1972)

977 THOMAS, EUGENE S., and CHRISTINE SORENSON. Youth's recipe for success with youth. Federal Probation 32(4):26-31 (1968)
Guidelines for juvenile court workers are offered.

Colorado

978 THOMAS, LESTER G. The Denver glue sniffing project. Juvenile Court Judges' Journal 18(2):46-49 (1967)

979 THOMAS, MASON P., Jr. Child abuse and neglect: historial overview, legal matrix, and social perspectives. North Carolina Law Review 50:293-349 (1972)
This article is the first part of a two-part treatment on child abuse and neglect. The quick responses of state legislatures in enacting child-abuse reporting laws reflect important legislative policy change in the legal framework for child protection. These laws may identify children who need protection, but do not provide a solution to the complex legal and social issues involved in child protection. (192 refs.)

980 THORNBERRY, TERENCE P. Race, socio-economic status and sentencing in the juvenile justice system. The Journal of Criminal Law and Criminology 64(1):90-98 (1973)

The purpose of this study is to examine empirically the validity of the assumption that members of minority groups, migrants, and persons with limited economic means are often the scapegoats of the frustrated police in local communities. (16 refs.)

California

981 THORNHILL, WILLIAM T. Inadequacies of the juvenile sealing procedure in California. California Western Law Review 7:421-437 (1971)

The inherent weaknesses within the California Welfare and Institutions Code Section 781, and the inadequacies in its application are illustrated in conjunction with their possible solutions. The importance of the need for the destruction of juvenile court records is stressed. (99 refs.)

Wisconsin

982 TILTON, DENNIS S. Law in the classroom. Juvenile Justice 23(3):37-41 (1972)

A discussion of the "Education in Law" course at the Urban Day School in Milwaukee, Wisconsin.

China(Rep.)

983 TING, T.Y. Causes of, and preventive measures for juvenile delinquency. Fa lü p'ing lun 36(8):16 (1970)

Japan

984 TING, T.Y. Japan's present measures for preventing and controlling juvenile delinquency. Fa lü p'ing lun 36(9):6 (1970)

China(Rep.)

985 TING, T.Y. Theory and practice of the system of reforming juveniles. Part I. Fa lü p'ing lun 37(1):16 (1971)

China(Rep.)

986 TING, T.Y. Theory and practice of the system of reforming juveniles. Part II. Fa lü p'ing lun 37(2):15 (1971)

987 TOBIAS, JERRY J., and PHILIP DENOMME. The affluent suburban delinquent. The Criminologist 8:22-30 (1973)

988 Torts - contribution and parental immunity - contribution action against parent joint tortfeasor allowed despite existence of parental immunity. The Georgetown Law Journal 60:1612-1618 (1972)

An analysis of two possible methods of attack where a party seeks contribution against a joint tortfeasor protected from the plaintiff by a parental immunity. (31 refs.)

New Hampshire

989 Torts - infants - suits between parent and child. New York Law Forum 13:182-188 (1967)

A discussion of the immunity between parent and child. (32 refs.)

Tennessee

990 Torts - minors - contributory or comparative negligence. Tennessee Law Review 39:747-755 (1972)

The utilization of comparative negligence principles in accidents which involve minors is discussed. (57 refs.)

991 Torts - parental immunity - unemancipated minor allowed to maintain negligence action against the parent. University of Kansas Law Review 16:562-566 (1968)

A discussion of Hebel v. Hebel, 435 P.2d 8 (Alaska 1967), and the doctrine of parental immunity. (38 refs.)

Virginia

992 Torts - parent-child immunity - reluctance to further abrogate the immunity rule. University of Richmond Law Review 7:571-579 (1973)

A discussion of Wright v. Wright, 213 Va. 177, 191 S.E.2d 223 (1972), and the doctrine of parental immunity. (52 refs.)

993 TROJANOWICZ, ROBERT C. The contrasting behavior styles of policemen and social workers. Public Personnel Review 32:246-251 (1971)

The author reports on the results of an exploratory study of the measured behavioral styles of persons in the police and social work professions.

994 TROJANOWICZ, ROBERT C. Juvenile delinquency and the middle-class parent. Police 15:29-32 (1971)

995 TURTON, JAMES R. Unequal protection of the illegitimate child. South Texas Law Journal 13:126-142 (1971)

The author shows that the statute has no effect in promoting the purpose of the statute (i.e. to promote family life), and that other less onerous and more effective alternatives to the statute are available to achieve the legislative purpose. (73 refs.)

Germany

996 ULRICH, H. Ein denkbar schlechter Leumund. Zentralblatt für Jugendwohlfahrt 57:121-128 (1970)

Oregon

997 Unfit parents - ORS 419.523 (2) (a). Willamette Law Journal 5:177-181 (1968)

Because a word such as "unfit" is difficult to define in strict and concise terms, a court is given great freedom to treat each case as its sentiment dictates. (24 refs.)

998 VALENTE, WILLIAM D. Student discipline in public schools under the constitution. Villanova Law Review 17:1028-1051 (1972)

This article considers the nature of the roles and tasks that school authorities and their counsel encounter by reason of recent landmark decisions. (123 refs.)

Czěchoslovakia

999 VALENTORIČ, Z. Some questions concerning the jurisdiction of Czechoslovak Courts in matters of education and maintenance of infants according to the law. No. 97/1963 Coll. Právny Obzor 55:401-416 (1972)

Illinois

1000 VALUKAS, ANTON R. The juvenile court in operation - substantial improvements needed. Chicago Bar Record 50:352-365 (1969)
The author discusses juvenile court due process, station house adjustments, intake, the need for legal counsel, sentencing procedure, supervision cases, and he makes recommendations to substantially improve the present system of justice for the juvenile. (61 refs.)

1001 VAN BROEKHOVEN, ROLLIN A. Intrafamily immunity and its present status. Baylor Law Review 20:27-70 (1967)
The author deals with the present status and trends of the law relating to: immunity or liability in suits by one spouse against the other spouse for tortious conduct; immunity or liability in suits by child against parent; and liability in suits as between siblings for tortious conduct. (150 refs.)

U.S.S.R.

1002 VAN DEN HEUVEL, MP. Praktische jeugd: de jonge generatie in de Sowjet-Unie. International Spectator 22:129-141 (1968)

Belgium

1003 VAN HEULE, H.F. Die nieuwe wet op de Jeugdbescherming. Rechtskundig Weekblad 31:1635-1666 (1968)

1004 VANDIVER, JAMES V. Juvenile records are justifiable. Police 15:41-42 (1970)
The author gives reasons in defense of the need for police juvenile record maintenance.

Virgin Islands

1005 VASALY, CHARLES E.K. Volunteers in court: observations on a new approach to juvenile delinquency and remarks on implementation in St. Croix. Virgin Islands Bar Journal 4:47-61 (1973)
A discussion of the Voluntary Service Program, one of the proposals recommended in the "New Criminal Justice System - Juvenile Study" report issued by the Virgin Islands Government in January, 1972. (11 refs.)

Canada

1006 VAZ, EDMUND W. Explorations in the institutionalization of juvenile delinquency. Journal of Criminal Law, Criminology and Police Science 62:396-406 (1971)
This paper explores the problem of the institutionalization of middle-class boys having committed selected delinquent acts. (13 refs.)

1007 Venue in juvenile courts. Washington University Law Quarterly 407-426 (1973)
This Note examines venue in the juvenile justice system, analyzes the relevant state statutes and case law, and reports on the findings of a nation-wide study. Possible bases for venue as a constitutional right are also discussed. (93 refs.)

Poland

1008 VLASOV, I.S. The legislative measures to suppress crimes as among minors in the Polish People's Republic. Ucheuye Zapiski 16:152-167 (1969)

1009 WADLINGTON, W. Minors and health care: the age of consent. Osgoode Hall Law Journal 11:115-125 (1973)
This Comment seeks to provide a comparison of court and legislative response to problems created by the parental consent requirement. (51 refs.)

1010 Waiver in the juvenile court. Columbia Law Review 68:1149-1167 (1968)
This Note considers the role which must be played by the juvenile, the parent and the court, if the child's rights are to be adequately protected. (121 refs.)

1011 WALD, PATRICIA M. The changing world of juvenile law - new vistas for the non-delinquent child - alternatives to formal juvenile court adjudication. Pennsylvania Bar Associaton Quarterly 40:37-46 (1968)
A discussion of supplementary community programs needed since juvenile courts, after Gault, are being urged to return to parents, schools and communities the responsibilities they have been delegating to the judicial system. (20 refs.)

Canada

1012 WALKER, PAMELA. The law and the young: some necessary extra-legal considerations. University of Toronto Faculty of Law Review 29:54-72 (1971)
A discussion of legal and extra-legal considerations which should be taken into account when dealing with legislation for young people. (84 refs.)

1013 WALKER, STEPHEN G. The lawyer-child relationship: a statistical analysis. Duquesne Law Review 9:627-650 (1971)
This article discusses the legal and social responsibilities of the lawyer who deals with delinquent, neglected and dependent children, and the many ramifications inherent in representing a child. The results of a questionnaire are given. (46 refs.)

1014 WALLACE, PHYLLIS. A perspective. Delinquency study project. Juvenile Court Judges' Journal 18(2):44-45 (1967)

Missouri

1015 WALSH, JAMES F. An urban riot - a juvenile court meets the challenge. Crime and Delinquency 14:306-314 (1968)
What is a juvenile court staff's role during a riot? A seven-step intake procedure is described.

1016 WALSH, JOSEPH T. The attorney and the dispositional process - attorney's role in formal disposition. St. Louis University Law Journal 12:644-658 (1968)
Should the attorney in the juvenile court use strong adversary tactics in an effort to obtain a complete release for his juvenile client, or should he act for the 'best interests' of the child? (76 refs.)

1017 WALSCH, KENNETH P. Parent-child – the right of the state to order surgery on a minor in a nonterminal situation despite the religious objections of the parent. Dickinson Law Review 77:693–698 (1973)

A discussion of the Green Appeal, 448 Pa. 338, 292 A.2d 387 (1972). (38 refs.)

1018 WANG, KECHIN. The continuing turbulence surrounding the parens patriae concept in American juvenile courts. Part I. McGill Law Journal 18:219–245 (1972)

The history of parens patriae and the development of the parens patriae concept in the United States. A discussion of intake, adjudication and disposition. (83 refs.)

1019 WANG, KECHIN. The continuing turbulence surrounding the parens patriae concept in American juvenile courts. Part II. McGill Law Journal 18:418–460 (1972)

A continuation of the discussion of trends in the juvenile court: right to counsel and waiver of counsel; trial by jury; right to treatment; right to bail; hearsay evidence; bifurcated hearings; different kinds of juvenile courts; untrained and understaffed personnel; due process procedures; constitutional safeguards; rehabilitation. (240 refs.)

1020 WANNER, DAVID L. The uniform juvenile court act. North Dakota Law Review 48:93–108 (1971)

Numerous questions arise concerning the stated purpose of the Uniform Juvenile Court Act. However, five issues appear to dominate in the area of constitutional safeguards for juveniles. This analysis examines the Act in relation to these five areas. (118 refs.)

Great Britain/Wales

1021 WARBURTON, B. The juvenile courts in England and Wales. International Journal of Offender Therapy and Comparative Criminology 16:187–193 (1972)

A brief description of the composition of the juvenile courts and how they function. Some typical cases are discussed.

1022 WARD, RICHARD H. The labeling theory: a critical analysis. Criminology 9: 269–290 (1971)

(25 refs.)

1023 WASSERMANN, SIDNEY. The abused parent of the abused child – understanding comes first in helping. Children 14(5):175–179 (1967)

The dangers of labeling persons as "battering parents" is discussed. The author states reasons why prosecuting the battering parent does not solve the problems of either the parent or the child. (6 refs.)

1024 WATERMAN, NAIRN. Disclosure of social and psychological reports at disposition. Osgoode Hall Law Journal 7:213–233 (1970)

The following questions are discussed: ought the social scientist to be able to present to the judge his professional assessment without reserve, or must he be equivocal because the subject of that evaluation will see the report and may take offense? On the other hand, ought the subject to be a helpless bystander while his character is being discussed by someone who has possibly known him for an hour or so? (57 refs.)

Great Britain

1025 WATSON, JOHN. The children and young person's act 1969. The Solicitor's Journal 114:159-160 (1970)
A discussion of the children and young person's act 1969 in Great Britain.

Hawaii

1026 WATTS, THOMAS T. Limits of family court jurisdiction under section 571-11(2) of the Hawaii revised statutes. Hawaii Bar Journal 10:41-50 (1973)
The author discusses three cases of neglect which, he feels, did not warrant state intervention. He suggests that courts should articulate some threshold level of home deficiency justifying judicial and social welfare intervention. (51 refs.)

Great Britain/Wales

1027 WEBB, A.M.F. The training of justices of peace in England and Wales. Canadian Journal of Corrections 9(2):105-114 (1967)
Only in the past 50 years has any consideration been given to training. Two syllabi were developed, one for newly appointed justices and the other for juvenile court justices, with an emphasis on the problems of punishment and treatment.

1028 WEBB, WILLIAM H., Jr. A probation officer speaks out: treatment referrals of delinquent children. Juvenile Court Judges' Journal 20(4):138-143 (1969) (2 refs.)

1029 WEBSTER, JAMES. Criminal law - juvenile courts - In Re Gault held to have retroactive effect so that juveniles convicted without representation by counsel are entitled to new trial. Notre Dame Lawyer 44:158-165 (1968)
In this Comment the author attempts to show why the Gault decision was incomplete. (52 refs.)

New York

1030 WEINER, NORMAN L., and CHARLES V. WILLIE. Decisions by juvenile officers. American Journal of Sociology 77:199-210 (1971)
This paper examines decision making by juvenile officers, and looks at the effect that race and the socio-economic status of the individual as well as the racial composition and socio-economic status of his neighborhood have on juvenile police disposition. (20 refs.)

California

1031 WEINKAUF, GEORGE A., Jr. The conflicts of parens patriae and constitutional concepts of juvenile justice. Lincoln Law Review 6:65-79 (1970)
This article uses California law, together with binding federal authority and illustrative examples from other jurisdictions as well as English common law to demonstrate the development of state and federal law in the juvenile field. (61 refs.)

1032 WEINSTEIN, NOAH, and CORINNE R. GOODMAN. The supreme court and the juvenile court. Crime and Delinquency 13:481-487 (1967)

The supreme court did not intend, in its opinion, to convert the juvenile court into a criminal court - at least not at this time. However, it is up to the community to provide the juvenile court with facilities and services which will enable it to function properly as a juvenile court rather than as a juvenile criminal court. (10 refs.)

1033 WEISS, JONATHAN. The poor kid. Duquesne Law Review 9:590-612 (1971)

The author traces the stages of the juvenile system as they impinge upon infants and the young as defined by the appropriate juvenile court statute. He analyzes what existing practices mean, and their effect. (104 refs.)

1034 WEISS, JONATHAN A. The emerging rights of minors. University of Toledo Law Review 4:25-42 (1972)

This article is primarily concerned with the rights of youths in the legal system, and the resulting effect upon society in general. The focus is to establish what traditional legal and social concepts combine to define how the state and adults treat the youth. The author examines how the interplay of concept, cliche, legal process, and reality define a world of privileges and dangers, potential protections and limited freedoms. There is a survey of rights achieved, and perhaps realizable, in this country. Attention is also given to parents who are deprived of their children. (70 refs.)

New York

1035 WEISS, JONATHAN, and OSCAR CHASE. The case for repeal of section 383 of the New York social services law. Columbia Human Rights Law Review 4:325-335

Parents who sign agreements surrendering custody of their children to state welfare agencies often sign these under duress and are unaware of the nature of document. In New York they may unknowingly relinquish their ability to unilaterally determine the child's future status. The author gives reasons why Section 383 of the New York Social Services Law should be repealed. (52 refs.)

1036 WEITZ, H. Summation in an infant trespasser case. Trial Lawyer's Quarterly 9(3):15-22 (1973)

1037 WELCH, THOMAS A. Kent v. United States and In Re Gault: two decisions in search of a theory. Hastings Law Journal 19:29-45 (1967)

A discussion of juvenile court procedure in conjunction with the background of the Kent and Gault decisions. (83 refs.)

California

1038 WENK, E.A., and R.L. EMRICH. Assaultive youth: an explorative study of the assaultive experience and assaultive potential of California youth authority wards. Journal of Research in Crime and Delinquency 9:171-196 (1972)

Austria

1039 WELSER, R. Die Neuordnung der Geschäftsfähigkeit und ihre Problematik. Versicherungs Rundschau 28:146-164 (1973)

California

1040 WEST, MARY B. Juvenile court jurisdiction over "immoral" youth in California. Stanford Law Review 24:568-586 (1972)

This article discusses the uses of the "immoral" clause in California, and analyzes the advantages and disadvantages according to the approach taken by the Supreme Court. Alternate solutions to eliminate abuses are given. (95 refs.)

Indiana

1041 WESTLEY, KENT H. Extending constitutional rights to juveniles - Gault in Indiana. Indiana Law Review 43:661-676 (1968)

This Note explores the impact of Gault, both as a present statement of law and as a portent of decisions to come, on the Indiana juvenile court system. (96 refs.)

1042 WEYHRICH, JOSEPH H. Representing the juvenile in the adjudicatory hearing. St. Louis University Law Journal 12:466-493 (1968)

This article is concerned with the various aspects of the adjudicatory hearing and the function of counsel in that hearing. (126 refs.)

Great Britain

1043 WHARAM, ALAN. Parent and child. New Law Journal 121:786-788 (1971)

A discussion of recovery of expenses incurred in consequence of an injury sustained by a child. (6 refs.)

1044 WHEELER, GERALD R. Children of the court: a profile of poverty. Crime and Delinquency 17:152-159 (1971)

A discussion of the relationship of child neglect and delinquency to poverty. (23 refs.)

Pennsylvania

1045 When is a criminal trial not a criminal trial? - The case against jury trials in juvenile court. St. John's Law Review 46:126-138 (1971)

A discussion of McKeiver and a juvenile's right to a jury trial. (74 refs.)

North Dakota

1046 WHITE, JAMES P. The juvenile and the court: a continuing dialogue. North Dakota Law Review 44:211-225 (1968)

Recent judicial decisions involving juveniles, and law review articles, create the need for a current assessment of the basic operation of the juvenile court in North Dakota (51 refs.)

Great Britain

1047 WHITE, STEPHEN. The presentation in court of social inquiry reports. Criminal Law Review 629-637 (1971)

In this study the author concludes that the presentation of social inquiry reports is an aspect of the legal process in which an unrepresented defendant is at a disadvantage. (25 refs.)

1048 WHITLACH, WALTER G. The Gault decision - its effect on the office of the prosecuting attorney. The Ohio Bar 41:41-51 (1968)

1049 WHITLACH, WALTER G. The juvenile court - a court of law. Western Reserve Law Review 18:1239-1250 (1967)

The juvenile court, as a court of law, has often come under attack on procedural and constitutional grounds. After stating that these attacks are probably due to a lack of public understanding of the court, the author explains why they are unjustified. The growth and development of the juvenile court is also traced. (62 refs.)

Ohio

1050 WHITLACH, WALTER G. Toward an understanding of the juvenile court process. Juvenile Justice 23(3):2-8 (1972)

A discussion of the social control or discipline which the juvenile court should exercise in cases involving violations of the criminal statutes and aberrant behavior of children. A court diversion program in Cuyahoga County, Cleveland, Ohio is discussed.

1051 WHITTEN, PATRICIA. Rights of foster parents to the children in their care. Chicago-Kent Law Review 50:86-102 (1973)

(68 refs.)

Gr.Br./U.S.

1052 WILHELM, S. Verträge Minderjähriger im anglo-amerikanischen Recht. Zeitschrift für Rechtsvergleichung 13:161-173 (1972)

1053 WILLESS, THOMAS N. Schools - constitutional law - hair regulations - regulation governing the length of hair is one that is not cognizable in the federal courts, nor is such right to be found within the plain meaning of the federal constitution. St. Mary's Law Journal 4:232-239 (1972)

With the eight to seven decision of Karr v. Schmidt, 460 F2d 609 (5th Cir. 1972), the apparent diversity of hair regulations is again demonstrated. The need for the Supreme Court to grant a writ of certiorari and resolve the problem, is discussed. (49 refs.)

1054 WINEMAN, DAVID, and ADRIENNE JAMES. The advocacy challenge to schools of social work. Social Work 14(2):23-32 (1969)

Schools of social work teach theories, technology, and ideals that often are rendered useless by the abusive and dehumanizing practices toward clients witnessed by students in field work agencies, especially in captor-captive settings. Social work schools must back their students in criticism of agency settings, and should attempt to change agency settings rather than resort to avoidance and denial of realities. (19 refs.)

Canada

1055 WINSHIP, P.J. Problems of youth. Royal Canadian Mounted Police 35(1):10-19 (1969)

1056 WIZNER, STEPHEN. The child and the state: adversaries in the juvenile justice system. Columbia Human Rights Law Review 4:389-399 (1972)

A discussion of adversary proceedings and a juvenile's right to counsel. (76 refs.)

1057 WIZNER, STEPHEN. Defense counsel: 'neither father, judge, probation officer or social worker'. Trial 7(5):30-31 (1971)
A discussion of the lawyer's role in juvenile court.

Great Britain

1058 WOOTTON, BARBARA. The white paper on children in trouble. Criminal Law Review 465-473 (1968)

1059 WREN, LAURANCE T. The Miranda doctrine and juvenile court. Juvenile Court Judges' Journal 18(4):115-120 (1968)
The author discusses the following questions: do the Miranda warnings apply to juvenile court? Did Gault incorporate this new concept of custodial interrogation into juvenile hearings, juvenile hall, and pre-adjudicatory questioning of juveniles? (13 refs.)

1060 The legal aspects, and the nature of, court-ordered rehabilitation aimed at improving character and changing criminal tendencies of minors. Vestuik Moskovskogo Universiteta. Pravo 1:73-81 (1971)

Canada

1061 YELAYA, S.A. The abused child: a reminder of despair. Canadian Welfare 49 (2):8, 10-11 (1973)

1062 YOUNG, DON J. Due process and the rights of children. Juvenile Court Judges' Journal 18(3):102-105 (1967)
The extension of the constitutional protections found in adult trial courts to juvenile dispositions is examined. The need for reform in juvenile courts is discussed.

1063 YOUNG, DON J. Is the juvenile court successful? Juvenile Court Judges' Journal 22(3):55-56 (1971)
A discussion of the juvenile court system.

1064 YOUNGER, EVELLE J. Stop and frisk: "say it like it is." The Journal of Criminal Law, Criminology and Police Science 58:293-302 (1967)
An analysis of the social and constitutional issues involved in the police investigative procedure of "stop and frisk." (32 refs.)

1065 Youthful offenders and adult courts: prosecutorial discretion vs. juvenile rights. University of Pennsylvania Law Review 121:1184-1193 (1973)
The author discusses the clash between prosecutorial discretion and the rights of offenders, and the need for the Supreme Court to prevent a doctrine aimed at ensuring prosecutorial fairness and flexibility from shielding potential arbitrary and inequitable handling of juvenile offenders. (54 refs.)

1066 ZAKOURO, JAMES P. Trial by jury in adjudicational stage of state juvenile court delinquency proceedings not constitutionally required. University of Kansas Law Review 20:369-376 (1972)

A criticism of the McKeiver decision and parens patriae. The author feels that the constitutional rights which were granted juveniles in Kent, Gault, and Winship have now been dealt a severe blow. (60 refs.)

1067 ZEHLER, RALPH P., Jr. Post-Gault - one judge's view of the juvenile court. Juvenile Court Judges' Journal 21(4):112-116 (1971)

Pre- and post-Gault juvenile court operation at dispositional hearings is discussed, and suggestions for improving juvenile court decisions are offered. (11 refs.)

1068 ZEKAS, JOSEPH P. Constitutional law - juvenile waiver statute - delegation of legislative power to judiciary. Wisconsin Law Review 259-268 (1973)

The possibility of increasing numbers of waiver proceedings, the fact that varying criteria are currently being applied in making waiver determinations, and the uncertainty over the limits of a juvenile court's discretion should force a re-examination of the criteria on which waivers to adult courts are based, states the author. (62 refs.)

Florida

1069 ZEWADSKI, WILLIAM K. Delinquency and denied rights in Florida's juvenile court system. University of Florida Law Review 20:369-385 (1968)

Analysis of a survey of procedural practices in delinquency cases before Florida's juvenile courts. (74 refs.)

1070 ZEWADSKI, WILLIAM K. Juvenile courts: the Gault case - new procedural rights for juveniles. University of Florida Law Review 20:120-126 (1967)

The Supreme Court's extension of procedural protections to juveniles in a delinquency hearing will not eviscerate the distinctive nature and purpose of the juvenile courts. (57 refs.)

Poland

1071 ZIELINSKI, A. Court procedure in the handling of juveniles after the first of January, 1970. Nowe Prawo 3:319-322 (1970)

1072 ZUCKERMAN, JACOB T. The family court - evolving concepts. Annals of the American Academy of Political and Social Science 383:119-128 (1969)

There are differences of opinion about the extent of the jurisdiction of the integrated family court. Questions have been raised concerning whether it should be a separate court or a division of the court of general trial jurisdiction. There is conflict over whether these courts require "specialized" judges. The trend seems to be toward an all-encompassing family court; with complete jurisdiction in all children's and family matters; a court which might well be a division of the highest court of original jurisdiction. Such a court needs to be manned by specialized judges who have the assistance of helping professionals such as well-trained case workers, psychiatrists, psychologists, and marriage counselors. (52 refs.)

BOOKS

B1 ADAMS, GARY B., et al. Juvenile justice management. Springfield, Charles C. Thomas, Publisher, 1969.

Great Britain

B2 ADAMS, PAUL, et al. Children's rights. Wellingsborough, England, Weatherby Woolnough, Ltd., 1971. 248p.

This series of papers from related disciplines dealing with the rights of children provides the opportunity for a thorough study of an important area.

B3 ADAMS, PAUL, et al. Children's rights: toward the liberation of the child. New York, Praeger Publishers, Inc., 1971. 265p.

B4 ADDAMS, JANE. The spirit of youth and the city streets. Urbana, University of Illinois Press, 1972.

B5 ADDAMS, JANE, et al. Child, the clinic, and the court. New York, Johnson Reprint Corp., 1971.

B6 AHLSTROM, WINTON M. Four hundred losers; delinquent boys in high school. San Francisco, Jossey-Bass, Inc., Publishers, 1971.

B7 AMBROSINO, LILLIAN A. Youth in trouble: runaways. Boston, Beacon Press, 1972. 150p.

W.Eur./Scand./U.S.

B8 AMEND, H. Organization und Zuständigkeit der Jugendgerichte und Vormundschaftsgerichte in Westeuropa, Skandinavien und der Vereinigten Staaten von Nordamerika. Marburg/Lahn, 1970. 112p.

Connecticut

B9 AMERICAN CORRECTIONAL ASSOCIATION. Consultant's report: institutional care of Connecticut's delinquent children. Washington, D.C., Law Enforcement Assistance Administration, 1970.

B10 THE AMERICAN HUMAN ASSOCIATION. Third national symposium. Protecting the abused, the neglected, and the sexually exploited child. nyp.1973.

Canada

B11 ANDREWS, H.T.G., ed. Family law in the courts. Toronto, The Carswell Company, Ltd., 1973. 232p.

It is the trend, throughout Canada, to provide in one court an organized tribunal which is competent to deal thoroughly with all family-related problems. The Family Court has become the most widely studied and discussed court system in Canada. However, there is not much published materials available. This book contains useful chapters on child neglect; illegitimate children; child custody proceedings; charges against children; assault as between parent and child; child welfare; etc.

Great Britain

B12 ANDRY, R.G. Delinquency and parental pathology. rev. ed. London, Staples, 1971. 189p.

B13 ANDRY, ROBERT J. Delinquency and parental pathology: a study in forensic and clinical psychology. New York, Russak Crane and Co., 1971.

Germany

B13a ARLET, D. Kinder töten Kinder. Hamburg, Kriminalistik Verlag, 1971. 140p.

B14 ARNOLD, WILLIAM R. Juveniles on parole: a sociological perspective. New York, Random House, Inc., 1970. 177p.

B15 BADEN, MARY A. Becoming a female delinquent. Ann Arbor, Xerox University Microfilms, 1971. 167p.

B16 BAKAN, DAVID. Slaughter of the innocents. San Francisco, Jossey-Bass, Inc., Publishers, 1971. 175p.

Switzerland

B17 BALDEGGER, W. Vormundschaftsrecht und Jugendfürsorge. Freiburg, Diss.-Freiburg, 1970. 125p.

B18 BALL, JOHN C. Social deviancy and adolescent personality; an analytical study with the MMPI. Westport, Greenwood Press, Inc., 1973. 199p.

B19 BATTEN, TONY. A'int gonna eat my mind. New York, Lawrence Hill and Co., Inc., 1974.

California

B20 BAY AREA SOCIAL PLANNING COUNCIL. Study committee on the San Francisco juvenile court. San Francisco juvenile court: three-phase report and recommendations of the study committee. San Francisco, Bay Area Social Planning Council, 1969. 60p.

B21 BAZELON, DAVID L. The juvenile court: from promise to frustration. Detroit, Michigan Society of Psychiatry and Neurology, 1969. 20p.

The gap between theory and practice in the juvenile court is discussed.

B22 BECK, CARL, ed. Law and justice: essays in honor of Robert S. Rankin. College Station, Duke University Press, 1970.

B23 BECKER, THOMAS T. Due process in child protective services - intervention on behalf of neglected children. Denver, The American Humane Association, Children's Division. No date. 24p.

The author discusses the implications of the mandate for due process as it applies to the neglect proceedings in juvenile court, defines the elements of due process, and interprets the precarious balance required to protect conflicting rights.

B24 BESHAROV, DOUGLAS J. Defending and prosecuting juveniles - practice in a unique court. New York, Practising Law Institute, 1973. 175p.

Great Britain

B25 BEVAN, H.K. The law relating to children. London, Butterworths, 1973. 522p.

The law with regard to children in Great Britain, as of October, 1972, is examined: juvenile court; procedure and orders in care proceedings and criminal proceedings in juvenile courts; children in the care of local authorities; the penal protection of children from physical and moral harm; legitimacy; custody; adoption; foster parenthood; guardianship; education and employment of children; financial provisions for children. Tables of cases are included.

New Zealand

B26 BLIZARD, P.J. Juvenile delinquency in New Zealand. Wellington, 1967.

B27 BLUM, JEFFREY D., and JUDITH E. SMITH. Nothing left to lose: studies of street people. Boston, Beacon Press, 1972.

B28 BLUMBERG, ABRAHAM S. Criminal justice. Chicago, Quadrangle Books, Inc., 1967. 206p.

A former constitutional and criminal lawyer documents charges that justice for the accused is being denied in American courts, particularly in criminal and juvenile courts. His sociological analysis of our criminal court system describes a disregard for due process in the name of bureaucracy.

B29 BLUMER, HERBERT, and PHILIP M. HAUSER. Movies, delinquency and crime. New York, Arno Press, Inc., 1970. 233p.

B30 BOCHES, RALPH E., and JOEL GOLDFARB. California juvenile court practice. Berkeley, California Continuing Education of the Bar, 1968. 264p.

This book is designed to give attorneys a fuller understanding of how to represent juveniles more effectively. The authors discuss the following: the role of the attorney; the theory of juvenile court law in California; the decision-making process; jurisdiction; venue and transfer; temporary custody by law enforcement officers; custody by probation officers; the detention hearing; representation by counsel; adjudication and disposition; proceedings after disposition; dependency cases.

B31 BOCK, RICHARD D., and ABIGAIL ENGLISH. Got me on the run: a study of runaways. Boston, The Beacon Press, 1973. 224p.

B32 BOTTOMS, A.E., and F.H. McCLINTOCK. Criminals coming of age: a study of institutional adaptation in the treatment of adolescent offenders. New York, Humanities Press, Inc., 1974.

B33 BOVET, LUCIEN. Psychiatric aspects of juvenile delinquency: a study. Westport, Greenwood Press, Inc., 1972. (Reprint of 1951 edition.) 90p.

B34 BREMNER, ROBERT H., ed. Children and youth in America. Cambridge, Harvard University Press, 1971, 2 vols., 836, 1546p.

Every facet of youth in America is covered, including the legal status of children in foster care, juvenile delinquency, etc. The second of three volumes covers the period from the end of the Civil War to the beginning of the New Deal.

B35 BROWNE, ELIZABETH W. Child neglect and dependency: a digest of case law. Reno, National Council of Juvenile Court Judges, 1973. 43p.

Senator Browne presents some of the problems of decision-making, and changes in case law in this publication.

B36 BUSS, WILLIAM G. Legal aspects of crime investigation in the public schools. Topeka, National Organization on Legal Problems of Education, 1971. 173p.

B37 CAIN, ARTHUR H. Young people and crime: the use and abuse of beverage alcohol. New York, John Day Co., Inc., 1968.

B38 CALDWELL, ROBERT G., and JAMES A. BLACK. Juvenile delinquency. New York, Ronald Press Co., 1971. 354p.

This textbook provides a view of juvenile delinquency in contemporary America. A definition of delinquency as a legal concept is followed by an examination of delinquency as a social problem.

California

B39 CALIFORNIA CONTINUING EDUCATION OF THE BAR. Benchbook - misdemeanor procedure. (California College of Trial Judges' Handbook), Berkeley, California Continuing Education of the Bar, 1971. 446p.

B40 CAPLAN, GERALD, and SERGE LEBOVICI, eds. Adolescence: psychosocial perspectives. New York, Basic Books, 1969.

B41 CAREY, J.T., et al. The handling of juveniles from offense to disposition. Washington, D.C., U.S. Department of H.E.W., no date. 63p.

B42 CAREY, WILLIAM L., et al. The complaint process in protective services for children. Governor's Commission on Youth. Portland, Oregon, Portland State University, 1971. 60p.

Great Britain

B43 CARSON, WESLEY G., and PAUL WILES, eds. Crime and delinquency in Britain: sociological readings. New York, Humanities Press, Inc., 1971. 258p.

B44 CAVAN, RUTH S. Readings in juvenile delinquency. 2d ed. New York, J.B. Lippincott, 1969. 499p.

B45 Challenge of youth service bureaus. Washington, D.C., U.S. Department of H.E.W., Youth Development and Delinquency Prevention Administration, 1973. 41p.

Italy

B46 Child law. Milano, Giuffré, 1968. 128p.

B47 CHILD WELFARE LEAGUE OF AMERICA. Committee on revision of CWLA standards for child protective service. Child Welfare League of America standards for child protective service. Rev. ed. New York, Child Welfare League of America, 1973. 85p.

China

B48 CHU, S.-C. The law dealing with juvenile cases in practice. Tapei, 1972. 326p.

B49 CICOUREL, AARON V. The social organization of juvenile justice. New York, John Wiley and Sons, Inc., 1968. 345p.

This book presents a detailed view of the everyday practices of the police, probation officials, and the courts, and points out how various agencies actually generate delinquency. Differences in the administration of justice are shown, and the way community political structure and departmental organization influence juvenile justice is presented.

B50 CLARK, HOMER H., Jr. The law of domestic relations in the United States. St. Paul, West Publishing Co., 1968. XI, 754p.

B51 COHEN, ALBERT K. Delinquent boys: the culture of the gang. New York, The MacMillan Company, 1971. 198p.

B52 COHEN, FRANK J., ed. Law enforcement institute – New York University. Youth and crime: proceedings. New York, International Universities Press, 1969.

B53 COLE, LARRY. Our children's keepers: inside America's kid prisons. New York, Grossman Publishers, Inc., 1972. 256p.

Colorado

B54 COLORADO. Legislative Council. Labor laws relating to women and children: report to the Colorado General Assembly. Denver, 1970. 44p.

B55 COMMINS, NIGEL. The essence of delinquency. Cambridge, Cambridge Aide to Learning (Publishing) Ltd., 1971. 42p.

B56 COMSTOCK, G.A., et al., eds. Television and social behavior. Vol. V. Television's effects: further explorations. Washington, D.C., U.S. Government Printing Office, 1972.

U.S.S.R.

B57 CONNOR, WALTER D. Deviance in a Soviet society: crime, delinquency and alcoholism. New York, Columbia University Press, 1972. 327p.

B58 CORTES, JUAN B., and FLORENCE M. GATTE. Delinquency and crime, a biophysical approach; empirical, theoretical and practical aspects of. New York, Seminar Press, Inc., 1972. 468p.

Puerto Rico

B59 CORTÉS-GARCÍA, E. A new approach to juvenile antisocial behavior in the Commonwealth of Puerto Rico. 3rd rev. Orford, Nitl., Equity, 1970. 139p.

B60 COTTRELL, LEONARD S., Jr., et al. On community, family and delinquency. Chicago, University of Chicago Press, 1973.

Europe

B61 COUNCIL OF EUROPE. Collected studies in criminological research. Strasbourg, 1967. 90p.

Europe

B62 COUNCIL OF EUROPE. European Committee on Crime Problem. Short-term methods of treatment for young offenders. Strasbourg, 1967.

B63 COUNCIL OF JUDGES OF THE NATIONAL COUNCIL ON CRIME AND DELINQUENCY. Provision of counsel in juvenile courts: a policy statement. New York, National Council on Crime and Delinquency. 1970. 34p.
(79 refs.)

B64 COWIE, JOHN, et al. Delinquency in girls. Cambridge, England, Institute of Criminology, Humanities Press, 1968. 220p.

B65 CRESSEY, DONALD R., and DAVID A. WARD. Delinquency, crime and social process. New York, Harper and Row, 1969. 1151p.

Middle-class delinquency is not a happenstance affair. Our youth might be captive to the obligation to accept the dictates, the suggestions, and the mores of their peers in our present youth culture. As growing identification with the latter is strengthened, these new prevailing attitudes, definitions and practices are assumed and learned, and the youth are trapped as they adopt a relatively unserious attitude towards delinquency and think of themselves as being immune. This seeming immunity, and the protection given by parents, confirms the teenager in his delinquent ways, and serves to sustain existing delinquent patterns which the parents and counsellors often perceive as "signs of maturity." Lawyers who serve the parents of such children may have an opportunity for a far wider range of practice than they either bargained for or trained for.

B66 Crime and delinquency literature. Paramus, National Council on Crime and Delinquency. Periodical, issued quarterly.

Great Britain

B67 DAVIES, M. Probationers in their social environment. London, H.M.S.O., 1969. 203p.

Argentina

B68 DEFLEUR, LOIS B. Delinquency in Argentina: a study of Cardoba's youth. Pullman, Washington State University Press, 1970. 164p.

B69 DE FRANCIS, VINCENT. Child abuse legislation in the 1970's. Denver, The American Humane Association, Children's Division, 1970. 134p.

The results of a study of child-abuse reporting legislation as of 1970. The changes in the laws over a five-year period, the status of the law in each of the states and territories is presented.

B70 DE FRANCIS, VINCENT. Community cooperation for better child protection. Denver, The American Humane Association, Children's Division. No date. 20p.

A discussion of the cooperative roles of the court, school, church, police and voluntary agencies, and how they may best contribute to the protection of children.

B71 DE FRANCIS, VINCENT. The court and protective services - their respective roles. Denver, The American Humane Association, Children's Division. No date. 19p.

A discussion of the purpose and functions of the two agencies - a recognition of their separate and mutual responsibilities.

B72 DE FRANCIS, VINCENT. The fundamentals of child protection. Denver, The American Humane Association, Children's Division. No date. 71p.

A manual on basic concepts, principles and practices for social work practitioners in this specialized field.

B73 DE FRANCIS, VINCENT. Protecting the child victims of sex crimes committed by adults. Denver, The American Humane Association, Children's Division. No date. 230p.

Major findings of a survey of each state and county in the U.S.A. reported on a state-by-state basis. An analysis and discussion, from a national perspective, of the different laws, policies and practices found to exist in the fifty states and the territories.

B74 DE FRANCIS, VINCENT. Protective services and community expectations. Denver, The American Humane Association, Children's Division. No date. 17p.

A discussion of community responsibility for providing protective services - the legal frame of reference for physical and emotional neglect - the problems involved in obtaining a legal finding of emotional neglect.

B75 DE FRANCIS, VINCENT. Termination of parental rights - balancing the inequities. Denver, The American Humane Association, Children's Division. No date. 20p.

An exploration of the problem of termination of parental rights and the legal complications which surround the process. Basic data are given with respect to the rights of parents and children, and variations on the theme of how parental rights are affected, are presented and discussed.

Netherlands

B76 DE RUITER, J., en J.A.M. SCHOUTEN. Hulp en Recht. Deventer, Kluwer, 1972. 77p.

Germany

B77 DEUTSCHE VEREINIGUNG FÜR JUGENDGERICHTE UND JUGENDGERICHTSHILFEN. Denkschrift über die Behandlung von kriminell stark gefahrdeten jungen Tätern in Vollzugsanstalten. Goettingen, Schwartz, 1970. 56p.

B78 DEXTER, LEWIS A. Elite and specialized interviewing: handbooks for research in political behavior. Evanston, Northwestern University Press, 1970.

The author discusses suggestions for obtaining, conducting and recording interviews. Interviewing procedures employed in law and psychiatry are discussed also.

B79 DICK, JONATHAN S., and IRENE M. ROSENBERG. Manual for new attorneys. New York, Legal Aid Society, 1971.

B80 DONOVAN, F.R. Wild kids: how youth has shocked its elders then and now. Harrisburg, Stackpole Books, 1967.

B81 DORMAN, MICHAEL. Under twenty-one. New York, Dell Publishing Co., Inc., 1971.

B82 DOUGLAS, JACK D. Youth in turmoil. Chevy Chase, National Institute of Mental Health, Center for Studies of Crime and Delinquency, 1970.

B83 DOWNIE, LEONARD, Jr. Justice denied: the case for reformation of the courts. New York, Praeger Publishers, 1971. 234p.

A criticism of the court system, including juvenile courts.

B84 DUSTER, TROY. The legislation of morality: law, drugs, and moral judgment. New York, Free Press, 1970. 274p.

The author examines the connection between laws and morals by tracing historically a specific case; the evolution of narcotics morality. He shows how narcotics morality was a direct consequence of legal change. He submits an analysis of the implications of his argument, not only for narcotics but for other current issues and problems.

B85 EISNER, VICTOR. Delinquency label: the epidemiology of juvenile delinquency. New York, Random House, Inc., 1969.

B86 ELDEFONSO, EDWARD. Law enforcement and the youthful offender: juvenile procedures. 2d edition. New York, John Wiley and Sons, Inc., 1973. 494p.

B87 ELDEFONSO, EDWARD. Youth problems and law enforcement. Englewood Cliffs, Prentice-Hall, Inc., 1972. 128p.

B88 EMERSON, ROBERT M. Judging delinquents: context and process in juvenile court. Chicago, Aldine Publishing Company, 1971. 304p.

This analysis of juvenile courts and their clients attempts to combine the sociological approaches of institutional analysis and societal reaction. It discusses the ways in which juvenile courts' judgments and responses to defendants are influenced by the external context, and by the internal dynamics of the court operation. It is based on field work conducted between January 1966 and May 1967.

B89 EMPEY, LAMAR T., and MAYNARD L. ERIKSON. Provo experiment; evaluating community control of delinquency. Lexington, Lexington Books, 1972. 321p.

B90 EMPEY, LAMAR T., and STEVEN G. LUBECK. Delinquency prevention strategies. U.S. Department of H.E.W., Social and Rehabilitation Service, Youth Development and Delinquency Prevention Administration. Washington, D.C., U.S. Government Printing Office, 1970.

B91 FAUST, FREDERIC L., and PAUL J. BRANTINGHAM, eds. Juvenile justice philosophy: readings, cases and comments. St. Paul, West Publishing Co., 1974. 600p.

The purpose of this volume is to present a single resource that will give further insight into the evolution of juvenile justice philosophy in the United States, and the impact of that philosophy upon the legal boundaries of juvenile court procedure. Six subject areas are dealt with.

B92 FLAMMANG, C.J. The police and the under-protected child. Springfield, Charles E. Thomas, 1970. 310p.

(99 refs.)

B93 FLAMMANG, C.J. Police juvenile enforcement. Springfield, Charles C. Thomas, Publisher, 1972. 284p.

Germany

B94 FLUCK, M. Der Jugendarrest als mittel zur Bekämpfung der Jugendkriminalität. Saarbrücken, Diss. Saarland, 1969. 214p.

B95 FONTANA, VINCENT J. Maltreated child; the maltreated syndrome in children. 2d edition. Springfield, Charles C. Thomas, Publisher, 1970. 96p.

B96 FONTANA, VINCENT J. Somewhere a child is crying: maltreatment - causes and prevention. New York, McMillan Publishing Co., Inc., 1973. 268p.

This study outlines a program for eliminating the causes of child abuse.

B97 FORER, LESTER G. No one will lissen: how our legal system brutalizes the youthful poor. New York, John Day, 1970. 352p.

An intimate firsthand account of a daily struggle by lawyers to make the legal system operate to give poor children the same fair treatment and due process that it gives to the middle-class adult.

B98 FOSTER, HENRY H., Jr. A "bill of rights" for children. Springfield, Charles C. Thomas, Publisher, 1974.

B99 FOX, SANFORD J. Cases and materials on modern juvenile justice. St. Paul, West Publishing Co., 1972. 1012p.

B100 FOX, SANFORD J. The law of juvenile courts in a nutshell. St. Paul, West Publishing Co., 1971. 286p.

This book contains sections on the jurisdiction of juvenile courts, waiver to the criminal courts, the role of police, the detention and pre-trial process, juvenile court hearings, sentencing and other forms of disposition, and appeals.

B101 FRANKENSTEIN, CARL. Varieties of juvenile delinquency. New York, Gordon and Breach Science, 1970. 252p.

B102 FREEMAN, J.L. The predelinquency jurisdiction of the juvenile court and constitutional liberties. Cambridge, Harvard University Press, 1969. 71p.

B103 GARABEDIAN, PETER G., and DON C. GIBBONS, eds. Becoming delinquent: young offenders and the correctional system. Chicago, Aldine Publishing Co., 1971. 304p.

B104 GARFF, REGNAL W. Handbook for new juvenile court judges. Reno, University of Nevada, 1973.

B105 GAZELL, JAMES A., and THOMAS GITCHOFF. Youth, crime and society. Boston, Holbrook Press, 1973. 345p.

B106 GEORGE, B. JAMES, Jr. Gault and the juvenile court revolution. New York, Practising Law Institute, 1968. 326p.

B107 GIALLOMBARDO, ROSE. Juvenile delinquency: a book of readings. 2d ed. New York, John Wiley and Sons, Inc., 1972. 613p.

The content of the first sections in this book has been substantially changed to include new areas of concern in the field of the juvenile delinquent.

B108 GIL, DAVID G. Violence against children; physical child abuse in the United States. Cambridge, Harvard University Press, 1970. 204p.

A documented study of child abuse in the U.S.A.

B109 GLASER, DANIEL. Crime in the city. New York, Harper and Row, 1970. 308p.

A treatise of the problem of urban crime and delinquency.

B110 GLAZIER, ALICE E., et al. Child abuse: a community challenge. New York, Henry Stewart, Inc., 1971. 169p.

B111 GLUECK, ELEANOR T., and SHELDON GLUECK. Identification of pre-delinquents: validation studies and some suggested use of Glueck table. New York, Intercontinental, 1972. 150p.

B112 GLUECK, SHELDON. Of delinquency and crime; a panorama of years of search and research. Springfield, Charles C. Thomas, Publisher, 1974.

B113 GLUECK, SHELDON, and ELEANOR T. GLUECK. Delinquents and nondelinquents in perspective. Cambridge, Harvard University Press, 1968.

B114 GOLD, MARTIN. Delinquent behaviour in an American City. Belmont, Wadsworth Publishing Co., Inc., 1970. 150p.

B115 GOLDSTEIN, JOSEPH, et al. Beyond the best interests of the child. New York, The Free Press, 1973. 169p.

Child custody, and placement of children for adoption is discussed.

Great Britain

B116 GOODMAN, L., ed. Clarke Hall and Morrison's law relating to children and young persons. 8th edition. Toronto, Butterworths, 1972. 1436p.

This book covers the English laws relating to children. Definitions and tables of statutes and cases are included.

India

B117 GOPALKRISHNAN, T.P. Hindu adoptions and maintenance act. 3rd ed. by J.A. Singhai. Allahabad, Law Book Company, 1969. 230p.

B118 GOSHEN, CHARLES E. Society and the youthful offender. Springfield, Charles C. Thomas, Publisher, 1973.

California

B119 GOSSLAND, RUTH. Juvenile rights in court. 1969 California Family edition. (?) Los Angeles, 1969. 31p.

B120 GOTTLIEB, DAVID, ed. Children's liberation. Englewood Cliffs, Prentice-Hall, Inc., 1973. 181p.

New York

B121 Gould staff editors. Family court act (New York). Looseleaf. Jamaica, New York, Gould Publications, 1973.

Great Britain

B122 GREAT BRITAIN. Home Department. Part I of the children and young persons act 1969: a guide for courts and practitioners. London, H.M.S.O., 1970. 63p.

Great Britain

B123 GREAT BRITAIN. Social Work Services Group. Children's hearings: notes on Part III of the social work (Scotland) act 1968. Edinburgh, H.M.S.O., 1970. 42p.

B124 GROSSER, CHARLES. Helping youth: a study of six community organization programs. U.S. Department of H.E.W. Washington, D.C., Government Printing Office, 1969.

Switzerland

B125 GUT, R.H. Die Erziehungsaustalt Aarburg mit Berücksichtigung des Aarganischen Jugenstrafsrechtes. Aaran, Keller, 1969. 149p.

B126 HAHN, PAUL H. The juvenile offender and the law. Cincinnati, W.H. Anderson Co., 1971. 416p.
(174 refs.)

B127 HALLORAN, J.D. Mass media and delinquent behavior. New York, Humanities Press, Inc., 1970. 168p.

B128 HARDY, RICHARD E., and JOHN G. CULL. Climbing ghetto walls: disadvantagement, delinquency and rehabilitation. Springfield, Charles C. Thomas, Publisher, 1973.

Germany

B129 HARTMANN, K. Theoretische und empirische Beiträge zur Verwahrlosungsforschund. Berlin, Springer, 1970. 149p.

B130 HASKELL, M.R., and L. YABLONSKY. Crime and delinquency. The Hague, Nijhoff's Uitgevers, 1970. 517p.

Switzerland

B131 HILTY-WANWEILER, A. Das Verhaltnis der Zivilrechtlichen zu den jugendstrafrechtlichen Erziehungs- und Fürsorgemassnahmen. Zürich, Juris Druck, 1970. 106p.

B132 HIRSHI, TRAVIS. Causes of delinquency. Berkeley, University of California Press, 1969.

B133 HIRSHI, T., and H.C. SELVIN. Delinquency research. New York, Free Press, 1967.

Germany

B134 HOFFMAN, T. Jugend im Gefängnis. München, Piper, 1967. 220p.

Canada

B135 HOLDEN, D.A. Child legislation, 1969. Toronto, Butterworths, 1970. 341p.

B136 HOLL, JACK M. Juvenile reform in the progressive era: William R. George and the junior republic movement. Ithica, Cornell University Press, 1971.

B137 HOPSON, DAN, Jr., et al. Juvenile offender and the law: a symposium. New York, Da Capo Press, Inc., 1968. 237p.

Great Britain

B138 HOWARD, DEREK L. Trouble with the law: notes for youth workers on the children and young persons act. London, National Association of Youth Clubs, 1971. 19p.

India

B139 HUSSAIN, S. Juvenile delinquency. Madras, Madras Book Agency, 1967. 83p.

Illinois

B140 ILLINOIS INSTITUTE FOR CONTINUING LEGAL EDUCATION. Illinois juvenile practice. Springfield, Illinois Institute on Continuing Legal Education, 1971. 250p.

Pakistan

B141 ILYAS KHAN, MOHAMMED. Juvenile law in Pakistan. Karachi, Lee Law Publications, 1970. 245p.

B142 INTERNATIONAL PENAL AND PRISON COMMISSION. Children's courts in the United States: their origin, development, and results. New York, AMS Press, Inc., 1973. 203p.

B143 IRWIN, THEODORE D. The rights of teenagers as patients. New York, Public Affairs Committee, 1972. 28p.

B144 JAMES, HOWARD. Children in trouble: a national scandal. New York, David McKay Co., 1971. 340p.

The author's primary focus is on bringing to light the cruel damage that is being done to troubled youngsters throughout the country in the name of juvenile courts, and through misdirected and ill-supported programs of treatment.

B145 JAMES, HOWARD. Crisis in the courts. Revised edition. New York, David McKay Co., Inc., 1971. 267p.

B146 JAMES, T.F. Children and the law. Elmsford, Pergamon Press, Inc., 1965.

Florida

B147 JEFFERSON, RUFUS O. Florida juvenile law. Atlanta, Harrison Company, 1972. 300p.

Fr./Ger./Gr.Br./Switz.

B148 JEUTSCH, G. Die Geschäftsfähigkeit Minderjähriger im deutschen, österreichischen, schweizerischen, französchen und englischen Recht. Bonn, diss. Universität zu Bonn, 1967. 244p.

B149 JORDAN, DANIEL C., and LARRY L. DYE. Delinquency - an assessment of the Juvenile Delinquency Prevention and Control Act of 1968. Amhurst, University of Massachusetts Press, 1970. 288p.

An assessment of the above-mentioned act. (177 refs.)

Germany

B150 Jugendwohlfahrtsgesetz. München, Beck, 1972. 2 vols. 851p.

B151 JURJEVICH, RATIBOR M. No water in my cup: experiences and a controlled study of psychotherapy of delinquent girls. New York, Libra Publishers, 1968.

B152 Justice for children: a guide to study and action on the juvenile system in your community. New York, National Council of Jewish Women, 1972. 101p.

B153 Juvenile and family courts, legal bibliography. Washington, D.C., U.S. Department of H.E.W., Youth Development and Delinquency Prevention Administration, 1971. 110p.

This issue contains the 1966 edition of legal bibliography for juvenile and family courts, and four annual supplements.

B154 Juvenile Court Digest. Reno, National Council of Juvenile Court Judges, 1967-

A monthly publication dealing with selected current court decisions in connection with juveniles, and summaries of law review articles as well as book reviews.

B155 Juvenile delinquency planning. A joint publication of the U.S. Department of H.E.W., Social and Rehabilitation Service, Youth Development and Delinquency Prevention Administration; and the U.S. Department of Justice, Law Enforcement Assistance Administration. Washington, D.C., U.S. Government Printing Office, 1971.

B156 Juvenile justice digest: a monthly summary of significant news events in the field of juvenile delinquency prevention. Washington, Washington Crime News Services, 1973. Periodical, issued monthly.

B157 Juvenile law litigation directory. Juvenile justice standards project. Institute of judicial administration. New York, New York University School of Law, 1972.

B158 Juvenile practice manual: public defender service. Washington, D.C., Juvenile Practice Institute, 1971. 180p.

District of Columbia

B159 Juvenile Practice Institute, 2d. Washington, D.C., 1971. 170p.

The following are discussed in this manual: opposition to commitment of the respondent to the custody of Welfare Services, juvenile proceedings in family court, interstate compact, disposition, PINS. Also included are: court forms for orders for commitment proceedings, to suspend proceedings, intermediate review, consent decree, medical or physical examination, for return to custody, detention order, shelter care order, conditional release, waiver of trial and plea of guilty.

B160 Juvenile traffic offenders. New York, National Council of Judges, 1969. 16p.

This pamphlet includes procedures for use in both juvenile court and traffic court.

B161 KAHN, ALFRED J., et al. Child advocacy: report of a national baseline study. New York, Columbia University School of Social Work, 1972. 184p.

California

B162 KAMM, ERNEST R., et al. Juvenile law and procedure in California. Beverly Hills, Glencoe Press, 1971. 372p.

B163 KATZ, SANFORD N. When parents fail. The law's response to family breakdown. Boston, Beacon Press, 1971. 251p.

The author examines, critically, the process of public intervention into the parent-child relationship, and into the procedures in the handling of neglect cases in the pre-court stage, the court hearing and court disposition steps. Serious questions are raised as to the validity of the entire process, and regarding foster care in specific custody cases. Important questions are examined regarding the role of judges, child-caring services, departments of welfare, departments of probation, etc. Professor Katz is deeply concerned about what he fears may be too powerful authorith, arbitrary action, and less than high calibre performance on the part of public and private agencies dealing with families and children; about what he sees as an insistance on the part of courts and agencies of the application of middle-class standards to low-class or non-conforming families; about what he sees as too vaguely drawn neglect statutes giving wide latitude of discretion to judges; about the use by agencies and courts of neglect statutes and custody statutes to police families rather than to further the best interests of children. He makes the point that the lower-class family and one-parent family is much more viable, and therefore much more vulnerable to the charge of neglecting their children. (Mod. of a review by Judge Florence M. Kelley).

B164 KEMPE, C. HENRY, and RAY E. HELFER. Helping the battered child and his family. Philadelphia, J.B. Lippincott Co., 1972.

B165 KENNEY, JOHN P., and DAN G. PURSUIT. Police work with juveniles and the administration of juvenile justice. 4th edition. Springfield, Charles C. Thomas, Publisher, 1971. 436p.

B166 KETCHAM, ORMAN W., and MONRAD G. PAULSEN. Cases and materials relating to juvenile courts. Mineola, Foundation Press, 1967. 558p.

The many dimensions of the complicated socio-legal problem of the administration of justice for juveniles are amply covered by Judge Ketcham and Dean Paulsen in this ten chapter book.

B167 KIESTER, DOROTHY J., ed. Training program juvenile probation service. Chapel Hill, University of North Carolina, Institute of Government, 1969. 86p.

Japan

B168 KIKUTA, K. The movement of juvenile law. Tokyo, Seibundō, 1971. 232p.

B169 KING, DONALD B. One hundred injustices to the child. St. Louis, St. Louis School of Law, National Juvenile Law Center, 1972. 120p.

B170 KLEIN, MALCOLM W. Street gangs and street workers. Englewood Cliffs, Prentice-Hall, Inc., 1971. 338p.

Germany

B171 KLOTZ, K.O. Die rechtstatsächliche und rechtpolitische Bedenkung der Vorschriften über die Anlage von Mündelgeld. Berlin, Duncker und Humbolt, 1966. 123p.

California

B172 KNIGHT, DOUG. Delinquency causes and remedies; the working assumptions of California youth authority staff. Sacramento, California Youth Authority, Division of Research and Development, 1972. 163p.

B173 KNUDTEN, RICHARD D. Crime in complex society: an introduction to criminality. Homewood, Illinois, Dorsey Press, 1970. 758p.
(1384 refs.)

B174 KOBETZ, RICHARD W. The police role and juvenile delinquency. Gaithersburg, Md., International Association of Chiefs of Police, 1971. 264p.
Policy guidelines for police-juvenile operations are outlined.

B175 KOBETZ, RICHARD W., and BETTY B. BOSARGE. Juvenile justice administration. Gaithersburg, International Association of Chiefs of Police, 1973. 770p.
This book explores the official agencies of the juvenile justice system - the police, courts, probation, corrections and social services. It contains recommendations made by interdisciplinary teams of juvenile justice practitioners for the improvement of juvenile justice administration.

B176 KOENIGIL, MARK. Movies in Society. New York, Robert Speller & Sons, Publishers, 1962.

B177 KORN, RICHARD R., ed. Juvenile delinquency. New York, Thomas Y. Crowell, 1968.

B178 KRAUSE, HARRY D. Illegitimacy: law and social policy. Indianapolis, Bobbs-Merrill Co., 1971. 379p.
Professor Krause has combined a fully documented account of the present law applicable to the illegitimate child with extensive criticism of that law, a brief examination of social attitudes toward it, and recommendations for thorough reform. The inconsistencies and inadequacies of the peculiar legal proceeding for the establishment of paternity, and some foreign laws, are also examined.

Germany

B179 KRIEGER, H. Anwendungsbereich und Wirksamkeit des Jugendarrests in Saarland. Saarbrücken, Diss. Saarland, 1970. 194p.

B180 KVARECEUS, WILLIAM C. Prevention and control of delinquency: the school counselor's role. Boston, Houghton Mifflin Co., 1971. 65p.

B181 LALLI, MICHAEL, and LEONARD SAVILZ. Delinquency and city life. Washington, National Institute of Law Enforcement, 1972. 67p.

B182 LARRICK, NANCY, and EVE MERRIMAN, eds. Male and female under 18. New York, Avon Books, 1973.

B183 Law and the Commonwealth. Fourth Commonwealth Law Conference. New Delhi, 1971.

Texas

B184 LEDBETTER, JACK W. Texas family law. rev. ed. Austin, University of Texas, Bureau of Business Research, 1970.

California

B185 LEE, EUGENE C., and WILLIS D. HAWKLEY, eds. The challenge of California - with a concise introduction to California government. Boston, Little Brown and Co., Inc., 1970.

Great Britain

B186 LEEDING, A.E. Child care manual for social workers. London, Butterworths, 1971. 167p.

B187 Legal rights of children. New York, Practising Law Institue, 1973. 128p.

B188 Legal rights of children: status, progress and proposals. Intr. by Rena K. Uviller. Fairlawn, N.J., R.E. Burdick, distr. by International Scholarly Book Services, Inc., ca.1973.

B189 Legislative guide for drafting state-local programs on juvenile delinquency. Washington, D.C., U.S. Youth Development and Delinquency Prevention Administration, 1972. 40p.

California

B190 LEMERT, EDWIN M. Social action and legal change: revolution within the juvenile court. Chicago, Aldine Publishing Co., 1970. 248p.

Based on a detailed analysis of change in the law and in the administration of justice affecting juvenile offenders in California, this book is addressed to three questions: how does law, particularly procedural law, develop on a long term basis? Under what conditions, and by what processes do revolutionary changes in law occur? To what extent can social change be directed or controlled by legislation? (320 refs.)

B191 LERMAN, PAUL. Delinquency and social policy. New York, Praeger Publishers, Inc., 1970. 488p.

(741 refs.)

B192 LEVINE, MARTIN. The current status of juvenile law. Los Angeles, University Of Southern California, Delinquency Control Institute, 1971. 95p.

B192 LEVINE, MARTIN. The current status of juvenile law. Los Angeles, University of Southern California, Delinquency Control Institute, 1971. 95p.

B193 LINDSAY, BEN B., and HARVEY O'HIGGINS. Beast. Seattle, University of Washington Press, 1970.

B194 LOEB, ROBERT H., Jr. Your legal rights as a minor. New York, Franklin Watts, Inc., 1973.

The author discusses the origin, purpose, and application of the most relevant legal rights of minors in the United States.

B195 LOTH, DAVID. Crime in the suburbs. New York, William Morrow, 1967.

B196 McDONOUGH, J. NORMAN, et al. Juvenile court handbook. South Hackensack, Fred B. Rothman & Co., 1970. 54p.

This juvenile court handbook covers practices and procedures in the juvenile court. Included are the roles of the lawyer, the social worker, and the court worker, and the nature, structure, and workings of the court. The appendices contain forms typically found in the juvenile court processes. (42 refs.)

B197 McLEAN, GORDON R. We're holding your son. Old Tappan, Fleming H. Revell Co., 1969.

France

B198 MADLENER, K. Das französische Unehelichenrecht. Bielefeld, Gieseking, 1969. 312p.

B199 MARTIN, JOHN. Toward a political definition of juvenile delinquency. Washington, D.C., U.S. Government Printing Office, 1970.

Maryland

B200 MARYLAND. Governor's Commission on young offenders. Report of the Commission on young offenders: bibliography. Baltimore, 1971. 48p.

Massachusetts

B201 MASSACHUSETTS. Governor's Committee on Child Abuse. Final Report. Boston, 1971.

Japan

B202 MATSUO, K., et al. Juvenile law: the present conditions and problems. Tokyo, Tasei shuppan-sha, 1972. 299p.

B203 MAYS, JOHN B., ed. Juvenile delinquency, the family and the social group: a reader. New York, Longman, Inc., 1973.

B204 MENNELL, ROBERT M. Thorns and thistles; juvenile delinquents in the United States 1825-1940. Hanover, University Press of New England, 1973. 231p.

Illinois

B205 MERCER, SHELLEY, and RICHARD FAHEY. Trial of juveniles as adults under the Illinois criminal code. Evanston, Chicago Law Enforcement Study Group, 1972. 35p.

The entire juvenile transfer process is examined with respect to actual practice, the statute governing action, and the alternatives to present practices. A survey was made of cases of youths who were transferred to criminal court to examine the standards and legal procedures behind the decision to transfer.

B206 MERRILL, EDGAR J., et al. Protecting the battered child. Denver, The American Humane Association, Children's Division. No date. 30p.

A report of a statewide study and an analysis of child abuse cases. Discussions of implications as viewed by experts in psychiatry, medicine, law and social work.

B207 MIDONECK, MILLARD L., and DOUGLAS J. BESHAROV. Children, parents and the courts; juvenile delinquency, ungovernability and neglect. New York, Practising Law Institute, 1972. 209p.

A discussion of practical questions of juvenile court administration; the troublesome problem posed by the gradual integration into the juvenile court procedures of constitutional requirements such as due process, equal confrontation, self-incrimination, etc.; the future development of juvenile courts in the context of our rapidly changing social environment; the hurry-scurry tendency, accelerated by court congestion; the lack of auxiliary services intended to staff juvenile courts as originally planned; the function of the jury trial in juvenile court proceedings; trials; sentencing or dispositional proceedings; post-dispositional proceedings; jurisdiction; theoretical bases for the juvenile court system; etc.

B208 MILLER, FRANK W., et al. The juvenile justice process: cases and materials on criminal justice administration and related processes. Mineola, The Foundation Press, Inc., 1971. 1411p.

The authors discuss parens patriae and constitutionalism; the substantive law of delinquency; confidentiality in the juvenile justice process; apprehension and investigation of the juvenile believed to be an offender; the decision whether to refer a child to juvenile court; the intake process; pre-trial detention; non-judicial adjustment of delinquency cases; the decision whether to transfer a case to criminal court; the adjudication hearing; arraignment and pleading; trial of contested cases; the disposition hearing; juvenile probation; treatment and control in the training school; right to care and treatment; transfers to "adult" institutions; release from training and aftercare.

Germany

B209 MOLINSKI, W. Unehelichen Kinder: rechtlose Kinder. Recklinghausen, Paulus, 1967. 96p.

B210 MONDALE, WALTER F. Justice for children. Washington, United States Government Printing Office, 1972. 33p.

B211 MORRIS, JOE A. First offender: a volunteer program for youth in trouble with the law. New York, Funk and Wagnall, 1970. 214p.

Germany

B212 MOSER, T. Jugendkriminalität und Gesellschaftsstruktur. Frankfurt-am-Main, Suhrkamp Verlag, 1970. 377p.

B213 MUELLER, GERHARD O.W. Delinquency and puberty - examination of a juvenile delinquency fad. New York University Criminal Law Education and Research Center. Distributed by Fred B. Rothman & Co., South Hackensack, N.J., 1971. 123p.

Puerto Rico

B214 MUELLER, GERHARD O.W., et al. The legal norms of delinquency; a comparative study. New York, Criminal Law Education and Research Center, New York University; distribution by Fred B. Rothman, South Hackensack, N.J., 1969. 76p.

Minnesota

B215 MULCRONE, R.T. A study into the feasibility of a Youth Services Bureau. Shakopee, Minnesota, Department of Court Services, 1970. 61p.

The report of a study on the feasibility of establishing a youth services bureau for two counties in Minnesota.

B216 MUMFORD, G.H.F. A guide to juvenile court law. 6th ed. London, Jordan, 1968. 334p.

B217 MUMFORD, GILBERT H.F. Guide to juvenile court law. 7th edition. Wheaton, Harold Shaw, 1970. 312p.

Great Britain

B218 NATIONAL COUNCIL FOR CIVIL LIBERTIES, LONDON. Children's Committee. The children and young persons act - a critique; the juvenile courts; children in the civil court; a children's ombudsman. London, National Council for Civil Liberties, 1971. 18p.

Great Britain

B219 NATIONAL COUNCIL FOR CIVIL LIBERTIES, LONDON. Children's Committee. Children in residential care and adoption (Children have rights, No.3). London, National Council for Civil Liberties, 1971. 8p.

B220 NATIONAL COUNCIL OF JUVENILE COURT JUDGES. Central resource summaries of pre-official court delinquency prevention programs. Reno, National Council of Juvenile Court Judges, 1972. 50p.

B221 NATIONAL COUNCIL OF JUVENILE COURT JUDGES. Ventures in judicial education. Chicago, Allen-Fisher Press, 1967. 168p.

B222 National strategy to prevent delinquency. U.S. Department of H.E.W., Social and Rehabilitation Service, Youth Development and Delinquency Prevention Administration. Washington, D.C., U.S. Government Printing Office, 1971.

B223 A national symposium on child abuse. Denver, The American Humane Association, Children's Division, 1972. 72p.

B224 The neighborhood youth corp: hope and help for youth. U.S. Department of H.E.W., Manpower Administration. Washington, D.C., U.S. Government Printing Office, 1969.

New Jersey

B225 NEW JERSEY. Administrative office of the courts. Disposition manual for juvenile courts. Trenton, 1971. 80p.

B226 NEW YORK (State). Commission on Mental Health Services Inside and Outside the Family Court in the City of New York. Juvenile justice confounded; pretensions and realities of treatment services. New York, National Council on Crime and Delinquency, 1972. 124p.

New York

B227 NEW YORK (State) Legislature. Committee on Social Services. Sub-committee on adoption practices. Report. Albany, December 15, 1970. 73p.

B228 NEWMAN, GEORGE G., ed. Children in the courts - the question of representation. I.C.L.E. Speciality Handbook No. 19. Ann Arbor, Institute of Continuing Legal Education, 1967. 571p.

These essays address themselves specifically to policy questions, and to problems to be faced by those charged with the responsibility of protecting and representing the interests of children in a variety of legal settings. A discussion on the lack of legal training in this specialized field of representation is included. (refs.)

B229 NORDIN, VIRGINIA D., ed. Gault: what now for the juvenile court? Ann Arbor, Institute of Continuing Legal Education, 1968. 218p.

This book is a collection of papers on the Gault decision, which were presented at three programs conducted in New York City, in Ann Arbor, and in Boulder in January and February, 1968.

B230 NORMAN, SHERWOOD. Standards and guides for the detention of children and youth. New York, National Council on Crime and Delinquency, 1969. 168p.

Standards and guides for juvenile detention in large juvenile court jurisdictions, and in smaller regional detention homes, are outlined.

Nigeria

B231 NWOGUGO, E.I. Family law in Nigeria. London, Heinemann Educational, 1973.

Texas

B232 OLM, JANE. Bibliography on juvenile delinquency in Texas. Austin, Tarlton Law

Library, 1970. 35p.

Oregon

B233 OREGON STATE BAR. Committee on Continuing Legal Education. Oregon Juvenile Law Handbook. Portland, Oregon State Bar, 1970. 1 volume, looseleaf.

B234 PAPPENFORT, DONNEL M., et al, ed. Child caring: social policy and the institution. Chicago, Aldine Publishing Co., 1973. 333p.

B235 PAULSEN, MONRAD G. Due process and the family court; comments, questions and tests. Unpublished paper, New York Academy of the Judiciary, 1968. 29p.

The following questions are examined: on what theory is the bill of rights binding on the states; what does due process require in a juvenile court delinquency case; how is Gault limited; what did Gault hold; what does Kent require; is Gault retroactive.

B236 PAULSEN, MONRAD G., and WALTER WADLINGTON. Statutory materials on family law. Mineola, Foundation Press, 1971. 169p.

Pennsylvania

B237 PENNSYLVANIA. General Assembly. Joint Government Commission. Proposed adoption act. Harrisburg, 1970. 18p.

B238 PHILBRICK, ELIZABETH. Treating parental pathology through child protective services. Denver, The American Humane Association, Children's Division. No date. 18p.

Great Britain

B239 PHILLIPSON, MICHAEL. Sociological aspects of crime and delinquency. Boston, Routledge and Kegal Paul, Ltd., 1971. 184p.

B240 PIZZATT, FRANK J. Behavior modification in residential treatment for children. New York, Behavioral Publications, 1973. 98p.

B241 Planning and designing for juvenile justice. Washington, D.C., Law Enforcement Assistance Administration, 1971. 158p.

B242 PLATT, ANTHONY M. The child savers. Chicago, University of Chicago Press, 1969. 230p.

The author indicts the juvenile courts as the expression of middle-class white protestants who used the instrumentality of the court to subject urban lower class youth to middle-class morals, and to deny them progress towards independence. He believes that the 19th century criminal law was not nearly as harsh to children as is widely believed, and he makes some major criticisms of the juvenile court.

Minnesota

B243 PLOETZ, RAYMOND C. Minnesota family law desk reference. Minneapolis, Minnesota Continuing Legal Education, 1971. 145p.

B244 The police-school liason program. Flint, The Mott Foundation, 1971.

B245 POLK, KENNETH, and WALTER E. SCHAFER. Schools and delinquency. Englewood Cliffs, Prentice-Hall, Inc., 1972. 282p.

B246 POOLEY, RICHARD C. Delinquency intervention in the high school. Carbondale, Center for the Study of Crime, Delinquency and Corrections, Southern Illinois University, 1969. 61p.

B247 PORTUNE, ROBERT. Changing adolescent attitudes towards police. Cincinnati, W.H. Anderson Company, 1971. 273p.

This book deals with one of the most annoying problems of our social revolution - the need for youth to recognize the authority and social responsibility necessary for an orderly society. Several police-juvenile programs for changing attitudes of youth toward law and law enforcement are also examined.

Netherlands

B248 PRINS, P.G., et al. Inleiding in het kinderrecht en de kinderbescherming. Alphen ann den Rijn, Samson, 1967. 140p.

B249 Proposed national policy objectives in the juvenile delinquency-youth development area. Washington, U.S. Interdepartmental Council to Coordinate all Federal Juvenile Delinquency Programs, 1972. 18p.

B250 Provision of counsel in juvenile courts. New York, Council of Judges, 1970. 40p.

An analysis of decisions and statutes governing the right to counsel, and waiver of the right to counsel.

B251 Public defender service. Juvenile practice manual. Washington, Juvenile Practice Institute, 1971. 180p.

B252 PURSUIT, DAN G., et al. Police programs for preventing crime and delinquency. Springfield, Charles C. Thomas, Publisher, 1972. 780p.

B253 RECKLESS, WALTER C., and SIMON DINITZ. The prevention of juvenile delinquency: an experiment. Columbus, Ohio State University Press, 1972. 253p.

Ohio

B254 RECKLESS, WALTER W., and WALTER C. RECKLESS. The initial impact of the Gault decision on juvenile court procedure in Ohio. Ohio Commission on Delinquency and Crime, 1967.

The results of a survey show that there has been a more rigorous application of procedural safeguards by the juvenile court in Ohio since Gault, and that the greatest amount of compliance with Gault in Ohio has been in the realm of the adversary procedure.

B255 REED, JOHN P., and FUAD BAALI. Faces of delinquency. Englewood Cliffs, Prentice-Hall, Inc., 1972. 420p.

Israel

B256 REIFEN, DAVID. Juvenile court in a changing society; young offenders in Israel. Philadelphia, University of Pennsylvania Press, 1972. 256p.

B257 REMINGTON, FRANK J., et al. Criminal justice and administration, materials and cases. Indianapolis, The Bobbs-Merril Co., 1969. 1504p.

Part three of this book deals with the administration of juvenile justice.

Germany

B258 REUTER, D. Kindesgrundrechte und elterliche Gewalt. Berlin, Duncker und Humbolt, 1968. 253p.

B259 RICHETTE, LISA A. Throwaway children. Philadelphia, J.B. Lippincott Co., 1969.

B260 Rights and responsibilities of youth. (UNESCO) New York, Unipub, Inc., 1973.

B261 Rights of youth and juvenile delinquency: developments and strategy for change. St. Louis, St. Louis University Press, 1970. 12p.

The rights of youth outside the context of juvenile courts are discussed.

Mexico

B262 ROSENQUIST, CARL M., and EDWIN I. MEGARGEE. Delinquency in three cultures. University Station, University of Texas Press, 1969.

B263 RUBIN, SOL. Crime and juvenile delinquency. Dobbs Ferry, Oceana Publications, 1970. 234p.

The following paragraph in Percy E. Russel's review of this book is of interest: "...Rubin makes a plea, and says that it is only a minority view that the defendant should have the right to see and, if necessary, controvert a part of the report. This is a strange reading to people in England who would see this as a fundamental right of the defendant, and his counsel, to have a copy of the report so that they can challenge any part of it with which they do not agree...."

B264 RUBIN, TED. Institute for court management. Three juvenile courts; a comparative study. Denver, University of Denver Law Center, 1972. 556p.

B265 RUBIN, TED, and JACK F. SMITH. The future of the juvenile court. Implications for correctional manpower and training. Commission on Correctional Manpower and Training, 1968. 67p.

This paper, which explores the problems and prospects of the juvenile court in the United States, is the first in a series of consultant's papers prepared at the request of the Joint Commission on Correctional Manpower and Training. The authors attempts to indicate the dimensions of the changes which will take place in the American juvenile courts and the dimensions of these changes, as well as their implications for manpower and training of juvenile court judges and staff, and for the lawyers who will represent an increasing number of clients in juvenile courts.

B266 SALEEBEY, GEORGE. Non-prison; a new approach to treating youthful offenders. Milwaukee, Bruce Publishing Co., 1970. 135p.

Austria

B267 SALURA, V. Jugend in Konflikt. Wien, Tyrolia-Verlag, 1972. 125p.

B268 SANDERS, WILEY R. Juvenile offenders for a thousand years: selected readings from Anglo-Saxon times to 1900. Chapel Hill, University of North Carolina Press, 1970. 453p.

B269 SCHAFER, STEPHEN, and RICHARD D. KNUDTEN. Juvenile delinquency: an introduction. New York, Random House, Inc., 1970.

The authors discuss the legalistic approaches to the problem of juvenile delinquency, as well as the psychological, the sociological, and the social welfare approaches. Topics include the causes of delinquent conduct, variations in delinquency sociocultural influences, law-enforcement and delinquency control, the treatment of juvenile delinquents and youthful offenders.

B270 SCHECHTER, HOWARD J. Defending kids: the public defender and the social organization of juvenile court. Ann Arbor, Xerox University Microfilms, 1972. 116p.

Ger./Gr.Br./U.S.

B271 SCHNEIDER G. Die Verletzung der Fürsorge- und Aufsichtspflicht über Kinder und Jugendliche im anglo-amerikanischen und deutschen Zivilund Strafrecht unter Berücksichtigung des deutschen Strafgesetzbuchentwurfs 1962. Hamburg, Diss.-Universität, 1967. 181p.

B272 SCHULTZ, L., ed. PINS: the juvenile status offenders. Cambridge, Ballinger Publishing Co., 1974.

B273 SCHUR, EDWIN M. Labeling deviant behavior - its sociological implications. New York, Harper & Row, Publishers, 1971. 177p.

Several authorities on "juvenile delinquency" are quoted by the author, who states that the juvenile court is a major arena for the labeling process. He blames this, in part, on the broad discretion afforded juvenile court judges who set procedures, tone and policies of the court, and whose ultimate authority dominates the proceedings; on the quite apparent absence of consistency and uniformity in the disposition of specific cases; and to the substantial discretion vested in control agents at several stages.

B274 SCHUR, EDWIN M. Radical nonintervention: rethinking the delinquency problem. Englewood Cliffs, Prentice-Hall, Inc., 1973. 180p.

B275 SCHWARTZ, LAWRENCE H., ed. Second juvenile practice institute manual. Washington, Juvenile Practice Institute, 1971. 180p.

B276 SEAGRAVES, ROY W., et al. Juveniles have rights, too. Belmont, Fearon Publishers, 1972.

B277 SHAFER, STEPHEN, and RICHARD D. KNUDTEN. Juvenile delinquency: an introduction. New York, Random House, 1970. 394p.
(1192 refs.)

Great Britain

B278 SHAW, O.L. Prisons of the mind. London, Allen and Unwin, 1969. 243p.

B279 SHERIDAN, WILLIAM H., and ALICE B. FREER. Juvenile and family courts: a legal bibliography for juvenile and family courts. Washington, D.C., U.S. Government Printing Office, 1971. 110p.

B280 SHERWOOD, NORMAN. The youth service bureau: a key to delinquency prevention. Paramus, National Council on Crime and Delinquency, 1972. 244p.
A description of the youth service bureau program.

B281 SLOAN, I.J. Youth and the law: rights, privileges and obligations. Dobbs Ferry, Oceana Publications, Inc., 1970. 122p.

B282 SMITH, PAULINE C. End of the line. Cranbury, A.S. Barnes and Company, 1970. 192p.

Germany

B283 Sonderfragen der elterlichen Gewalt. Berlin, Schweitzer, 1967. 946p.

B284 SPERGEL, IRVING A. Community problem solving: the delinquency example. Chicago, University of Chicago Press, 1969.

South Africa

B285 SPIRO, ERWIN. Law of parent and child in South Africa. 3rd edition. Johannesburg, Juta and Company, Ltd., 1971.

B286 STAPLETON, W. VAUGHN, and LEE E. TEITELBAUM. In defense of youth; a study of the role of counsel in American juvenile courts. New York, Russel Sage Foundation, 1972. 243p.

B287 STOENNER, HERB. Plain talk about child abuse. Denver, The American Humane Association, Children's Division. No date. 24p.

Six articles from the Denver Post which expose the myths and stereotypes popularly accepted about parents who neglect or abuse children. An interpretation for the general public of the nature and dimensions of neglect and abuse, its causation and treatment.

B288 STROUSE, JEAN. Up against the law: the legal rights of people under 21. New York, New American Library, 1970. 269p.

Georgia

B289 STUBBS, ROBERT S. Second summary of the Georgia law of children. Charlottesville, Michi Company, 1969.

India

B290 SUBRAHMANYAN, E.S. Law of minors. Allahbad, Law Book Company, 1968. 197p.

California

B291 SUNDEEN, RICHARD ALLEN, Jr. A study of factors related to police diversion of juveniles: departmental policy and structure, community attachment, and professionalization of police. Dissertation. Ann Arbor, University Microfilms, 1972. 163p.

The author explains the wide variations in juvenile dispositions. Results of a survey in Los Angeles County are discussed.

B292 SUSSMAN, F.B., and F.S. BAUM. Law of juvenile delinquency. 3rd edition. Dobbs Ferry, Oceana Publications, 1968. 110p.

B293 SZUREK, S.A., and I.N. BERLIN, eds. The antisocial child: his family and his community. Palo Alto, Science and Behavior Books, 1969.

Japan

B294 TANAKA, K. Leading cases on parent and child law. Tokyo, Nihon Kajo Shuppan, 1968. 291p.

B295 TEELE, JAMES E. Juvenile delinquency: a reader. Itasca, Illinois, F.E. Peacock Publishers, Inc., 1970. 461p.

(1027 refs.)

North Carolina

B296 THOMAS, MASON P., Jr. Juvenile corrections: a brief history; and juvenile jurisdiction: North Carolina's laws and related cases. Chapel Hill, Institute of Government, University of North Carolina, 1972. 53p.

B297 THOMAS, MASON P., Jr. Juvenile corrections - five issues to be faced. U.S. Department of H.E.W., Washington, D.C., U.S. Government Printing Office, 1971.

California

B298 THOMPSON, HOMER B. California juvenile court deskbook. Berkeley, California Continuing Education of the Bar, 1972. 300p.

B299 TOMPKINS, DOROTHY C. The confession issue - from McNabb to Miranda. Berkeley, University of California, Institute of Governmental Studies, 1968.

B300 TROJANOWICZ, ROBERT C. Juvenile delinquency: concepts and control. Englewood Cliffs, Prentice-Hall, Inc., 1973. 354p.

Not only does this book provide an overview of the many variables related to delinquency, it points out the duties, responsibilities, and functions of the agencies in the criminal justice system that deal with the juvenile delinquent.

B301 TRUDEAU, ELAINE. Digest of state and federal laws: education of handicapped children. Arlington, Council for Exceptional Children, 1971.

Tennessee

B302 TURNER, KENNETH A. Juvenile justice: juvenile court problems, procedures and practices in Tennessee. Charlottesville, Michie Company, 1969.

B303 Uniform laws annotated. Matrimonial, family and health laws with annotations from state and federal courts. St. Paul, West Publishing Co., 1973. 975p.

This new volume 9 of the Master Edition of Uniform Laws Annotated, contains the text, amongst others, of the following uniform acts: Abortion Act; Adoption Act; Child Custody Jurisdiction Act; Juvenile Court Act.

B304 U.S. CONGRESS. House committee on education and labor. General subcommittee on education. Juvenile delinquency prevention and control act. Hearing on H.R. 14816 and H.R. 14817. 92d Cong. Washington, D.C., U.S. Government Printing Office, 1972. 77p.

B305 U.S. CONGRESS. Senate committee on labor and public welfare. Child abuse prevention and treatment act. Report to accompany S.1191. 93rd congress. U.S. Government Printing Office, July 10, 1973. 12p.

B306 U.S. CONGRESS. Senate committee on labor and public welfare. Subcommittee on children and youth. Child abuse prevention act, 1973. Hearing on S.1191. 93rd Congress 1st sess. Washington, D.C., U.S. Government Printing Office, 1973. 695p.

District of Columbia

B307 U.S. CONGRESS. Senate Committee on the District of Columbia. Subcommittee on public health, education, welfare and safety. District of Columbia youth act. Hearing on S.2693. 92d Cong., 2nd sess. Washington, D.C., U.S. Government Printing Office, 1972. 870p.

B308 U.S. CONGRESS. Senate committee on the judiciary. Report of subcommittee on juvenile delinquency on S.521. 92d Cong. Washington, D.C., U.S. Government Printing Office, 1972. 211p.

An argument for the development of juvenile legal rights and minimum standards of justice for juvenile courts is included.

B309 U.S. CONGRESS. Senate committee on the judiciary, subcommittee on improvements in judicial machinery. Eighteen-year-old jurors. Hearing. 92d Cong., 1st Sess. on S.1975. Washington, D.C., U.S. Government Printing Office, 1971. 37p.

A hearing on the bill to lower the minimum age qualification for serving as a juror in federal courts from 21 years of age to 18 years of age.

B310 U.S. President's commission on law enforcement and administration of justice. The challenge of crime in a free society. Washington, D.C., U.S. Government Printing Office, 1967. 340p.

B311 U.S. President's commission on law enforcement and the administration of justice. Task force report: juvenile delinquency and youth crime. Washington, D.C., U.S. Government Printing Office, 1967. 428p.

B312 U.S. SURGEON GENERAL. Scientific advisory committee on television and social behavior. Television and growing up: the impact of televised violence. Report to the Surgeon General. Rockville, National Institute of Mental Health, 1972. 169p.

A report on studies on the impact of televised violence.

B313 VAN DOREN, J., et al, ed. Juvenile court hearing officers training manual. New York, Practising Law Institute, 1965. 952p.

The material in this training manual was developed for those whose professional activities bring them into contact with juvenile court matters.

Canada

B314 VAN STOLK, MARY. The battered child in Canada. Toronto, McLelland and Stewart, 1972. 127p.

India

B315 VARMA, PARIPURNANAND. Pathology of crime and delinquency. Agra, India, Sahitya Bhawan, 1972. 527p.

Great Britain

B316 VAUGHAN, MARK. Rights of children. Report of the first National Conference on Children's Rights, held in London on March 11-12, 1972, and jointly sponsored by the National Council for Civil Liberties and the London Co-operative Society's Education Department. London, National Council for Civil Liberties, 1972. 42p.

B317 VAZ, EDMUND W., ed. Middle class juvenile delinquency. New York, Harper & Row, Publishers, 1967.

B318 VEDDER, CLYDE B. Juvenile offenders. Springfield, Charles C. Thomas, Publisher, 1971. 264p.

B319 VEDDER, CLYDE B., and DORA B. SOMERVILLE. The delinquent girl. Springfield, Charles E. Thomas, Publisher, 1970. 166p.

Australia

B320 VICTORIA. Australia - laws, statutes, etc. Bourke and Fogarty's maintenance, custody and adoption law. 3rd edition. Melbourne, Butterworths, 1972. 345p.

Virginia

B321 VIRGINIA. Regional juvenile and domestic relations courts. Uniform rules of court for Virginia regional juvenile and domestic relations courts. Charlottesville, Michie Co., 1970. 42p.

Germany

B322 VON GRETHLEIN, G., und R. BRUNNER. Jugendgerichtsgesetz. 3rd edition. Berlin, De Gruyter, 1969. 497p.

Germany

B323 VON JANSEN, L., und G. KNOEPFEL. Das neue unehelichen gesetz. Frankfurt, Metzner, 1967. 498p.

East Germany

B324 VON OEHMKE, E., und D. SANDER. Schutz der Kinder und Jugendlichen. Berlin, Staàtsverlag der Deutschen Demokratischen Republik, 1970. 94p.

B325 VOSS, HARWIN L., ed. Society, delinquency, and delinquent behavior. Boston, Little, Brown, and Co., Inc., 1970. 458p.

A selection of articles dealing with the sociological aspects of juvenile delinquency. (1020 refs.)

B326 VOSS, HARWIN L., and DAVID M. PETERSEN. Ecology, crime and delinquency. New York, Appleton-Century-Clofts, 1971. 328p.

B327 WALKER, ROBERT N. Psychology of the youthful offender. 2d edition. Springfield, Charles C. Thomas, Publisher, 1973.

California

B328 WARD, MILBURN R. California juvenile laws. 2d edition. Los Angeles, Legal Book Corp., 1970. 404p.

Great Britain

B329 WATSON, JOHN A. The juvenile court - 1970 onward: a guide to the children and young person's act 1969 for magistrates, police, child-care officers and others. London, Shaw and Sons, 1970. 88p.

Great Britain

B330 WATSON, J.A.F. Which is the justice? London, Allen and Unwin, 1969. 242p.

B331 WEINSTEIN, NOAH. Legal rights of children. Reno, National Council of Juvenile Court Judges, 1973. 28p.

B332 WEINSTEIN, NOAH. Supreme court decisions and juvenile justice. Reno, National Council of Juvenile Court Judges, 1973. 25p.

B333 WEISSMAN, HAROLD H., ed. Justice and the law in the mobilization for youth experience. New York, Association Press, 1969. 220p.

Great Britain

B334 WEST, D.J. The young offender. London, Duckworth, 1967. 333p.

B335 WEST, DONALD J. Present conduct and future delinquency: an inquiry into behavior problems of primary schoolboys. New York, International Universities Press, Inc., 1969.

B336 White House conference on youth. Washington, D.C., U.S. Government Printing Office, 1971. 310p.

Great Britain

B337 WILDE, EDWARD. The forgotten years: dealing with the young offender. London, Bow Group, 1971. 28p.

B338 WILKERSON, ALBERT E., ed. The rights of children: emergent concepts in law and society. Philadelphia, Temple University Press, 1973. 313p.

This book's twenty essays are grouped into three sections. Among the major issues articulated are: rights in custody decisions, rights to support and inheritance, rights in conflict with the law, the right to legitimacy, the right to stable and protective care, and the rights of the unborn.

B339 WILKERSON, D.R. Parents on trial: why kids go wrong, or right. New York, Hawthorne Books, 1967. 188p.

B340 WINSLOW, ROBERT W. Juvenile delinquency in a free society: selections from the President's Commission on Law Enforcement and Administration of Justice. 2d edition. Encino, Dickenson Publishing Co., Inc., 1973. 271p.

B341 With justice for all; comprehensive plan and program for improving the Missouri justice system and the reduction of crime and delinquency, 1969-1976. Missouri Law Enforcement Assistance Council, 1971. 224p.

B342 ZARECKY, GARY. Moot; a simulation of legal procedures derived from juvenile and adult law cases. Lakeside, California, Interact, 1972. 35p.

B343 ZUKERMAN, J.T. Support and custody of children. International Bar Association. International conference of the legal profession. Proceedings. 12:160-332 (1968)

SUBJECT INDEX

references are to abstract numbers